PROPHETIC BIRTHING

PREPARING PROPHETS AND PROPHETESSES FOR PROFOUND PROPHECIES

BY DR. RANDY E. SIMMONS

For DENISE BORCHERS
THE GIRAFFE

Thanks for the inspiration
Thanks for bringing me from my cocoon

ACKNOWLEDGMENTS

Special thanks to the following people, who without their inspiration and help, this book would not be possible.
Thanks for the inspiration!

~

Prophetess Holly Sharp
Prophetess Denise Borchers
Handmaid Wendy Young
Handmaid Emily Moobi
Prophetess Grace Becky
Handmaid Liandha Madondo

~

And to the many friends from face book whose comments and encouragement made it all possible.

Elias Mirabi; Yolandae Brown; Yolanda Irons, Lorraine Gannointed; Jossy Johnson; Prophetess Betty Sims;
Dr. Dorothia Lee; Sis Leisa Wilcox;

Copyright© 2014 BY Dr. Randy E. Simmons,
7070 42 Way N. #1227 West Palm Beach, Fl. 33404
All rights reserved.

No part of this book may be reproduced in any form or by any electronic or mechanical means, including information storage and retrieval systems, without permission in writing from the publisher, except by a reviewer who may quote brief passages in a review

Published in the United States of America
Library of Congress Cataloging-in-publication
Data Available

ISBN-13: 978-1499680546
ISBN-10: 1499680546

"………..and some Prophets…..
For the perfecting of the saints, for the work of ministry, for the edifying of the body of Christ:"

(Ephesians 4:11-12)

PROPHETIC WORD: SPIRITUAL IMPREGNATION

"My son, the church is willing to talk about birthing, but because of their fleshly minds they are afraid to talk about the process of impregnation. The Holy Spirit (which is the word of God-sword of the Spirit) impregnated Mary (a virgin) with Himself and bore Himself (for God is one-Father, Son, and Holy Spirit). Life and creation is a process. Except a grain of wheat fall into the ground and die, it abideth alone. But if it dies, it bringeth forth much fruit. The church is barren, their wombs miscarry and their breasts are dry (Hos.9:11-17). Unless the water of life begins to spring up in them for whom I designed it (Handmaids/Wo-man, man with a womb) and their purpose (to bear seed through the process of incubation) then the church will die. I will not let this happen. The very gates of hell will not withstand my purpose. **What I need, my son, are men with seed...men with vision. The first three letters of seed is 'see'! See this, my son, without vision the people perish; without seeing they have no vision.** I said in Joel that young men shall see vision...they shall 'seed' vision. Therefore, without seed the ground lies dormant...break up the fallow ground! It's time to plant seed!" – **(01-17-10)7:25am**

PROPHETIC WORD: IMMACULATE CONCEPTION

"My son, when the Holy Spirit came upon the virgin Mary, earthly flesh from the earthly ground received Spiritual, Holy seed to conceive my son Jesus. Who but God could do such a thing? This is the mystery of Immaculate Conception; God in you! Now Spirit meets with spirits for greater impregnation...Spirit to spirit for birthing of my end time sons and daughters into the kingdom. Jesus spoke of greater works...this, my son, is the season of greater works!

Many hand maids today will prophecy (produce, give birth) not to the natural word of God, but to the word of God spread abroad within the hearts of men. They shall give birth to new revelation, new vision, and new life within the body of Christ. Truly the children have come to birth but 'there is not strength to bring forth'. But I will strengthen the wombs of the daughters of Zion and they shall give birth to the word of God. Their hearts will burn within them like the disciples on the Emmaus road. And, like the woman at the well, it shall spring up in them a well of water of life. No longer will I curse the wombs of the daughters of Zion. And once again, the true sons of God will look through spiritual eyes at the daughters of men and find them fair. Only this time their seed shall be pure, holy and undefiled."
- **(02-18-10) 8:00pm**

PROPHETIC WORD: THE SEED MAN

"My son, the enemy fights against the seed because the seed is my first and only promise that would come to crush his head. He tries to contaminate the seed, as in the time of Noah when he produced an impure seed of giants. He tried to confuse my purpose in the seed when Sarai gave an Egyptian hand maid to Abram to produce an heir. The enemy tries to discourage the seed giver and thwart my purpose as in the case of the daughters of Lot, thus rising up Ammon and Moab to be thorns in the flesh of my people Israel.
Discouragement of seed producing is the greatest weapon of the enemy, that's why he creates barrenness and abortion. He would rather kill innocent babies, as in the case of the time of Moses (through Pharaoh) and even in the time of my son, Jesus (through Herod). I will always protect my seed as I did then, so will I do now. The promise of the seed (the word-Jesus) brings truth, faith, and hope. For faith (which is the substance of things hoped for (Heb.11:1) cometh by hearing and hearing by the word (seed-Jesus) of God (Rom.4:17). The entrance (impregnation or Impartation) of the word (seed-Jesus) brings light (life). All truth is parallel. As is in the case of the natural, so is the Spiritual. Satan tried to destroy the faith and hope of Eve by killing (by the hand of Cain) the first righteous seed (Abel). His blood still cries out today because his seed did not fulfill its purpose. So Eve said

that God had given her 'another'(seed) - Seth. I, the Lord God, killed a man because he refused to rise up seed to his brother. I hated the fact that he split the seed on the ground rather than in the womb of his dead brother's wife where it would've produced life. He dishonored the purpose of the seed. Life producing seed (for this is the purpose of seed) is far better off in the womb of a woman (for this is her purpose) than barrenness and abortion. That is why I allowed Tamar to have sons by her father-in-law Judah, from which earthly Tribe of Israel my very son Jesus came. Even a harlot named Rahab carried the righteous seed of the lineage of Jesus in her womb. I allowed a young virgin to suffer ridicule and (near justice under the law for adultery) just to bring my son Jesus (the seed of the woman) into life. As they cannot hear without a preacher, neither can a woman produce without a seed giver (for this is what a man is). All truth is parallel my son. As in the natural so is the Spiritual." - **(02-18-10)9:20pm**

PROPHETIC WORD:
THE WOMB-MAN...WOMAN

"My son, when I created woman (the Womb Man) I created the greatest life producing entity in the universe...there was no other like her anywhere. Within the womb of Eve was all the life producing seed to replenish the earth. All mankind was in her womb. So wonderfully made was woman (the Womb Man) that even the very sons of God looked upon her daughters and saw that they were fair and took them wives of all that they desired (Gen.6). This too, my son is another mystery of how spirit interacted with flesh impregnating them and giants were born unto them. This was Satan's first attempt to contaminate my seed. All truth is parallel, my son. As is the natural so is the spiritual. These teach. Within the spiritual wombs of the daughters of Zion is this same life producing womb seed. 'Upon my hand maids will I pour out of my Spirit and they shall **PROPHECY**...' Note the prefix **'PRO...' PRODUCE...PROCREATES**...BRING TO LIFE!' A woman has the power to birth a vision or abort a vision. Whatever you impregnate her with, she will give life to it. If joy...she will birth joy. If chaos...she will birth chaos. Within her spiritual womb is the ability to bring anything to life the same way as she brings to natural birth. All truth is parallel. As is the natural so is the spiritual. Life is in the womb...spiritual or natural! 'As the earth brings forth life, so does the Womb Man. The words that I speak...they are spirit and they are life. As I am the God that calleth those things which be not as though they were, so I call the things which be not as though they are. Before Abraham had a natural son I compared his seed to the stars in heaven and the sand on the seashore. Are natural sons and daughters stars? Are they sand? Yet people accept this statement. I call Gentiles the seed of Abraham (Gal.3:11-14). Are they really in the natural? They could only be spiritual seed or children. So if Abraham and Sarah can have spiritual sons and daughters, cannot the Womb Man procreate (prophecy) spiritual sons and daughters today? I am not a respecter of persons." - **(02-19-10)3:00pm**

PROPHETIC WORD: HAND MAID (MAID AT HAND)

"My son, a Hand Maiden (Maid at hand) is one given to a mistress to do and fulfill the complete will and bidding of that mistress. Anything asked of her or <u>demanded of her by the mistress she was under total obligation to perform</u>. The word of the Master or Mistress was law. <u>As in the case of Hagar, it was no problem for her to obey Sarai in bearing a son for Abram. This was</u> her duty. Custom dictated every action and there was never any thought not to obey. As in the case of the hand maids of Rachael and Leah, it was their understanding that they were <u>seed producers</u>. It was their responsibility to bear children in the stead of their mistresses. There was never a thought that they would do otherwise. The Virgin Mary was the ultimate Hand maiden. When the angel declared that she would bear the son of God (the seed word) it was no problem for her to obey. <u>She knew the responsibility of the Hand Maiden</u>. She declared: 'so be it according to your word'. Despite her disposition and betrothal to Joseph, she valued the duty of Hand Maiden. 'In the last days I will pour out my Spirit...upon my Hand Maids...and they shall prophecy. To be a <u>Hand Maid is to be a **PRODUCER, PRO CREATOR, and PROPHETESS**-one who brings to life or one who prophesies forth the word of God</u>. All truth is parallel. As is the natural, so is the Spiritual. Mary **Produced, Pro created,**

prophesied forth the actual word of God, Jesus my only begotten son. She gave life and prophesied forth the actual word of God, Jesus. The word of God in the spiritual sense is still being birthed forth or **PROPHESIED** by my Hand Maids today. This was spoken by Joel the Prophet and declared to be truth by Peter the Apostle in the book of Acts Chapter 2:18. All truth is parallel. As is the natural, so is the spiritual." - **02-20-10/11:30am**

PROPHETIC WORD:
SPIRITUAL CONNECTIONS

"My son, the day will come when more will be done through spiritual connections than natural connections. As men become more and more busy and technology increases, social interaction will cease as we know it today. Men will learn to connect with each other through their spirits...through their minds. You have heard of the gifts of premonition; well is it real? The ability to know men in the spirit as people know me in the spirit will be increased. Think it not strange to believe that two people can connect through spiritual intervention. It is done every day. The heart of man (wherein is his soul) is a wonderful thing. Women fall in love and they 'feel connected' to their husbands; children are connected to parents; etc. I will increase the spirits of men in these last days and they shall know even as they are known...IN SPIRIT. I will remove the dark glass and they shall see through a clear glass. They will know the power of SPIRIT...the true realm of existence:

"For we know in part, and we prophesy in part. But when that which is perfect is come, then that which is in part shall be done away. When I was a child, I spake as a child, I thought as a child: but when I became a man, I put away childish things. For now we see through a glass, darkly: but then face to face: now I know in part; but then shall I know even as also I am known."(1 Cor.13:9-12)

To connect in spirit is to bring two spirits together and to know each other as never before. Like social interaction on the internet, or the matrix, so shall men learn the gift of spiritual interaction or connection. These things ponder and let it not go". - **(02-22-10)8:15pm**

PROPHETIC WORD: THE TABLE IS PREPARED

"I sense that a new season is upon us. It is a season of rest and plenty. It is a season of bounty and glory from the Lord. It is a season where I believe that God will truly bless the works of our hands. I heard in the Spirit this morning: '**THE TABLE IS PREPARED**'! Truly God has set the table. The providential care of God is at hand and some things can and will be done only by miracles; the supernatural ability of God to produce something from nothing...**THIS IS A MIRACLE!** He is the God which calleth those things which be not as though they are (Rom. 4:17).

I rejoice this day. I feel as if for a brief moment that the creation has stopped groaning and travailing. I feel that for a brief moment as if the earth has stopped spinning and instead has stood still just to give birth, today I feel as if a Son of God has been birthed by a thousand daughters of Zion; and today I feel that creation is laughing with joy because a male child has come forth: "A woman when she is in travail hath sorrow, because her hour is come: but as soon as she is delivered of the child, she remembereth no more the anguish, for joy that a man is born into the world."(John 16:21)

THIS IS A MOMENT IN TIME OF GREATNESS. THIS IS A MOMENT IN TIME OF BLESSINGS. THIS IS A MOMENT OF TIME IN VICTORY. THIS IS A MOMENT OF

TIME IN THE MANIFESTATION OF ALL THINGS.

At two am this morning, I found myself speaking to the wind; I found myself speaking to the city of Brunswick, Georgia to release its hidden treasures of darkness and its riches of secret places (Isa. 45:3). I walked the floor and spoke to the wind to blow away the dross and reveal the resources. This morning I saw the earth tilt on its axis and pour its resources into the hands of the people of God, that we may establish his covenant upon the earth and to do kingdom business (Deut.8:18).

This day I saw, and this day it shall be. I stand on the word and Brunswick, Georgia and the world shall know that there are prophets in their midst.

Be blessed today…**THE TABLE HAS BEEN PREPARED!**" –07-30-10

CONTENTS

PREFACE
THE NEED FOR SPIRITUAL BIRTHING……………………………Pg. 1

FOREWORD
"DELIVERY IS OVER: CUT THE CORD" EZEKIEL 16:4………Pg. 4

INTRODUCTION
"PREPARING PROPHETS AND PROPHETESSES FOR PROFOUND PROPHECIES"…………………………………………………………….Pg. 8

CHAPTER ONE
THE PROCESS: SPIRITUAL IMPREGNATION OR IMPARTATION……………………………………………………….. Pg.19

CHAPTER TWO
BIRTHING YOUR GIFT: "BELIEVING IT CONCEIVES IT"……..Pg.56

CHAPTER THREE
SPIRITUAL INTERPENITRATION: MOTHER-FATHER-MIDWIFE………………………………………………………………Pg.81

CHAPTER FOUR
THE BIRTH: "AND ADAM KNEW EVE….AND SHE CONCEIVED" ……………………………………………………………………….Pg. 100

CHAPTER FIVE
THE NURSERY: THE NANNY-'FAMILY'-FRIENDS ……………Pg. 115

CHAPTER SIX

THE NURSERY: TRAINING-MENTORING-TUTORING……Pg. 133

CHAPTER SEVEN

THE ROYAL SEED: PRINCE AND PRINCESS - SPIRITUAL COURTSHIP…………………………………………………………..Pg. 163

CHAPTER EIGHT

THE ROYAL PRIESTHOOD: THE SEED AND THE CALL…Pg. 184

CHAPTER NINE

REBIRTH: THE PROCESS REPEATS ITSELF……………Pg.207

CHAPTER TEN

SPIRITUAL INTIMACY: GOD DESIRES TO KNOW YOU….Pg.236

CHAPTER ELEVEN

THE COVERING AND COVENANT OF INTIMACY…………..Pg. 277

CONCLUSION

IT IS FINISHED: "DON'T CAP THE FLOW!"………………Pg. 297

PREFACE

THE NEED FOR SPIRITUAL BIRTHING:

Spiritual birthing is yet a tender and delicate subject within the body of Christ. So often it is misunderstood. When we request a spiritual 'mid-wife', we responded to a natural human need to be assisted or helped in all our endeavors. This is a frailty and weakness found only in humans. Yet man says: "for the children have come to the birth, and there is not strength to bring them forth"(2 Kings 19:3). BUT GOD SAYS: "Shall I bring to the birth, and not cause to come forth? Shall I cause to bring forth, and shut the womb?"(Isa. 66:9)

I am glad the Holy Spirit shows us the instinct of animals...they need no 'mid-wife', they need no help. When God created animals he put within them an 'animalistic' instinct and natural ability to have sex, get pregnant, and then give birth. As soon as that is over, the process begins again, and often time not with the same mate. We humans and Christians would frown upon that because we don't understand nor can we accept the natural (and spiritual) processes that God put in place. That is simply because of our sin nature. We became dependent...the man is dependent on the ground from whence he came, the woman's desire is to the man (her husband) she can't have sons or daughters without his seed. Hence the need to be born again so that we may understand the things of the Spirit (John 3:1-21).

Spirit needs neither midwife nor direction to conceive or bring about... (It blows here it listeth..."John 3:8) it's a spiritual process...it's a spiritual thing. Let me go deeper, and please spare my ignorant indulgence. God saw a virgin in Israel; he needed a vessel to bring His son, Jesus into flesh. And according to Galatians 4:4-5 'in the fullness of time...' It happened. But let's examine the process. An angel appeared, spoke to a virgin who had never known a man, told her she would conceive, and the Holy Spirit came upon her, and nine months later she had a baby in a stable, in a manger in Bethlehem...all by herself and her husband; no indication of a midwife, or crying or any such thing. She had it among the animals...and they understood. The child in her was HOLY. Again forgive my depth of ignorance (Luke 1:26-40; 2:1-21).

Last year I was about to publish this book called: "PROPHETIC BIRTHING". I cancelled the project because the Holy Spirit spoke and said: "this generation of believers is not ready or prepared for such things". We associate everything with flesh and that is how we, even as Christians, judge all things. Such things should not be. For 'that which is born of flesh is flesh; and that which is born of the Spirit is spirit'(John 3:6) I hope some of this may help. I would say more, but I prefer to allow the Spirit to speak to you instead. There is much that we in the body must learn if we are to win a generation not yet born to Christ Jesus.

1/22/15

SPIRITUAL BIRTHING IS A PROCESS THAT ONLY THE HOLY SPIRIT CAN BRING ABOUT. IT HAS NOTHING TO DO WITH OUR FLESH…

IT IS DESIGNED TO BRING ABOUT SPIRITUAL THINGS INTO THE NATURAL…

THE KINGDOM OF HEAVEN TO MANKIND…

THE WILL OF THE FATHER BE DONE ON EARTH AS IT IS IN HEAVEN…

THE RESTORATION OF ALL THINGS AND DOMINION BACK TO MAN AS GOD GAVE IT…

TO BRING HONOR TO GOD THE FATHER AND HIS SON JESUS CHRIST…

THE BLESSINGS OF ABRAHAM TO THE GENTILES…

THESE THINGS ARE SPIRITUALLY DISCERNED… BE BLESSED.

Dr. Randy E. Simmons
(09-01-11)

FOREWORD

DELIVERY IS OVER: CUT THE CORD - EZEKIEL 16.4

When it comes to spiritual matters there are things that are similar to natural things, take for example a woman giving birth which is spoken of in the Bible concerning End Time events that shall come upon the Earth before the return of our Lord and Savior Jesus Christ. It shows that just like a woman, the Earth will go through pains, travails, and breakings to bring forth that which God has prepared. So too, when it comes to a person saved and delivered it is likened to a baby being born including those things that take place afterwards. Take for example what the text that has been chosen is speaking about. It says "as for thy nativity..." meaning the day you were born, it's not speaking of a natural birth, but a spiritual one. When we are saved from our sins and brought into the Kingdom of God it is likened to us being "BORN AGAIN". When a person is saved they go through a similar birthing process as does a baby in the natural; you have a place of conception (your heart), birth pangs (convictions), body becoming disfigured (you no longer fit in worldly situations and circumstances), needing to push (Pray Until Something Happens), and then finally delivery (you are birthed into the Kingdom). Now many have gotten to that place in their lives, but as we read further and for those that know about natural child birth, there is more to it that we have neglected.

Once the baby has been delivered (birthed out) and is brought into the world, the next thing that must take place is the cutting of the umbilical cord. In the spirit the umbilical cord is symbolic to those things that you were once attached to in your old lifestyle. The Scripture text says "the day thou wast born thy naval cord was not cut", or those things, those people, and those situations that use to bring you sustenance, satisfaction, relief, and joy in the world you have not gotten to the place where you cut them loose. A lot of times we have people who are BORN AGAIN, but they have yet to experience full DELIVERANCE. These are the kind of people that they go to church, but still lie, still cuss people out, still watch pornography, still commit adultery/fornication, etc. Though these people have come to church, gone to the altar, recited the Sinner's Prayer, and asked Jesus into their lives; they have not gone on to true DELIVERANCE which requires the cutting away of those things that their flesh desires.

Another thing about natural child birth that is similar to a person going through full DELIVERANCE is that the text says "neither wast thou washed in water". Now according to Scripture "water" is symbolic to The Word because the Scripture declares "now are you washed by the water of the WORD". This says that although you have been born again you refuse to allow the Word to wash you of those old things, old natures, old ways, and old mindsets to be cleansed from you. Too many people in the church are walking around with old stuff on them. The reason it is needful for the Word to wash us is because just like the stuff a natural baby is washed from, if we don't allow the Word to wash us off, if it gets too old we begin to stink and become putrid. You have seen people doing the exact same thing they have been doing since they were young and now it's beginning to stink. I'm sure you've heard people say "that person has a STANK attitude, that person has a STANK disposition, that person has a STANK way of thinking, etc." We can't expect to go to other dimensions in God carrying nasty, rotten, disgusting, and unwashed things in our lives.

Next we read "thou wast not salted at all", now at first you may not understand this, but in the old Jewish culture after a baby was born and washed, they would salt the baby's skin so that it would toughened against diseases and germs. In other words it would preserve the baby's skin to keep it nice and smooth. This pertains to a person that refuses to allow the Word to make them stronger and instead they walk around with a chip on their shoulder allowing any and everything to offend them. These are the people that get hurt because "they talking about me, nobody spoke to me when I walked in the room, someone took my favorite seat in the church, the pastor didn't recognize me for the job I did in the service, and so on". God has not called us to be wimps in the Spirit, but to be true soldiers of Jesus, because we're not fighting against flesh and blood, but against spiritual forces. If we can't handle going up against other people what makes you think that you can handle anything that the devil throws at you?

Finally the text says "nor was swaddled at all" which means that the baby now is covered in cloth and wrapped tightly to not only be safe, but again to keep the baby's skin soft and since it was salted to help the skin to be toughened. This speaks of the next level of a person going through true DELIVERANCE; they have now gone to the point of being completely covered in the spirit. In other words God brings spiritual leaders who are submitted under His authority to be your spiritual covering. Many people think that they don't need a pastor, but you must understand that God has a set order in His Kingdom. The Bible declares to us to be "submitted unto those who have ruler ship over you", when it comes to the church it is the Pastor, because God has set them up to shepherd His flock. When you walk without true DELIVERANCE you make the decision to walk without covering. A Pastor is a covering that helps protect your spiritual well-being against spiritual attacks, spiritual diseases, and anything else the enemy would try in the spirit. Understand that without the CUTTING<WASHING<SALTING<COVERING in the spirit you are open to fall right back into your old filthy and stinking lifestyle; or as the Bible says "the dog has returned to his own vomit." It's time that the people of God get not only saved for real, but also get FULLY DELIVERED. CUT THE CORD!!!

WILL JENNINGS
FLORIDA METROPOLITAN UNIVERSITY
JACKSONVILLE, FLA.

INTRODUCTION

"PREPARING PROPHETS AND PROPHETESSES FOR PROFOUND PROPHECIES"

In an email to my dearest friend on July 31st 2010, I wrote the following:

"So that you really understand the clarity and importance that the saying from the Prophetess(Denise Borchers) and her husband Rex about Mentoring her is, that it brought clarity to the purpose of many of the teachings and revelations that I've had all last year(2009) on 'spiritual impregnation'. As I said earlier in my email, Americans don't seem to understand the strength and relevance of all this. Mostly when you speak to most American women about spiritual impregnation, they immediately go to their flesh or start thinking that I'm supposed to be their husband. Auuugh! What a thought.

For the past few day I've watched a prophetess being born and watched her husband confirm every step of the way. When you read the entire discourse you will understand why I say this. This was the second time, you being the first, that I've had a deep discussion with a woman of God and deep use of words, and came away feeling pure and clean and not as if I'd done anything wrong or as you like to say picked up and STDs (Spiritually Transmitted Demons). Our conversation was strong, yet basic and based on a truth of revelation.

Also for the first time I can use the words 'spiritual impregnation' and not wonder if I just cursed or did something bad. It is amazing how people from around the world and Africa understand so well this concept. God also made it clearer to me this evening why he had given me the teachings. As I used a few revelations briefly in my interchange with both Prophetess (Holly Sharp and Denise Borchers), they confirmed them to be truth. The Prophetess who was birthed posted most of our conversation on her fb page and prophets the world over hailed her rise that already knew of her gift. I heard immediately as I said from Kenya. This evening I heard also from Albania. Wow! My picture was posted next to the comments on her page and now my face and name is known among the Sons of the prophets as a leader in Prophetic Birthing. Who would've thought of it?

God broke down however the process to me this night and I will share it with you first and none other till the time is at hand: I heard the words: **"PROPHETIC BIRTHING"**
This is the purpose of spiritual impregnation. And I came to believe that it should be a book. I will have it ready by time you get here. It will be huge on the worldwide market.

 1. **THE PROCESS - SPIRITUAL IMPREGNATION**: - Hence the teachings God gave me last year to describe the scriptural process. "For I long to see you, that I may impart unto you some spiritual gift, to the end that ye may be establish", says Paul in Rom.1:11. "For

we know that the whole creation groaneth and travaileth in pain together until now."(Rom. 8:22). PAUL TRAVAILS IN BIRTH A SECOND TIME TO RECLAIM THE GALATIAN SAINTS TO CHRIST AND HIS GRACE. THE GREEK WORD; 'ODINO' IS USED HERE AND IT MEANS: BIRTH PANGS; TRAVAIL (WHICH SAME WORD IS USED IN GALATIANS 4:27. EVEN THE VERY CREATION IS PREGNANT WAITING FOR THE MANIFESTATION OF THE SONS OF GOD (Rom. 8:22-23).

2. **BIRTH YOUR GIFT: -** BIRTH YOUR MIRACLE! MIRACLES ARE LIKE GIVING BIRTH. You have the capacity to birth your gift or miracle. There was an old saying among Christians when I came into the church in the seventies: "IF YOU CAN BELIEVE IT...YOU CAN CONCEIVE IT! "Who hath heard such a thing? Who hath seen such things? Shall the earth be made to bring forth in one day? Or shall a nation be born at once? For as soon as Zion travailed, she brought forth her children. Shall I bring to the birth, and not cause to bring forth? Saith the LORD: shall I cause to bring forth, and shut the womb? Saith thy God?"(Isa.66:8-9).THE INTIMACY OF GOD IS REFLECTED IN THE INTIMACY OF MAN AND WOMAN. THE FAITH OF GOD IS REFLECTED THROUGH HIS CHURCH, THE WIFE OF JESUS CHRIST. THIS IS THE MYSTERY OF ONE FLESH.

3. **SPIRITUAL INTERPENITRATION**:-
   When people of Like spirits connect, whether in the case of a harlot as Paul describes in the book of Corinthians (1 Cor.6:15-20); or when two people 'connect' in the spirit, we develop INTERPENETRATION. A Discourse or interaction between a Prophet and Prophetess can lead to the unfolding of great revelations and confirmations of the word of God; See Isaiah chapter eight and Hosea chapter one. Now I understand why my discussions at first with Holly sharp, after I had posted 'the table is prepared', led to such great revelations. She and I were like the 'husband' and 'wife' or mid-wives preparing the prophetess to be birthed. '….Shall be in him a well springing up into everlasting life", says Jesus in John 4:14. The woman at the well understanding this to be like a water bag said: "Sir, give me this water…." (John 4:15). Again the disciples on the road to Emmaus, "And they said one to another, did not our heart burn within us, while he talked with us by the way, and while he opened to us the scriptures?"(Luke 24:32)……**EMOTIONAL INTERACTION**!

4. **THE BIRTHING**: - The Prophetic Birthing itself. Birthing is a process. It begins with the impregnation of a seed; Conception, spiritual embryo; morning sickness; incubation period; first trimester, second trimester, third trimester; and delivery – THE GIVING OF

BIRTH!. This is how the process of Spiritual Birthing also seems to unfold. The angel discussed with Mary her birthing of Jesus the word of God; "And, behold, thou shalt conceive in thy womb, and bring forth a son, and shalt call his name Jesus…..Then said Mary unto the angel, How shall this be, seeing I know not a man?...and she brought forth her firstborn son…."(Luke 1:31, 34; 2:7)

5. **THE NURSERY- THE NANNY-FRIENDS-FAMILY**: - This is the after birth process. This is like the nursery process. Family comes to visit, friends offer well wishes. Remember Mary went to Elizabeth before the birth for comfort (Luke 1:39-56); the prophet Simeon blesses the birth of Jesus (Luke 2:25-32); the Prophetess Anna gives thanks (Luke 2:36-38). A nanny is essential to the growth of a baby, spiritually or otherwise. Someone should always be prepared to speak into their lives. Miriam the sister of the great Prophet Moses recognized this also and said to Pharaoh's daughter: "Shall I go and call thee a nurse of the Hebrew women, that she may nurse the child for thee?"(Ex.2:7)

6. **THE NURSERY-TRAINING-MENTORING-TUTORING**: - The nurturing begins here. Wow what a process! A Prophetess said to me one day after this process: "Randy, the baby is born; now all you have to do is feed it

and change its diapers". She was correct. Even Jesus the son of God knew that there would be a training, mentoring, tutoring process: "And he went down with them, and came to Nazareth, and was subject unto them....And Jesus increased in wisdom and stature, and in favour with God and man".(Luke 2:51-52). Samuel understood nurturing and training: "And Samuel told him every whit, and hid nothing from him...And Samuel grew, and the Lord was with him, and did let none of his words fall to the ground. And all Israel from Dan even to Beersheba knew that Samuel was established to be a Prophet of the Lord".(1 Samuel 3:18-20)

 **SPIRITUAL COURTSHIP**: - There seems to be a time when Prophets become Princes and Prophetess become Princesses. "But ye are a chosen generation, a royal priesthood, an holy nation, a peculiar people; that ye should show forth the praises of him who hath called you out of darkness into his marvelous light;" so say peter 2:9. The Prophetic office is unique and there is a place in God where I've learnt God's intimacy. Females seem to understand this better and try to teach it to the male. The anointing is attractive and there is a dance that seems to go on between a male and female Prophet...a flirtation in the spirit if you please!

8. **THE ROYAL PRIESTHOOD-THE SEED-THE CALL**: - Every Prophet or Prophetess is called for a time and a season, for this is how God operates. When Earth demands a change, God will send a Prophet. It would seem that every Prophet with a great calling came from a Royal family or were taken care of by Royalty until their appointed time.
Moses, the future heir of Egypt chose "rather to suffer affliction with the people of God, than to enjoy the pleasures of sin for a season; esteeming the reproach of Christ greater riches than the treasures in Egypt: for he had respect unto the recompense of the reward." (Heb.11:25-26)

9. **REBIRTH-THE PROCESS REPEATS ITSELF**: - We conceive, we travail, we give birth, we rest, we conceive again, and the process repeats itself. The intimacy with the Lord is first that...intimate! We are excited about what is to be birthed. Even in our zeal, some spiritual pregnancies do not see fruition and there is deep sadness, even a sense of unworthiness or embarrassment. However, even the loss, the miscarriage does not eliminate the desire to conceive, so we try again and again and again, until the time is upon us. "My little children, of whom I travail in BIRTH AGAIN until Christ be formed in you, I desire to be present with you now and to change my voice; for I stand in doubt of you" (Gal.4:19-20)

10. **SPIRITUAL INTIMACY**: - God desires to 'KNOW' you. God is indeed calling you and me to a greater intimacy with him and he has been slowly teaching us how to be intimate with him. The intimacy with the Lord is first that...Intimate! Intimacy is precious...sacred! The cougars come looking for seed, they claim to be able to birth, but they rape away the anointing for their own pleasure. OH HOW I SEEK DAILY THE INTIMACY OF GOD!!! Paul said it this way: "That I may know him, and the power of his resurrection, and the fellowship of his sufferings, being made conformable unto his death..." (Phil 3:10).

11. **THE COVERING AND COVENANT OF INTIMACY**: - "God is the greatest covenant maker of all and the greatest warrior. He made a covenant with another warrior Abraham; and because he could swear by no other he swore by himself. That is an ultimate covenant. He made a covenant with Adam; one given to subdue the earth and when he was defeated by Satan; God gave him a promise, HIS OWN SEED! Wow what a covenant of Love... 'For God so loved the world', says John 3:16...wow!

12. **CONCLUSION- "DON'T CAP THE FLOW!"**: - I found the source of my communication today. It's like an oil well that gushes. Jeremiah likened it to fire, mine is like the oil spill in the gulf that is

not easily capped. Working on the cap. But how do you cap God when you know he is exposing truth. And really why would anybody cap God. Paul spoke till the man fell out the window, than raised him up.

MAY THIS BE OUR RESOLVE!

As I contemplate and meditate over all this something wonderful came into my spirit. What if around the world there were set up: PROPHETIC IMPREGNATION CENTERS (P.I.C.)

Wouldn't that be wonderful?"

Dr. Randy E. Simmons
Global Visions Ministries Intl. Inc.
July 31, 2010

CHAPTER ONE

THE PROCESS: -
SPIRITUAL IMPREGNATION OR IMPARTATION

THE PROCESS: - SPIRITUAL IMPREGNATION. Hence the teachings God gave me last year to describe the scriptural process. "For I long to see you, that I may impart unto you some spiritual gift, to the end that ye may be establish", says Paul in Rom.1:11. "For we know that the whole creation groaneth and travaileth in pain together until now."(Rom. 8:22) PAUL TRAVAILS IN BIRTH A SECOND TIME TO RECLAIM THE GALATIAN SAINTS TO CHRIST AND HIS GRACE. THE GREEK WORD; 'ODINO' IS USED HERE AND IT MEANS: BIRTH PANGS; TRAVAIL (WHICH SAME WORD IS USED IN GALATIANS 4:27. EVEN THE VERY CREATION IS PREGNANT WAITING FOR THE MANIFESTATION OF THE SONS OF GOD (Rom. 8:22-23).

CHAPTER ONE

THE PROCESS: SPIRITUAL IMPREGNATION OR IMPARTATION

Romans 1:11-13

GOD IMPARTED AUTHORITY:

"For I long to see you, that I may impart unto you some spiritual gift..." (Romans 1:11)

1. MEN OF GOD HAVE THE POWER AND AUTHORITY TO IMPART GIFTS (ROM.1:11; 1 TIM.4:14; 2 TIM.1:6; HEB.6:2)).
2. ALTHOUGH THE HOLY SPIRIT IS THE AGENT OF IMPARTATION/IMPREGNATION, WE ARE THE VESSELS IN DOING SO.
3. IT IS NOT TAKING GOD'S GLORY, OR HIS PLACE.
4. THE GIFT OF THE PROPHET IS SUBJECT TO THE PROPHET.

Paul had the fullness of God (Rom.15:29) and could impart spiritual gifts by the laying on of hands (Rom.1:11; 1 Tim. 4:14; 2 Tim.1:6; Heb.6:2).

MEN OF GOD TRAVAIL IN BIRTH:

"My little children, of whom I travail in birth again until Christ be formed in you..." (Galatians 4:19)

Paul travails in birth a second time to reclaim the Galatian saints to Christ and his grace. the Greek word; 'odino' is used here and it means: birth pangs; travail (which same word is used in Galatians 4:27 concerning a woman who has not had children; and in rev.12:1-2 concerning Israel, as a woman about to give birth).Paul had labored in preaching, prayer, and tears to win them to Christ, so he considered them his children. They were very dear to him; Now he had to travail in birth again until they would come back to God and Christ be formed in them again.

"I desire to be present with you now, and to change my voice; for I stand in doubt of you." (Galatians 4:20)

PURPOSE OF IMPARTATION/IMPREGNATION:

"...to the end ye may be established; that is, that I may be comforted together with you by the mutual faith both of you and me." (Romans 1:11b-12)

1. "...to the end ye may be established..."(Rom.1:11)
2. "...that I may be comforted together with you..."(Rom.1:12)
3. "...by the mutual both of you and me."(Rom.1:12)
4. "...that I might have some fruit among you also, even as among other Gentiles."(Rom.1:13).

The purpose of all Spiritual gifts is to establish the body of Christ (1 Cor.1;7; 12:4-11,28-30; 14:1-40; Rom.12:3-8; 1 Tim.4:14; 1 Pet.4:11).

DEFINITION:

IMPREGNATE:

New concise dictionary defines as: to make pregnant; to saturate; to imbue.

To saturate: <u>to fill completely</u>; to cause (a substance) to become impregnated to the point where it can absorb no more.

To imbue: <u>to fill</u>, especially with moisture; to fill, e.g. <u>with an emotion</u>.

IMPARTATATION:

New Concise dictionary defines as: To give of share of (something); to make known, or to communicate.

To impregnate is simply to impart; to fill completely (with emotion); to saturate; or may be understood as to plant as in the case of a seed! And the Holy Spirit accomplishes all of the above. we speak of being 'filled with the spirit'; we feel emotions when the spirit comes upon us; etc.

METHODS OF IMPREGNATION/IMPARTATION:

1. By the preaching of the word of God
2. By the laying on of Hands.
3. By the Holy Spirit coming upon and within us.
4. By speaking with an anointed man of God, as in the case of the disciples on the road to Emmaus with Jesus.
5. By desiring and asking as in the case of Elisha (2 kings chp. 2) and the woman at the well (John chp. 4).
6. By being blown upon by an anointed man of God, as in the case of Jesus upon the disciples (John chp. 20).
7. By a prophet going in and knowing a prophetess, thus confirming a prophetic utterance (Isaiah chp. 8; Hos. Chp. 1)
8. By a spoken word from an angel or man of God, as in the case of Sarah, Hanna, Elizabeth, Mary, Etc.
9. By becoming 'one spirit' with someone. Whoever you connect with, you receive of that persons spirit, whether through impartation or impregnation (1 Cor. 6:17).
10. By the quickening of the Holy Spirit.

THE VERY CREATION IS PREGNANT!
(Rom. 8:22-23)

EVEN THE VERY CREATION IS PREGNANT WAITING FOR THE MANIFESTATION OF THE SONS OF GOD.

"For we know that the whole creation groaneth and travaileth in pain together until now. And not only they, but ourselves also, which have the first fruits of the Spirit, even we ourselves groan within ourselves, waiting for the adoption, to wit, the redemption of our body."(Rom.8:22-23).

Note the connection between the groanings of the children of God and that of creation. So if the creation travails, as in pregnancy, then we also travail in spiritual pregnancy. "For we know that the whole creation groaneth and travaileth in pain together until now.
And not only they, but ourselves also, which have the first fruits of the Spirit, even we ourselves groan within ourselves, waiting for the adoption, to wit, the redemption of our body.'(Rom.8:22-23)

THE HOLY SPIRIT IMPREGNATES!

THE HOLY SPIRIT UNDERSTANDS SPIRITUAL IMPREGNATION BECAUSE HE IS THE AGENT OF SPIRITUAL IMPREGNATION:

"Likewise the Spirit also helpeth our infirmities: for we know not what we should pray for as we ought: but the Spirit itself maketh intercession for us with groanings which cannot be uttered.'(Rom.8:26).

Note the word **'LIKEWISE'**. Any English major will tell you that it means: **in the same way or manner; or just like**. IN THE SAME WAY OR MANNER...JUST LIKE...the earth groans and travails and we also groan in our bodies; the Holy Spirit does the same.

THREE IMPORTANT GREEK WORDS:

i. **Sunantilambanomai;** 'helpeth'...joint help. It is the assistance afforded by any two persons to each other, who mutually bear the same load or carry it between them (Rom.8:26).
ii. **Huperentugchano**; to apply one's self to intercede for another (as in a midwife or surrogate mother; Rom.8:26).
iii. **Stenagmos**; unutterable gushings of the heart (which only a pregnant mother can make because she understands the importance of the birthing of a son or daughter) "And Adam was not deceived, but the woman being deceived was in the transgression. Notwithstanding she shall be saved in childbearing, if they continue in faith and charity and holiness with sobriety."(1 Tim.2:14-15)

"THE BEGINNING OF SORROWS":

Jesus, in Matthew 24: uses the same analogy as does Paul in Romans 8:22, "For we know that the whole creation groaneth and travaileth in pain together until now." 'Groaneth' and 'Travaileth' are signs of a woman giving birth.

Paul said, because of the sins that he mentions in previous chapters (one, two, and three) for example; the whole earth was subjected unto sin. And the burden of this sin is like giving birth. Jesus saw the same thing as he spoke of the end time in the great mount Olivet Prophecy:

"And Jesus answered and said unto them, Take heed that no man deceive you.

For many shall come in my name, saying, I am Christ; and shall deceive many.

And ye shall hear of wars and rumours of wars: see that ye be not troubled: for all these things must come to pass, but the end is not yet.

For nation shall rise against nation, and kingdom against kingdom: and there shall be famines, and pestilences, and earthquakes, in divers places.

All these are the beginning of sorrows." (Matt.24:4-8)

'All these are the beginning of sorrows....' 'The beginning of birth pang…..' 'The beginning of contractions…….' 'The beginning of travail'. Clearly Jesus was thinking of the 'TRAVAIL' of Israel as he spoke these words. He references it in verses following:

"When ye therefore shall see the abomination of desolation, spoken of by Daniel the prophet, stand in the holy place, (whoso readeth, let him understand :) Then let them which be in Judaea flee into the mountains: Let him which is on the housetop not come down to take

anything out of his house: Neither let him which is in the field return back to take his clothes.
And woe unto them that are with child and to them that give suck in those days!
But pray ye that your flight be not in the winter, neither on the Sabbath day: For then shall be great tribulation, such as was not since the beginning of the world to this time, no, nor ever shall be.
And except those days should be shortened, there should no flesh be saved: but for the elect's sake those days shall be shortened.
Then if any man shall say unto you, Lo, here is Christ, or there; believe it not." (Matt.24:15-23)

This is the same analogy as used by God of the great tribulation in the following passage below:

"For thus saith the LORD; we have heard a voice of trembling, of fear, and not of peace. Ask ye now, and see whether a man doth travail with child? Wherefore do I see every man with his hands on his loins, as a woman in travail, and all faces are turned into paleness? Alas! For that day is great, so that none is like it: it is even the time of Jacob's trouble, but he shall be saved out of it. For it shall come to pass in that day, saith the LORD of hosts, that I will break his yoke from off thy neck, and will burst thy bonds, and strangers shall no more serve themselves of him: But they shall serve the LORD their God, and David their king, whom I will raise up unto them. Therefore fear thou not, O my servant Jacob, saith the LORD;

neither be dismayed, O Israel: for, lo, I will save thee from afar and thy seed from the land of their captivity; and Jacob shall return, and shall be in rest, and be quiet, and none shall make him afraid." (Jer.30:5-10; Isa. 66:7-8; Dan.7:23-27; 8:9-14, 23-26; 9:27; 11:40-45; 12:1,7; Micah 5:3; Zech.12:10-14:21; Rom.11:25-27; Matt.24:15-22).

JESUS THEREFORE UNDERSTOOD SPIRITUAL PREGNANCY AND SPIRITUAL BIRTHING...FOR UNTIL THE EARTH GIVES BIRTH, THEN THE TRAVAIL AND PAINS OF SIN SHALL NO DOUBT CONTINUE. THE WHOLE EARTH WILL CONTINUE TO GROAN UNTIL IT GIVES BIRTH OR SEES THE MANIFESTATION OF THE SONS OF GOD.

IMMACULATE CONCEPTION OR SPIRITUAL RAPE?

DEFINITION:

IMMACULATE...new concise dictionary says; impeccably clean; having no fault.

SO THE HOLY SPIRIT UNDERSTANDS SPIRITUAL IMPREGNATION. And because Mary was a virgin... "Seeing I know not a man" (Lk. 1:34); "the Holy Ghost shall come upon thee, and the power of the highest shall over shadow thee :..."(Lk.1:35); it was her impeccable purity that allowed this transaction. After all it was He who impregnated the Virgin Mary. Did the Holy Spirit rape her? No, of course not, she simply complied and submitted to His will: "And Mary said behold the handmaid of the

Lord; be it unto me according to thy word..." (Lk.1:38) The question then becomes: how can a woman, a virgin give birth to a child seeing that she has never known a man? It is a spiritual thing. "For with God nothing shall be impossible" (Lk.1:37). When the Holy Spirit came upon the Virgin Mary, earthly flesh from the earthly ground received Spiritual, Holy seed to conceive God's son, Jesus. Who but God could do such a thing? This is the mystery of Immaculate Conception; God in you; ".....therefore also that Holy thing which shall be born of thee shall be called the son (word) of God." (Lk.1:35). "And the Word was made flesh, and dwelt among us, (and we beheld His glory, the glory as of the only begotten of the Father,) full of grace and truth (Jn. 1:14; Isa. 7:14; 9:6; Matt.1:18; Lk.1:35; Rom.1:3; 8:3; Gal.4:4; 1 Tim.3:16; Heb.1:5).

Now Spirit meets with spirits for greater impregnation...Spirit to spirit for birthing of God's end time sons and daughters into the kingdom. Jesus spoke of 'greater works...' (Jn.14:12). This is the season of greater works! Many Hand Maids today will prophecy (Joel 2:28; Acts. 2:17-18(produce, give birth) not to the natural word of God, but to the word of God spread abroad within the hearts of men. They shall 'give birth' to new revelation, new vision, and new life within the body of Christ.

Truly '...the children are come to the birth, and there is not strength to bring forth' (2 kings 19:3). But God will strengthen the wombs of the daughters of Zion and they shall 'give birth' to the word of God. Their hearts will burn within them like the disciples on the Emmaus road. (Lk. 24:13-32); and like the woman at the well, '...but the water that I shall give him shall be **in him a well of water springing up into everlasting life.**' (Jn.4:14). As a woman, she understood the significance of water (placenta) springing up (conception), into...life (giving birth). No wonder she said: 'Come, see a man..., (Jn.4:29).

No longer will God curse the wombs of the daughters of Zion (Hos.9:11-17). And once again, the true sons of God will look through spiritual eyes at the daughters of men and find them fair. Only this time their seed shall be pure, holy and undefiled.'

We must crawl out of our fleshly carnal thinking and think in the Spirit. Remember 'whatsoever things are...true...pure...think on these things'(Phil.4:8-9).

TO NOT BELIEVE IN SPIRITUAL IMPREGNATION IS NOT TO BELIEVE IN THE VIRGIN BIRTH (IMMACULATE CONCEPTION) FOR IT WAS THE GREATEST SPIRITUAL IMPREGNATION AND BIRTHING OF ALL CREATION!

THE DIFFERENCE BETWEEN MEN AND WOMEN:

1. MEN ARE FROM MARS; WOMEN ARE FROM VENUS!
2. MEN AND WOMEN RECEIVE AND INTERPRET DIFFERENTLY!
3. MEN HEAR 'IMPARTATION'; WHILE WOMEN HEAR 'IMPREGNATION'!

4. MEN SEE 'SEED SOWING'; WHILE WOMEN SEE 'BIRTHING'

THIS IS HOW GOD ORDAINED AND SET UP HIS CREATION. AS IS THE NATURAL, SO IS THE SPIRITUAL. THERE IS NOTHING LEWD OR STRANGE ABOUT IT. IT IS SIMPLY OUR FLESH THAT CANNOT RECEIVE THE TRUTH OF THE SPIRIT, BECAUSE THESE THINGS ARE SPIRITUALLY DISCERNED (1 COR.2:14).

THE CASE OF THE SOWER:

SPIRITUAL IMPREGNATION (AS IN THE CASE OF A HAND MAID) OR IMPARTATION (AS IN THE CASE OF MEN) IS THE SAME AS A SOWER SOWING SEED. IN THE PARABLE OF THE SOWER, A SOWER WENT FORTH TO SOW SEED INTO THE GROUND.

"And when much people were gathered together, and were come to him out of every city, he spake by a parable: A sower went out to sow his seed: and as he sowed, some fell by the way side; and it was trodden down, and the fowls of the air devoured it. And some fell upon a rock; and as soon as it was sprung up, it withered away, because it lacked moisture. And some fell among thorns; and the thorns sprang up with it, and choked it. And other fell on good ground, and sprang up, and bare fruit an hundredfold. And when he had said these things, he cried, He that hath ears to hear let him hear. And his disciples asked him, saying, what might this parable be? And he said, unto you it is given to know the mysteries of the kingdom of God: but to others in parables; that seeing they might not see, and hearing they might not understand. Now the parable is this: The seed is the word of God. Those by the way side are they that hear; then cometh the devil, and taketh away the word out of their hearts, lest they should believe and be saved. They on the rock are they, which, when they hear, receive the word with joy; and these have no root, which for a while believe, and in time of temptation fall away. And that which fell among thorns are they, which, when they have heard, go forth, and are choked with cares and riches and pleasures of this life, and bring no fruit to perfection. But that on the good ground are they, which in an honest and good heart, having heard the word, keep it, and bring forth fruit with patience." (Luke 8:5-15)

NOTICE IN THE PASSAGE IN LUKE CHAPTER EIGHT, THE SOWER WENT FORTH TO SOW SEED. THE WORD, **SEED** IS VERY IMPORTANT IN THIS PASSAGE. GOD HAS SPOKEN OF THE **SEED** THROUGHOUT TIME AND ETERNITY. WITHIN THE **SEED** OF A THING IS THE LIFE OF A THING.

"And God said let the earth bring forth grass, the herb yielding seed, and the fruit tree yielding fruit after his kind, whose seed is in itself, upon the earth: and it was so.
And the earth brought forth grass and herb yielding seed after his kind, and the tree yielding fruit, whose seed was in itself, after his kind: and God saw that it was good….

And God said, Behold, I have given you every herb bearing seed, which is upon the face of all the earth, and every tree, in the which is the fruit of a tree yielding seed; to you it shall be for meat." (Gen.1:11-12, 29)

IF THE SEED OF NATURAL LIFE IS WITHIN ITSELF, THEN SO IS THE SEED OF SPIRITUAL LIFE. IF NATURE PRODUCES AFTER ITSELF, THEN SPIRIT PRODUCES AFTER ITSELF; IF TREES BECOME PREGNANT, AND IF ANIMALS AND MANKIND BECOMES PREGNANT, THEN WHY SHOULD WE NOT THINK THAT THERE IS SPIRITUAL IMPREGNANATION. THE BIBLE IS CLEAR ON THIS ISSUE.

Jesus said: "verily, verily, I say unto you, except a corn of wheat fall into the ground and die, it abideth alone: but if it die, it bringeth forth much fruit.' (John 12:24)

A SOWER SOWS GRAIN INTO THE EARTH AND EXPECTS A CROP. THE SPIRIT OF GOD ALSO SOWS HIS SEED EXPECTING A CROP. MEN PLANT A SEED WITHIN THE WOMB OF A WOMAN EXPECTING A CHILD, THE HOLY SPIRIT IMPREGNATES EXPECTING THE 'WORD OF GOD' TO BE BORN WITHIN US. DEATH OF A SEED WITHIN THE GROUND OR THE WOMB OF A WOMAN IS WHAT BRINGS FORTH LIFE. THE WORD OF GOD PLANTED WITHIN THE BELLY OF A PERSON IS THAT TO WHICH BIRTH IS GIVEN ...AS WAS THE CASE OF MARY IN THE NATURAL, SO IS THE CASE OF THE DAUGHTERS OF ZION IN THE SPIRITUAL.

BIOLOGY SUPPORTS THE BIRTHING PROCESS:

Now let me show you how it happens naturally between a man and a woman. The man has within him seed (He is the sower). The woman has a womb filled with eggs (She is the ground); and as she was made from the earth, her womb is just like the ground. The man sows his seed into her womb (the earth); the seed connects with an egg (the enzymes in the soil); they form a zygote (symbol of death) and repel all other seed. During the time of forming the zygote (death) conception (life) happens; producing an embryo **(which the New Concise Dictionary defines as: an animal organism during the early stages of growth and development; a human individual from the time of implantation to the eighth week after conception).** The seed dies in her womb but instead of bringing death it brings life and nine months later a child is born. The seed died so it brought forth much more life. If a male child is born, he becomes a seed giver or sower. If a female child is born, she becomes an egg producer of incubator **(man with a womb)** full of enzymes like the soil. Now, understand it in the Spirit. When a preacher preaches or teaches the word, he is just like a sower of seed. He is sowing the seed of the word. When he prays or lays hands upon someone he is imparting seed (as in the case of a man); and impregnating into the womb (as in the case of a woman; or handmaiden). All truth is relative. As is the case of the natural, so is the Spiritual. Men receive different than women.

Men are imparted with seed and then their desire is to sow just like the preacher or sower. It is man's nature to want to impregnate. God created him that way, with the ability to give forth seed. On the other hand a woman will hear the same word, but her nature is to produce (prophecy) life. She automatically begins to conceive and thinks how can she 'birth' something forth. She has a womb and whatever impregnates her womb, her natural and spiritual desire is to give birth. There is nothing lewd or fleshly in this, it's just the way God made her. She is like the earth crying for seed to bring forth. The water (placenta) in her womb is waiting for a seed to bring forth life. All truth is relative. As is the natural, so is the spiritual.

THE SEED MAN: (Gen.3:15)

The enemy fights against the seed because the seed is God's first and only promise that would come to crush his head (Gen.3:15). He tries to contaminate the seed, as in the time of Noah, when he produced an impure seed of giants (Gen.6:4; 2 Pet.2:4; Jude 6-7). He tried to confuse God's purpose in the seed when Sarai gave an Egyptian hand maid to Abram to produce an heir (Gen.16:1-6). The enemy tries to discourage the seed giver and thwart God's purpose as in the case of the daughters of Lot, thus rising up Ammon and Moab to be thorns in the flesh of God's people Israel (Gen.19:30-38). Discouragement of seed producing is the greatest weapon of the enemy, that's why he creates barrenness and abortion. He would rather kill innocent babies, as in the case of the time of Moses, through Pharaoh (Ex.1:15-22); and even in the time of God's son, Jesus, through Herod (Matt.2:16-18). God will always protect his seed as He did then, so will He do now.

The promise of the seed (the word-Jesus) brings truth, faith, and hope. For faith (which is the substance of things hoped for Heb.11:1) cometh by hearing and hearing by the word (seed-Jesus) of God (Rom.10:17). The entrance (impregnation or impartation) of the word (seed-Jesus) brings light or life (Ps.119:130). All truth is parallel. As is in the case of the natural, so is the Spiritual. Satan tried to destroy the faith and hope of Eve by killing, by the hand of Cain, the first righteous seed, Abel (Gen.4:3-15). His blood still cries out today because his seed did not fulfill its purpose (Heb.11:4; 12:24). So Eve said that God 'hath appointed me another seed instead of Abel whom Cain slew'- Seth (Gen.4:25-26). The Lord God killed a man because he refused to rise up seed to his brother. God hated the fact that he split the seed on the ground rather than in the womb of his dead brother's wife where it would've produced life. He dishonored the purpose of the seed (Gen.38:7-10)

Life producing seed; for this is the purpose of seed (Gen.1:29-30) is far better off in the womb of a woman (for this is her purpose Gen.3:16) than barrenness and abortion. That is why God allowed Tamar to have sons by her father-in-law Judah, from which earthly Tribe of Israel God's very son Jesus came

(Gen.38:11-30). Even a harlot named Rahab carried the righteous seed of the lineage of Jesus in her womb (Josh. 2:12-24; 6:28; Matt.1:5; Heb.11:31; James 2:25) God allowed a young virgin to suffer ridicule and near justice under the law for adultery just to bring His son, Jesus; the seed of the woman Gen.3:15; the Light of the World and the Word made flesh (John 1:9-14) into life in the fullness of time (Matt.1:18-25; Luke 1:26-38; Gal.3:19; 4:4). As they cannot hear without a preacher, neither can a woman produce without a seed giver (for this is what a man is). All truth is parallel, as in the natural so is the Spiritual.

THE WOMB MAN -WOMAN: (Gen.2:22-23)

When God created woman (the Womb Man) He created the greatest life producing entity in the universe...there was no other like her anywhere. Within the womb of Eve was all the life producing seed to replenish the earth. All mankind was in her womb (Gen.1:26-28; 2:19-24; 3:20)

OBSERVE THE TEXT IN GENESIS 2:22-23:

"And the rib, which the LORD God had taken from man, made he a woman, and brought her unto the man. And Adam said, this is now bone of my bones, and flesh of my flesh: she shall be called Woman, because she was taken out of Man." (Gen.2:22-23)

The Hebrew word used here is: **Ish Shah**, feminine of **Ish**, of man. It literally means **she-man; womb-man; man with a womb; or female-man,** because she was taken out of man (Gen.2:23; 1 Cor.11:3-12; 1 Tim.2:9-15).

So wonderfully made was woman (the Womb Man) that even the very sons of God looked upon the daughters of men and saw that they were fair and took them wives of all that they desired(Gen.6:1-4). This too, is another mystery of how spirit interacted with flesh impregnating them and giants were born unto them (Gen.6:4; 2 Pet.2:4; Jude 6-7). This was Satan's first attempt to contaminate God's seed. All truth is parallel, as is the natural so is the spiritual.

Within the spiritual wombs of the daughters of Zion is this same life producing womb seed. As Sarah was the daughter of Eve and the handmaids of today are the daughters of Sarah, then it follows to say that as Eve and Sarah produced seed, so shall the daughters of today Produce seed after its kind (Gen.3:20; 1 Tim.2:9-15; 1 Pet.3:5-7)

'Upon my hand maids will I pour out of my Spirit and they shall prophecy...' (Joel 2:29; Acts 2:18)Note the prefix 'PRO...' PRODUCE...PROCREATE...BRING TO LIFE!'

A woman has the power to birth a vision or abort a vision. Whatever you impregnate her with, she will give life to it. If joy...she will birth joy. If chaos...she will birth chaos. Within her spiritual womb is the ability to bring anything to life the same way as she brings to natural birth. All truth is parallel. As is the natural so is the spiritual. Life is in the womb...spiritual or natural! As the earth brings forth life, so does the Womb Man. The words that Jesus spake...they are spirit and they are life (John 6:63). As he is the God that quickened the dead and calleth those things which be not as though they were, so He calls the things which be as though they are (Rom.4:17).

THE WOMAN...THE WOMB MAN.... THE CHALICE....THE HOLY GRAIL!

Many great artistic minds, like Leonardo Da Vinci ("....one of the keepers of the secret of the Holy Grail"); Sir Isaac Newton; and others believed that Constantine was"...a lifelong pagan who was baptized on his deathbed, too weak to protest. In Constantine's day, Rome's official religion was sun worship-the cult of Sol Invictus, or the invisible sun-and Constantine was its head priest. Unfortunately for him, a growing religious turmoil was gripping Rome. Three centuries after the crucifixion of Jesus Christ, Christ's followers had multiplied exponentially. Christians and pagans began warring, and the conflict grew to such proportions that it threatened to rend Rome in two. Constantine decided something had to be done. In 325 A.D., he decided to unify Rome under a single religion, Christianity."
"During the fusion of religions, Constantine needed to strengthen the new Christian tradition, and held a famous ecumenical gathering known as the Council of Nicaea."

"The Holy Grail is a person?" "…A woman in fact."

The modern icons for male and female "……are not the original symbols for male and female. Many people incorrectly assume the male symbol is derived from a shield and spear, while the female symbol represents a mirror reflecting beauty. In fact, the symbols originated as ancient astronomical symbols for the planet-god mars and planet-goddess Venus.

The symbol for male '….A rudimentary Phallus……This icon is formally known as the blade, and it represents aggression and manhood. In fact, this exact phallus symbol is still used today on modern military uniforms to denote rank…."

"Moving on, the female symbol, as you might imagine, is the exact opposite…..This is called the chalice…resembles a cup or vessel, and more important, it resembles the shape of a woman's womb. The symbol communicates femininity, womanhood, and fertility."
"The Grail is literally the ancient symbol for womanhood, and the Holy Grail represents the sacred feminine and the goddess, which of course has now been lost, virtually eliminated by the Church. The power of the female and her ability to produce life was once very sacred, but it posed a threat to the rise of the predominantly male Church, and so the sacred feminine was demonized and called unclean. It was man, not God, who created the concept of 'original sin,' whereby Eve tasted of the apple

and caused the downfall of the human race. Woman, once the sacred giver of life, was now the enemy."

"...that this concept of woman as life-bringer was the foundation of ancient religion. Childbirth was mystical and powerful. Sadly, Christian philosophy decided to embezzle the female's creative power by ignoring biological truth and making man the Creator. Genesis tells us that Eve was created from Adam's rib. Woman became an offshoot of man. And a sinful one at that. Genesis was the beginning of the end for the goddess."

"The Grail....is symbolic of the lost goddess. When Christianity came along, the old pagan religions did not die easily. Legends of chivalric quests for the lost Grail were in fact stories of forbidden quests to find the lost sacred feminine. Knights who claimed to be 'searching for the Chalice' were speaking in code as a way to protect themselves from a church that had subjugated women, banished the Goddess, burned nonbelievers, and forbidden the pagan reverence for the sacred feminine."

The Holy Grail was ".....A woman who carried with her a secret so powerful that, if revealed, it threatened to devastate the very foundation of Christianity!" -**SOURCE: THE DA VINCI CODE, BY DAN BROWN.**

STARS, SAND AND ABRAHAM: (GEN. 15:5; 22:17)

"And he brought him forth abroad, and said, look now toward heaven, and tell the stars, if

thou be able to number them: and he said unto him, so shall thy seed be.
That in blessing I will bless thee, and in multiplying I will multiply thy seed as the stars of heaven and as the sand which is upon the seashore; and thy seed shall possess the gate of his enemies." (Gen. 15:5; 22:17)

Before Abraham had a natural son God compared his seed to the stars in heaven and the sand on the seashore (Gen.15:1-6; Gen.22:16-18). Are natural sons and daughters stars? Are they sand? Yet people accept this statement. God called Gentiles the seed of Abraham (Gal.3:11-14); are they really...in the natural? They could only be spiritual seed or children. So if Abraham and Sarah can have spiritual sons and daughters, cannot the Womb Man procreate (prophecy) spiritual sons and daughters today? God is not a respecter of persons.

THE CASE OF THE TREE: (GEN. 1:29)

Job understood the power of the seed and the power of recreation. He stated that a tree will be dead, but at the scent of water it will spring to life immediately. As in every living thing, **"and every tree, in the which is the fruit of a tree yielding seed"** (Gen.1:29); so is the seed and the word in the womb of a woman. Adam recognized that in Eve was the seed of all procreation and replenishing of the earth, for he called her the mother of all the living (Gen.3:20).

"For there is hope of a tree, if it be cut down, that it will sprout again, and that the tender branch thereof will not cease.
Though the root thereof wax old in the earth, and the stock thereof die in the ground; Yet through the scent of water it will bud, and bring forth boughs like a plant." (Job.14:7-9)

THE WOMAN AT THE WELL: (John 4:1-42)

The woman at the well understood this concept of spiritual impregnation and birthing when Jesus said: 'it will be in you as a well of water springing up unto eternal life'. As a woman, she understood that within her was a water bag, and at the time of pregnancy this water bag held the life of a child in it. No wonder she cried out: 'ever more give me this water'. Her first instinct was to go tell the good news, thus giving 'birth' to her people. 'Come, see a man...' Was her cry (John 4:29). We hear from Isaiah 12:3 these words: "Therefore with joy shall ye draw water out of the wells of salvation". This woman, this harlot, this outcast sure found out that day what an experience it was.

THE CASE OF NICODEMUS: (JOHN 3:4)

Nicodemus confused spiritual pregnancy and new birth with natural birth. He exclaimed: 'shall a man reenter his mother's womb ad be born...? (John 3:4). He understood the concept of birthing and pregnancy only in the natural. Jesus had to explain to him that: 'they that are born of flesh are flesh but they that are born of Spirit are Spirit...' He had to break it down for thus great religious teacher of the law. It was not natural birthing that he was speaking of, it was spiritual. All truth is parallel, as is the natural, so is the spiritual. Jesus was speaking concerning spiritual impregnation resulting in a spiritual new birth. As in the natural, so is the spiritual. In order for birthing to take place, there had to be an impregnation by the spirit just as there would be an impregnation in the natural by a man to a woman resulting in conception and finally in birthing. Nicodemus understood the concept of spiritual birthing, he was just thinking in his flesh, as do so many in the church today.

DRY BREAST AND MISCARRYING WOMBS! (HOS. 9:11-14)

Many have miscarrying wombs and dry breasts as God stated in Hos.9:11-14, but He never intended it to be so. Jesus came that men should have life and have it more abundantly. Here we have one of the strongest mentions of the birthing process in scriptures. It is clear here that God intended for Israel to be a fruitful nation as he did all mankind from the Garden of Eden, according to Gen.1:28:

"And God blessed them, and God said unto them, be fruitful, and multiply, and replenish the earth, and subdue it: and have dominion over the fish of the sea, and over the fowl of the air, and over every living thing that moveth upon the earth."

Therefore, to have miscarrying wombs and dry breast, whether in the natural or spiritual, is to be cursed and not fulfill the purpose or intent for which God created a man and a woman. They were made to PRODUCE…TO PROCREATE….TO PROPHESY! Man with a womb and man with a seed were displayed to confirm that the life of a thing is within itself. Only in the Spirit can we understand spiritual things, to try and discern them with our flesh is ludicrous. It is by the Spirit of God that we understand how Ephraim can have 'dry breast and miscarrying wombs'!

NATURAL IMPREGNATION CONFIRMS PROPHECY:

THE CASE OF THE PROPHET ISAIAH: (ISAIAH 8:1-4)

"Moreover the LORD said unto me, take thee a great roll, and write in it with a man's pen concerning Mahershalalhashbaz.
And I took unto me faithful witnesses to record, Uriah the priest, and Zechariah the son of Jeberechiah.
And I went unto the prophetess; and she conceived, and bare a son. Then said the LORD to me, call his name Mahershalalhashbaz.
For before the child shall have knowledge to cry, My father, and my mother, the riches of Damascus and the spoil of Samaria shall be taken away before the king of Assyria." (Isaiah 8:1-4)

Here God spoke to Isaiah that he should prophesy and write it in a scroll that he was to have a son by the prophetess, his wife, and that he should name the child Maher-shalal-hash-baz as a sign to Israel. He did so and had the prophecy properly recorded before faithful witnesses who could affirm that the prophecy was given before he even went in to the prophetess, so that Judah might believe it was of God. **STRANGE EVENTS HAPPEN IN THE MIND OF GOD TO BRING TRUTH TO LIGHT. WHY NOT A PROPHET GOING INTO THE PROPHETESS, HIS WIFE, WITH SEED TO CONFIRM A TRUTH THAT GOD WAS ABOUT TO REVEAL?**

THE CASE OF THE PROPHET HOSEA: (HOSEA 1:1-11)

"Go, take unto thee a wife of whoredoms….So he went and took Gomer the daughter of Diblaim; which conceived, and bare him a son. And the Lord said unto him, call his name Jezreel;
And she conceived again, and bare a daughter. And God said unto him, call her name Lo-ru-ha'mah: Now when she had weaned Lo-ru-ha'mah, she conceived, and bare a son. Then said God, call his name Lo-am'mi:" (Hos. 1:2-4, 6, 8).

Again God uses the connection of a Prophet with His wife, a seed carrying incubator, for this is what her womb was, to prove his word. It is amazing how the word of God and the seed are so closely associated. God's word is the seed, for this was the promise that he made to Eve in Gen. 3:15; and we know for a fact that the seed that came was Jesus Christ the only begotten son of God, our Saviour and redeemer.

TRIBULATION EQUALS IMPREGNATION EQUALS TRAVAIL (OR BIRTH PANGS): (JER. 30:5-10; ISA. 66:7-9)

"For thus saith the LORD; we have heard a voice of trembling, of fear, and not of peace. Ask ye now, and see whether a man doth travail with child? Wherefore do I see every man with his hands on his loins, as a woman in travail, and all faces are turned into paleness? Alas! For that day is great, so that none is like it: it is even the time of Jacob's trouble, but he shall be saved out of it. For it shall come to pass in that day, saith the LORD of hosts, that I will break his yoke from off thy neck, and will burst thy bonds, and strangers shall no more serve themselves of him: But they shall serve the LORD their God, and David their king, whom I will raise up unto them. Therefore fear thou not, O my servant Jacob, saith the LORD; neither be dismayed, O Israel: for, lo, I will save thee from afar, and thy seed from the land of their captivity; and Jacob shall return, and shall be in rest, and be quiet, and none shall make him afraid." (Jer.30:5-10; Isa. 66:7-8; Dan.7:23-27; 8:9-14, 23-26; 9:27; 11:40-45; 12:1,7; Micah 5:3; Zech.12:10-14:21; Rom.11:25-27; Matt.24:15-22).

MOSES AND ELIJAH TAUGHT SPIRITUAL IMPARTATION (IMPREGNATION): (NUM.11:16-17, 25-29)

Spiritual impartation (impregnation) is clearly taught throughout the Old Testament. However, because of a male dominated society and because women were not allowed to speak in public, especially of intimate things, this freedom of expression was not given to them. God said to Moses: 'Take of thy spirit...and put upon them' (Num. 11:16-17, 25-29). The Spirit 'upon' them here is the same as the Spirit 'within' them in the New Testament. Jesus said that:

"If any man thirst let him come unto me, and drink. He that believeth on me, as the scripture hath said, out of his belly shall flow rivers of living water. (But this spake he of the Spirit, which they that believe on him should receive: for the Holy Ghost was not yet given; because that Jesus was not yet glorified.)" (John 7:37-39).

Note that Jesus quoted the scriptures. Well there could only be the Old Testament scriptures. So the Spirit would be 'in them' as Jesus stated in John 14:16-17:

"And I will pray the Father, and he shall give you another Comforter, that he may abide with you forever; even the Spirit of truth; who the world cannot receive, because it seeth him not, neither knoweth him: but ye know him; for he dwelleth with you, and shall be in you."
If a woman was allowed this freedom and the ability to be a leader, the 'spirit upon them' or

'within them', to her would clearly have come to mean impregnation. She would've understood it in the same manner as 'the spirit coming upon Mary and she was found with child' in Luke 1:27-38. Women understand things differently. She was created with a womb and to her was to **'CARRY'** or **'BARE'** seed which eventually produced children. So in many cases this is how a woman thinks….**IMPREGNATION!** And all truth is parallel.

Elijah IMPARTED of his anointing to Elisha: (2 Kings Chap 2:1-15)

THE WRONG KIND OF SPIRITUAL IMPREGNATION: (1COR.6:15-20)

In the book of first Corinthians (6:15-20) Paul warns against spiritual fornication and the wrong kind of impregnation. He never said that spiritual impregnation was wrong, he simply warned against becoming 'ONE FLESH' with a harlot. So strong was this belief of Paul's that he compared it the same as being joined unto the Lord and becoming 'ONE SPIRIT' (1Cor.6:17).

Observe: NOTICE THAT PAUL SAYS 'ONE FLESH' WITH THE HARLOT; YET THE 'ONE FLESH' IS THE SAME AS BECOME 'ONE SPIRIT' WITH THE LORD OR THE SAME AS BECOMING 'ONE FLESH' AS IS THE CASE OF A MAN AND A WOMAN IN MARRIAGE (Gen.2:24)**.**

If sexual intercourse with a harlot leads to becoming 'one spirit' with her, then the opposite is also true of spiritual impregnation of a Hand Maid of God. As we, in the church believe, that you can be 'connected' with the spirits of others. For example we believe that if your partner sleeps with many people, then you are joined with those spirits. Why do we believe this? Because we believe in 'SPIRITUAL INTERPENETRATION'; THE ENTERING IN OF ONE STRONGER SPIRIT INTO THE WEAKER SPIRIT OF ANOTHER.

Satan entered Judas in Luke 22:3; the legion of demons entered the pigs in Luke 8:26-39; and the fact that Jesus said when a man's house is swept and clean, the devil that left returns to see it clean with seven devils more and the end of that man is worse than the beginning (Luke 11:24-26).

THEREFORE, IF SPIRITUAL 'IMPARTATION' IS REAL AND IF SPIRITUAL 'INTERPENETRATION' IS REAL; WHY NOT SPIRITUAL 'IMPREGNATION'?

Clearly Paul was addressing a spiritual condition here and not a natural.

THE SONS OF GOD AND SPIRITUAL IMPREGNATION: (Gen.6:1-7)

Clearly this is a unique development of spiritual invading the natural. Sons of God (angels) looking upon the daughters of men (Adam's race) AND SAW THAT THEY WERE FAIR and took wives unto themselves and having children by them. Spiritual beings desiring natural women. Whether through possessing men's bodies as Satan did the serpent we do not know; or did they take the form of men as did the angels who visited Abraham (Gen.19) and Lot (Gen.19) we cannot say. But this we do know that these same angels which kept not their first estate are reserved in chains of darkness, to be reserved unto judgment (1 Pet.3:18-20; 2 Pet. 2:4). We know that this is the time of Noah because Peter goes on to explain the flood in 2 Pet.2:5; and also in 1 pet.3:19-21; and compares their sins to that of Sodom and Gomorrah (2 Pet.2:6-9); which sin was that they left 'the natural use of the woman, burned in their lust one toward another; men with men working that which is unseemingly,' according to Romans 1:27. The angels left their Spiritual state and impregnated natural 'daughters of men', just as the men of Sodom left their 'natural use of the woman'. All truth is parallel. Hence angels understood 'SPIRITUAL IMPREGNATION'

However the truth is still relative. If spirit beings can impregnate natural beings to contaminate the pure seed of God-thus resulting in a breed of Giants, then spiritual impregnation is indeed a fact. These Sons of God left God's order of things to imitate God's program of bringing the seed of the woman into the earth (for Satan is an imitator of God). According to Peter, these same angels who kept not their first estate are reserved in chains :"...(2 Pet. 2:4)

Let's be real if the Holy Spirit can impregnate a natural virgin, would not Satan try the same? And if spiritual impregnation of the actual Word of God-Jesus took place; cannot then the spiritual impregnation of God's Hand Maids take place with the Rhema Word of God? And if the creation groans and travails to bring forth, cannot also the daughters of Zion? This is so, my son: 'That the righteousness of the law might be fulfilled in us, who walk not after the flesh, but after the Spirit. For they that are after the flesh do mind the things of the flesh; but they that are after the Spirit the things of the Spirit. For to be carnally minded is death; but to be spiritually minded is life and peace. Because the carnal mind is enmity against God: for it is not subject to the law of God, neither indeed can be. So then they that are in the flesh cannot please God.'(Rom.8:4-8).

Dakes confirms that these **'SONS OF GOD' WERE INDEED ANGELS**!

"Seth did not have a son until 235 years after creation; and his son did not have a son until 325 years after creation (Gen.5:3,6,9). Where did these SONS come from? They could not have been sons of Seth, for these marriages took place when men began to multiply – in the very beginning of the race before Seth had sons of marriageable age. The term 'sons of God' proves that they were the product of God, not Seth. They were the fallen angels of 1 Pet. 3:19; 2 Pet. 2:4; Jude 6-7."
This fact is also confirmed in the Septuagint; Josephus, page 36; Ante-Nicene Fathers, Vol.VIII, page 273; and Giants and sons of God page 62.

THE ERROR OF SODDOM AND GOMORRAH:
(Gen.18:16-33)

God destroyed the men of Sodom and Gomorrah, not simply because they were Homosexual(although this was a part of it) but more so because "...likewise also the men, leaving the natural use of the woman (which was to give life to seed, thus replenishing the earth), burned in their lust one toward another; men with men working that which is unseemly(contaminating and wrongfully spilling the seed which God had designed to enter into the womb of a woman and die, thus bringing life(John 14:24), and receiving in themselves that recompense of their error which was meet"(Rom.1:27).The Greek word for 'error' used here in Romans 1:27 is: **'Plane, wondering – wrong action'.** The men of Sodom took a wrong action, contrary to nature and God's divine order of things. A man was not designed to produce life; he was designed to be a seed giver. **SEED WRONGFULLY PLACE BECOMES CONTAMINATED**. Homosexuality is an abomination because it contaminated the plans of God and goes against nature.

THREE THINGS HAPPENED:

    i. They dishonored their bodies (Rom.1:24)
    ii. They took on vile affections in their souls (Rom.1:26)
    iii. Their minds became reprobate (Rom.1:28)

THE QUESTION IS: WAS THERE NO GAY OR LESBIAN WOMEN IN SODOM AND GOMORRAH? WERE THERE NO GAY AND LESBIAN WOMEN IN THE WORLD? AND IF SO, WHY DID THE BIBLE NOT SAY THAT GOD DESTROYED THEM ALSO?

We know that there were Gay and Lesbian women. Romans 1:26 tells us so: "for even their women did change the natural use into that which is against nature:"

THEY WERE SLEEPING WITH THE SAME SEX. THE DIFFERENCE IS, THAT EVEN A GAY WOMAN CAN STILL PRODUCE CHILDREN...SHE CAN STILL CARRY OUT HER PURPOSE (AS WE SEE TODAY SO MANY WOMEN THAT ARE GAY STILL DESIRE TO HAVE CHILDREN). GAY MEN CANNOT PRODUCE CHILDREN NO MATTER HOW MUCH SEED YOU PUT INTO THEM. LESBIAN WOMEN CAN AT THE DROP OF A SEED. THUS THE MATTER OF CONTAMINATION AND DOING THAT WHICH IS AGAINST NATURE. NO WHERE IN THE TEXT OF SCRIPTURE DO WE SEE GOD DESTROYING WOMEN BECAUSE THEY WERE LESBIANS!

LET'S CONCLUDE:

SPIRITUL IMPREGNATION IS CLEARLY TAUGHT IN THE SCRIPTURES. WE MAY NOT WANT TO ACKNOWLEDGE IT, BUT IT IS CLEARLY SEEN. OPEN OUR MINDS AND SPIRITS TO THE SPIRIT OF GOD. IF WITCHES AND DEMONS EXIST AND THEY POSSES PEOPLE, THEN SPIRITS (GOOD OR BAD) CAN STILL IMPREGNATE, JUST BE CAREFUL WHO IMPREGNATES YOU!

CHAPTER TWO

BIRTHING YOUR GIFT:
"BELIEVING IT…CONCEIVES IT!"

MIRACLES ARE LIKE GIVING BIRTH. You have the capacity to BIRTH YOUR GIFT….BIRTH YOUR MIRACLE! There was an old saying among Christians when I came into the church in the seventies: "IF YOU CAN BELIEVE IT…YOU CAN CONCEIVE IT!

"Who hath heard such a thing/ who hath seen such things? Shall the earth be made to bring forth in one day? Or shall a nation be born at once? For as soon as Zion travailed, she brought forth her children.
Shall I bring to the birth, and not cause to bring forth? Saith the LORD: shall I cause to bring forth, and shut the womb? Saith thy God?"(Isa.66:8-9).

THE INTIMACY OF GOD IS REFLECTED IN THE INTIMACY OF MAN AND WOMAN. THE FAITH OF GOD IS REFLECTED THROUGH HIS CHURCH, THE WIFE OF JESUS CHRIST. THIS IS THE MYSTERY OF ONE FLESH.

CHAPTER TWO

BIRTHING YOUR GIFT: - "BELIEVING IT...CONCEIVES IT!"

Miracles are like giving birth. You have the capacity to BIRTH YOUR GIFT....BIRTH YOUR MIRACLE! There was an old saying among Christians when I came into the church in the seventies: "IF YOU CAN BELIEVE IT...YOU CAN CONCEIVE IT!" Faith is the impregnation process..."except a grain of wheat fall into the ground..." Jesus said! "If ye have faith as a grain of mustard seed..." He further said! Then ye shall ask what you will and it shall be done unto you! So faith is the seed that begins the birthing process. The earth or your spirit man or woman is the ground into which the seed of faith is planted and it is there, within your heart a thing is conceived. It's up to you what!

Once the grain of seed falls into the ground, then it begins a process of germination...acts of faith are like germination. The more we see God do, the more we believe. The more we see faith in action or read of great acts of God, the sharper our faith becomes...germination has taken place. This 'little' grain of wheat has begun to produce life. And just like within the womb of a woman, you are now beginning an incubation period...THE BIRTHING OF YOUR GIFT OR MIRACLE!

THE INTIMACY OF GOD IS REFLECTED IN THE INTIMACY OF MAN AND WOMAN. THE FAITH OF GOD IS REFLECTED THROUGH HIS

CHURCH, THE WIFE OF JESUS CHRIST. THIS IS THE MYSTERY OF ONE FLESH.

GOD IMPREGNATED THE EARTH WITH HIMSELF: (Gen. 1:2)

God looked upon the earth in genesis chapter one, and saw that it was "without form and void". So God became pregnant with an idea, "WHAT IF I CAN RECREATE THE PROCESS...GIVE BIRTH TO NEWNESS AND BRING ABOUT A NEW BABY?" So God himself hovered over the face of the deep and God himself impregnated the earth with himself and began the birthing Process. The Bible says: "......and the Spirit of God moved upon the face of the waters."(Gen.1:2). The act of moving here is the same act that the angel of the Lord told Mary the virgin in Luke chapter 1:35; "......The Holy Ghost Shall come upon thee, and the power of the Highest shall over shadow thee..." THE PROCESS OF IMPREGNATION! So God impregnated the earth as he impregnated the Virgin Mary and the result in both cases ended up in the birthing of life.

GOD IMPREGNATED ADAM AND EVE WITH HIMSELF: (Gen.1:26-31)

THE BIBLE SAYS:

"And God said; let us make man in our image, after our likeness: and let them have dominion over the fish of the sea, and over the fowl of the air, and over the cattle, and over all the

earth, and over every creeping thing that creepeth upon the earth.
So god created man in his own image, in the image of god created he him; male and female created he them.
And God blessed them, and God said unto them, be fruitful, and multiply, and replenish the earth, and subdue it: and have dominion over the fish of the sea, and over the fowl of the air, and over every living thing that moveth upon the earth.
And God said, behold, I have given you every herb bearing seed, which is upon the face of all the earth, and every tree, in the which is the fruit of a tree yielding seed; to you it shall be for meat.
And to every beast of the earth, and to every fowl of the air, and to everything that creepeth upon the earth, wherein is life, I have given every green herb for meat: and it was so." (Gen.1:26-31)

Observe what God did in this process; Gen.1:27 says: "So God created man in his own image, in the image of God created he him; male and female created he them". God birthed himself into a male and female and put within them the power to birth after their kind. But let's look deeper at this. Romans 3:23 says that: "For all have sinned, and come short of the Glory of God". So if man came 'short' of something, then it must mean that he was 'full' of that something before. Man had the full 'Glory of God' before sin entered the world. God made Adam and Eve just like himself…. "in our image, after our likeness…"(Gen.1:26). Therefore if God has the capacity to 'hover'

over the face of the deep and recreate life; if he is the God which calleth those things which be not as though they were (Rom.4:17); if he can bring to the birth and cause to come forth (Isa.66; 8-9) then you and I, created in his image and likeness, now returned to the glory, can do the same. Here's how Isaiah puts it:

"Who hath heard such a thing/ who hath seen such things? Shall the earth be made to bring forth in one day? Or shall a nation be born at once? For as soon as Zion travailed, she brought forth her children.
Shall I bring to the birth, and not cause to bring forth? Saith the LORD: shall I cause to bring forth, and shut the womb? Saith thy God?"(Isa.66:8-9).

God has spoken...Isaiah has declared;
`…..SHALL I CAUSE TO BRING FORTH, AND SHUT THE WOMB? The answer is 'NO'! If you can believe it ...you can conceive it! God put within man the capacity to create and to bring forth and to birth, both naturally and spiritually. He gave the man and the woman a seed within themselves bearing fruit. He said: "Be fruitful, and multiply, and replenish the earth, and subdue it :"(Gen.1:28). All of these being creative powers to produce life and bring to birth anything possible. BIRTH YOU GIFT OR MIRACLE!

GOD IMPREGNATES MAN (ADAM) WITH HIMSELF: (Gen.2:7)

"HOW DID God impregnate man with himself"? You may ask.

A great question, so let's take a look! There are two occasions where we see God performing an act of creation or birthing upon the man. First it was when he created or birthed forth the first man (without a womb) Adam. Observe:

"And the LORD God formed man of the dust of the ground, and breathed into his nostrils the breath of life; and man became a living soul."(Gen.2:7)

The 'Lord God formed", **heb, yatsar**, to mould or squeeze into shape as a potter does. This means, that God began AN ACT OF FAITH...AN ACT OF BIRTHING...AN ACT OF CREATION! God saw something and he began to give birth to it. He saw himself in the image of a man that could serve him and glorify him. In the same manner we see our miracle; we see our healing; we see our gift already formed in our spirits, because that is who we first our. We see like God sees we see in the spirit. The problem now becomes as to how we birth it forth into the natural. 'Of the dust of the ground"; **heb, aphar, mud, rubbish, earth, ashes, powder.** So God took dust or rubbish and saw the great possibility of life. He saw a thing of beauty...no wonder he gives beauty for ashes (Isa.61:3)! See the gift...find the rubbish...look at the dust ....take the powder and create a beautiful gift, create a miracle and you would know, and only you alone that this was your baby…your child! "And breathed into"….AN ACT OF IMPREGNATION! The heb word used here is **naphach**, to breathe out, puff, inflate, and blow hard. These are all words that denote an action. So God impregnated man with himself; he breathed into or blew hard as in an act of love making the sperm of the spirit, if you please. Look at the previous act of God "And the Spirit of God moved…" (Gen.1:2; **heb, rachaph**, to brood, relax, and flutter; similar to **naphach**); and the future act of God as in the case of Mary "….and the power of the highest shall overshadow thee ;"(Luke 1:35). Each of these act resulted in an act of creation or birthing. It stands to reason therefore that God impregnated Adam with himself, and put within Adam all the creative forces necessary to produce or birth forth anything that he saw fit to the glory of God. God gave him dominion over all things….INCLUDING BIRTHING HIS GIFTS!

GOD IMPREGNATES ADAM WITH EVE: (Gen2:21-25)

The second most dynamic impregnation of God that resulted in birthing forth was the creation of Eve, perhaps God's most impressive creation of the two. Within this man God decided to put a womb-the capacity to conceive and incubate life until it came to birth. We must first understand that God is Spirit and all that he does is in the spirit. Man is first spirit and then flesh but because of sin, we think only in the flesh and this is not how

God intended it to be. "God is a Spirit: and they that worship him must worship him in spirit and in truth" so says John 4:24. Therefore if we see Spirit we know that nothing is impossible, God is Spirit and he does the impossible….we are first spirit, therefore we can do the impossible….BIRTH FORTH YOUR GIFT!

"And the Lord God caused a deep sleep to fall upon Adam, and he slept: and he took one of his ribs, and closed up the flesh instead thereof;" (Gen.2:21)

The first operation ever… "God caused….he took"! The man was asleep and God began the process of birthing another man. Look into the spirit to see the actual process. Remember God had just breathed into Adam the breath of life and Adam became a living soul. Now for a brief moment God wanted to perform another miracle, another birthing, another life. SO HE USED THE LIFE OF ONE TO CREATE THE LIFE OF ANOTHER! EVERYTHING YOU NEED TO CREATE YOUR MIRACLE, EVERYTHING YOU NEED TO BRING TO BIRTH YOUR GIFT IS ALREADY INSIDE OF YOU. Just follow God's example. Take of that which you know and form another of its kind, give it a womb so that you can continue to give birth to the next thing…THIS IS THE GENIUS OF GOD!

"And the rib….made he a woman…" MAN WITH A WOMB! The reason for and the process of creation. The reason for and the process for birthing! The reason for and the process of incubating a thing! The reason for and the process of bringing to birth and causing to come forth....WOMAN! She was God's greatest and most beautiful creation, EVE! When Adam saw her he knew that she had come from him, but more than that he knew that he had been impregnated with her and she had been impregnated with him.

"And Adam said, this is now bone of my bones, and flesh of my flesh: she shall be called woman (womb man), because she was taken out of man."

One birthed the other so that the other could birth from hence forth. This truth is found in the fact that after the fall, Adam knew that he would have to depend on eve to be the birth vessel...the procreator...the incubator of all his faith and future...the one to whom he was go to plant a grain of wheat into so that it may die and bring forth life...SHE WAS CALLED EVE AFTER THE FALL... "And Adam called his wife's name Eve; because she was the mother of all living."
WOW! HE PREDICTED AND SAW IT, EVEN BEFORE IT WAS AND THAT IS THE FAITH OF GOD WHICH CALLETH THOSE THINGS WHICH BE NOT AS THOUGH THEY ARE!

Women tend to understand spiritual impregnation and birthing far better than men, mainly because of the fact that they possess a womb. The woman possess the female essence of the man God created even though God did make them one:

"Therefore shall a man leave his father and his mother, and shall cleave unto his wife: and they shall be one flesh" (Gen.2:24)

This is the greatest mystery of birthing of all. How can two become one flesh? The act of love making is a divine act; just like faith is a divine act. It comes from God. When a man and a woman come together in the bonds of holy matrimony it is for the purpose of worshipping God in the greatest act of worship known to mankind. So sacred is this that Paul compared the Church as the bride of Christ and the relationship as a marriage. THE INTIMACY OF GOD IS REFLECTED IN THE INTIMACY OF MAN AND WOMAN. THE FAITH OF GOD IS REFLECTED THROUGH HIS CHURCH, THE WIFE OF JESUS CHRIST. THIS IS THE MYSTERY OF ONE FLESH. Man and woman coming together in an act of lovemaking, resulting in a creation...a child! This child carries within himself the same gene pool of the father and the mother, who carry the gene pool of Adam, who carries the gene pool of God. We therefore become the tools by which God purposes to produce and birth forth. No other creation of God has this ability. Not even Angels. ANGELS DON'T NEED FAITH, THEY LIVE IN THE GLORY!

You have come to the birth and like Mary said to the Angel, 'how can these things be, seeing that I know not a man?" you probably ask the same question. Look deep within. You have been pregnant for quite a while now, and you have come to birth feel the process...see the signs of your pregnancy...look at your gift and ask how do I bring it forth? Within you is the seed of life...the nature of God. You are his child; created in his own image and likeness...DO AS GOD DOES...BRING TO BIRTH AND CAUSE TO COME FORTH

THE BIRTHING OF A HAND MAID:

"And Mary said, Behold the handmaid of the Lord; be it unto me according to thy word....and on my handmaidens I will pour out in those days of my Spirit; and they shall prophesy."(Luke 1:38; Acts 2:18).

"My son, a Hand Maiden (Maid at hand) is one given to a mistress to do and fulfill the complete will and bidding of that mistress. Anything asked of her or demanded of her by the mistress she was under total obligation to perform. The word of the Master or Mistress was law. As in the case of Hagar, it was no problem for her to obey Sarai in bearing a son for Abram. This was her duty. Custom dictated every action and there was never any thought not to obey. As in the case of the hand maids of Rachael and Leah, it was their understanding that they were seed producers. It was their responsibility to bear children in the stead of their mistresses. There was never a thought that they would do otherwise. The Virgin Mary was the ultimate Hand maiden. When the angel declared that she would bear the son of God (the seed word) it was no problem for her to obey. She knew the responsibility of the Hand Maiden. She declared: 'so be it according to your word'. Despite her disposition and betrothal to Joseph, she valued the duty of Hand Maiden. 'In the last days I will pour out my Spirit...upon my

Hand Maids...and they shall prophecy. To be a Hand Maid is to be a PRODUCER, PRO CREATOR, and PROPHETESS-one who brings to life or one who prophesies forth the word of God. All truth is parallel. As is the natural, so is the Spiritual. Mary PRODUCED; PRO CREATED; PROPHESIED forth the actual word of God, Jesus my only begotten son. She gave life and prophesied forth the actual word of God, Jesus. The word of God in the spiritual sense is still being birthed forth or PROPHESIED by my Hand Maids today. This was spoken by Joel the Prophet and declared to be truth by Peter the Apostle in the book of Acts Chapter 2:18. All truth is parallel. As is the natural, so is the spiritual." **Prophetic word: 02-20-10/11:30am**

WHAT IS A HANDMAID?

A HANDMAID IS A BOND MAID (Gen. 16:1-6 with Gen. 21:9-12; Gal.4:22-24). It is mentioned, HANDMAID, forty five times in scripture; HANDMAIDEN, one time (Luke 1:48); HANDMAIDENS, three times (Gen.33:6; Ruth 2:13; Acts 2:18); HANDMAIDS, eight times (Gen.33:1-2; 2 Sam. 6:20; Isa.14:2; Jer.34:11, 16; Joel 2:29).

1. Handmaid of Sarah: (Gen.16:1; 25:12)
2. Handmaid of Leah: (Gen. 29:24; 35:26)
3. Handmaid of Rachael: (Gen.29:29; 30:4; 35:25)
4. Handmaid of the Lord: (Luke 1:38)

THE HANDMAIDEN'S PATH AND BURDEN:

"LORD, I pray that we might be empowered with wisdom from on high specifically to walk out this journey circumspectly, not as fools but as wise redeeming the time. I pray we do our part to stay in position, to walk under an open heaven that ...you have provided. To give forth rain abundantly, and oil to make our face to shine through the night seasons of our lives. In Jesus name!" – **August 14, 2010 @ 12:44pm**

"Thank you Dr. Simmons for pushing me to look at how I'm walking through posting what God instructs. See More Nevertheless, there were (2) points I wanted to make in regards to Dr. Simmons use of... the word strait, that made me ponder the birthing process. And the process God designed to reconcile us to himself.

(1) THE PATH AN INFANT MUST TAKE TO ENTER LIFE.

First: Often as Christian's we go through a period of struggling with who we are because we don't look like ourselves right away. It's during those stages many believers are aborted just like the fetus in the womb, because its value is not measured as priceless. Despite the risk the infant will face through unwise midwives standing in the mouth of the way. The infant's greatest challenge will be growing up.
God has provided for the church to move the babe from A- to-Z, so the child will be in

position to enter the next season of its life, which is not optional. There comes a point in our lives when we have to move to the next level or we become over ripe on the vine. The harvest is white (ripe) already. Overdue on the vine. Because folks are not moving along the continuum of life spiritually. Many have become complacent with carnality.

(2) THE BURDEN A CAMEL HAD TO UNLOAD IN ORDER TO ENTER THE GATES OF THE CITY.

The second point was just to share a historical throw back from my biblical visits to Jerusalem. How that a traveler coming into a city would have his camel loaded with his goods. But after the city gates were closed for the night, to ensure the safety of the city's inhabitants, travelers looking for lodging would have to unload their beast of burden and have them lower down (a humbling position literally); Yet needful for them to come through a narrow gate way. That common practice shed much light for me on why Jesus said it would be easier for a camel to go through the eye of a needle than for a rich man to enter the Kingdom of Heaven. ["Rich man" is indicative of attitude for the purpose of this point]. Rich in opinions, values and traditions as we all are naturally. But the richness of our state of mind should never supersede the mind of Christ that was shapened in humility when he had to come model how to overcome the birthing process to be birthed according to God's will spiritually (Luke 4:14).

We have been raised to carry baggage. We often carry a lot of baggage and we can't carry that stuff with us to where God is trying to take us. "Stuff" has the ability to hinder us from crossing over into the abundant life Jesus died for us to have. So we must learn to cast our cares -those goods we have packed, to the side of the road. So we can run the race set before us. Even Jesus had been set up, purposed by God to be led by the Spirit.

It's no different than the gate that was set before the camel; and the birth canal set before the infant. This was not set by the parent of the child or the owner of the camel. But the God who said "the earth is the Lord's and the fullness thereof and all they that dwell therein". The gate being there is not of our doing. The opening of the gate is not by our might. But to be ready to move when the birthing begins is key to defeating "Stillbirth's" in the body of Christ.

It's time to step outside our comfort zone. Into a God zone were we have to be led by the Spirit to overcome our number one enemy "Self" (not for nothing, God said a man's foes would be those of his own household, I'm just saying). This birthing puzzled Nicodemus, and the birthing process puzzled the five foolish virgins and continues to puzzle Christians today. And I believe it's because of our perspective. We think we're okay. But we can't continue, to see believers go through "C"-section deliveries verses natural deliveries. Because the children have come to the birth, without strength to push through, because of the, STRAIT / NARROWNESS of the Way they must come!

WE MUST TRAIN UP THE BRIDE OF CHRIST FOR DELIVERY.

I thank God for the 5-fold ministry gifts to the body. Set up by God for the development of his seed. Thank you doc for following in the footsteps of Jesus the great physician. And many thanks to my brothers and sisters who are ensuring we have enough oil, while we are able to share and make a difference for anyone who may need to run and make a purchase now- in Jesus name. - **August 14th 2010 @6:12pm**

THE CASE OF WENDY YOUNG:

"Woman of God, Wendy:
I sense the time of your conception and spiritual birthing is at hand…begin preparing the nursery for you shall bring forth! **Dr. Randy E. Simmons August 8th 2010 @6:57pm**

"Speechless… (Full)…my life is in HIS Hands…thank you sir. Already I know the LORD; my Lord is working with me…Jer. 9:17-24; Mark 16:15-20; Deut.32:1-3.
Shalom, Shalom….**Wendy Young August 8th 2010 @8:32pm**

"Dearest woman of God, hand maid…for this is who you are. Think upon all that he has been showing you. Look deep within the spirit and under the pull that is in your heart. Sense this your time of conception and then ask: "what is it you desire of your Hand Maid in this season?" Then remember the prophecy of Joel chapter two and reinforced in Act 2:18 by the Apostle Peter. There you will find your answers. What you are birthing is greater and bigger than you realize. This is the day of "greater works" that Jesus spoke about in John 14:12. You dear Hand Maid are birthing "Greater Works"! -**Dr. Randy E. Simmons August 8th 2010 @8:44pm**

"Greeting's Dr. Simmons. I am honored to have you in my life. I have pondered our FB interaction and the doors of fellowship that have been opened. That may sound trivial but it's not.

Mary pondered what the angel said to her because it would have a significant impact on her life. So much so God intervened to speak to Joseph who had to be instructed not to put her away. God was planning a big move through her, and all he needed was her willingness to have the Christ child and call him Jesus.

As I ponder what has been spoken over my life. The under current (pull) has always been "will you" & "if you". And lately I am burdened with a personal call to fast that is followed by this question:

'If you knew you were going to die what would you be doing? Do it. If you only had several more days to live? What would you be doing? Do it! What do you love doing more than anything else in life? Do it! Talk! Talk! Talk! Open your mouth and I will fill it!'

Doc that's the pull. I am alive literally "only" when I am talking about God. Outside of that, I live a mere existence of life. I work, eat, sleep, write poetry for open mic and serve in the church, when I'm not taking classes; I live out a structured routine. It's a good life. But it's not life, I feel like Joseph in captivity. Please understand I am not complaining about my life. Many feel I am blessed. What they can't see, is the me I see inside. I see in me another life, I see a person that talks freely through various modes with people from all walks of life. This seems contradictory to me, because I am often challenged with what to say.

Doc, I was led to share this with you for (2) reasons.

1. To confess my anxiety about talking, thus breaking its yoke. I talk a lot but apparently not enough for God.

2. To step out on faith and follow God's leading.

Months ago the words "You Are a Golden Goose" dropped into my spirit man. I believed God was telling me how he would be providing for me. Doc, I am salary, 50+ years of age with no turning back spirit. Pray for me! As I step out of my comfort zone. Bear with me. Becoming pregnant prior to marriage was Mary's storm. Reality is my storm...I am seeking to wake up the Jesus in me...and he is telling me to speak to the storm of doubt, by faith. Doc, does this make sense? Because talking is time consuming. But God views it as seedtime that will yield a harvest. I don't want to let God down, or try to figure out the how to's. I want the manifested demonstration of obedience in my life regarding the will of God uttered to me. And clarity to distinguish his will from my zeal. So as not to mess up. Man of God I've said a lot and I'm not sure if it's crossed from my heart through this text accurately. Nevertheless, I pray my honesty and openness has spoiled the devil...in Jesus name who has promised to fulfill Mark 16:20 with me." -**Wendy Young: August 13 2010 @9:31pm**

"WOG Wendy;

For two day now I've sat and pondered how to reply to you. I feel the pull of your spirit woman. Your uncertainty is so noted. Mary knew her purpose, yet in flesh and reason she asked the angel: "how can these things be seeing that I know no man?" His reply: "The Holy Ghost shall come upon thee, and the power of the Highest shall overshadow thee...For with God nothing shall be impossible."(Lk.1:35, 37).

My dear Wendy, the questions that you ask are reasonable for man or woman in the natural and to distinguish from zeal to anointing is so very important. The Holy Spirit shall come upon you. The will of God is our highest and most honored thing that we can offer to him. It is with this in mind that God chooses us. Ask the question of yourself; 'were there no other virgins in Israel in the days of Mary?' I'm sure there were, but she was chosen because she had made herself a Hand Maid of the Lord. This

is as you are. Think of the times you sought him.
Ponder the experiences that you've had in the secret chambers of your closet and heart. Ponder the times when the anointing came upon you and you felt as if in your belly you were pregnant. You were. God was even then planting a grain of wheat into the ground of your spirit woman that it may die and bring forth much fruit. Even then you pondered, as did Mary: 'what meaneth these things?'

Yes and the rational person that you are, you will continue the debate.
Therefore I say to you ask of the Lord a sign. And I will answer you as did Isaiah: 'ask thee a sign of the Lord thy God; ask it either in the depth, or in the height above...Therefore the Lord himself shall give you a sign; behold a virgin shall conceive, and bear a son, and shall call his name Immanuel.'(Isa. 7:14). You my dear handmaid are a spiritual virgin. You shall conceive and you shall birth the gift. Ponder now these things;" -**Dr. Randy E. Simmons**: **August 15th 2010@3:12pm**

"Dear Dr. Simmons, your labor of luv has not been wasted. I thank God for you. You are an answer to repeated prayers I have made to God regarding fellowship of the body. Awkward as it may be God is teaching me transparency. He is desirous of HIS light getting through me. I have been challenged with how to let my inner light shine before men that they might see God, and glorify him. Yet my (developed) opaque views were preventing the flow of light that glowed naturally within me. Let me take a moment to share: I felt it was a person's prerogative to go to hell, if they so choose. But God has caused me to see that many are ignorant of the choices they were and are making. Many people make decisions based on the desires of the flesh, designed to satisfy their earth suit (body), not their soul or spirit man.

To get past my disdain for stupidity GOD had to do a work in my heart to develop compassion, kinda like what he did with Jonah (Jonah 4:1-4) this was my dialogue with God for real. I was tired of sin and its effect on the life of me and others. I was disgusted with Christians afraid to tell the truth about sin because of their net profit in carnality, as they fed the babes with a milky alternative substance of the Gospel promoting mixed messages. Messages about sinning saints that had purchased "Life Assurance with Fire protection coverage."

I couldn't understand why God had impregnated me with seed Word for people he was okay with. Doc, I'm just keeping it real. These were my thoughts; till, like Jonah I was thrown out of life, arrested by the will of God. Pregnant with purpose, confused about the difference I could make in a lost and dying world; and it was during my state of brokenness God made known to me the end of Jonah's story (4:6-11).

God does so love the world. He is not a lover or fan of the world's system that enslaves mankind. Nevertheless, because of Adam mankind is trapped in sin and influenced by the

~~king of this world, just like the people under the King of Nineveh. The difference is Satan has committed the unpardonable sin, and God has chosen to give mankind a second chance under the second Adam, King Jesus.~~

So God's question to me was "Wendy, should I not spare sinful mankind. Persons that cannot discern between their right hand and their left hand; ignorant of the truth, lacking knowledge as were you and many other believers who were sold out to sin through lack of knowledge?"

God helped me realize just like the knowledge impregnated in Jonah, that Jonah was unable to abort, changed the course of the Ninevite people so shall what HE placed in my belly. Out of my belly shall flow rivers of living waters so that His people can make intelligent decisions to live and not die.

Doc, like Jonah I sought to abort this baby due to rejection because I did not have a title, nor did I fit the mold. Trust me when I say, I wanted to fit the mold. What God would have me say often made me an outcast. Needless to say I was humbled by rejection, and hardened by self-pity. So I purposed in my heart (for which I have since repented of that) I would be a single mother and raise this child just as I had my natural babies. There was just one huge problem. God was not an absentee Father. He would not let me dismiss him. This was his baby and he would raise his child. (tears...what kind of love is this! I was soon to learn.)

Doc, I don't think more highly of myself than I ought. Yet I believe all things are possible with God and to those that will believe, the Word of GOD. I no longer run from God but to him. You are right about many things. You have spoken into my life and I will ponder what God gave you to say to me, till God is satisfied that it has watered his seed. I acknowledge Fatherhood and the anointing that comes with this season of my life. I am encouraged because not only did Mary find herself to be with child, God worked out the plans to ensure her safety and that of the child's that HIS will might be fulfilled on earth as it was and is being fulfilled in heaven.

God has chosen you to be his disciple, the one that he loves. You are being used as iron: "Iron sharpeneth iron; so a man sharpeneth the countenance of his friend". God is developing my tongue to be the pen of a ready writer. He has placed you as a sharpener. And that's not all. "As in water face answereth to face, so the heart of man to man." You and the ministry have a place in my heart. I will be honest with my interactions, and responses. Please, please never think I am being forward. If ever I say something you are challenged by, please just tell me to chill out; also, so that you and Prophetess Dee may know. I have never spent this much time texting. Did I tell you I hate texting? Everybody that knows me knows that about me; but GOD has a way of having his way in every avenue of our lives. I am thankful to God he intercepted my closing the door to texting. It really is an awesome way to pour oil into his vessels. Oil to make

folks face to shine and bread (of life) to strengthen folks heart. GOD richly bless you and make your face like flint, ever pointed towards him for instructions to get to his warriors in the field (world) in Jesus name I pray. Your daughter in the body of Christ." –
Wendy Young: August 17 2010 @11:49am

CHAPTER THREE

SPIRITUAL INTERPENETRATION (IMPREGNATION) BIRTHING MOTHER-FATHER-MIDWIFE

SPIRITUAL INTERPENITRATION (IMPREGNATION):- When people of Like spirits connect, whether in the case of a harlot as Paul describes in the book of Corinthians (1 Cor.6:15-20); or when two people 'connect' in the spirit, we develop INTERPENETRATION. A Discourse or interaction between a Prophet and Prophetess can lead to the unfolding of great revelations and confirmations of the word of God; See Isaiah chapter eight and Hosea chapter one. Now I understand why my discussions at first with Holly sharp, after I had posted 'the table is prepared', led to such great revelations. She and I were like the husband and wife or mid-wives preparing the prophetess to be birthed. '….Shall be in him a well springing up into everlasting life", says Jesus in John 4:14. The woman at the well understanding this to be like a water bag said: "Sir, give me this water…." (John 4:15). Again the disciples on the road to Emmaus, "And they said one to another, did not our heart burn within us, while he talked with us by the way, and while he opened to us the scriptures?"(Luke 24:32)……EMOTIONAL INTERACTION!

CHAPTER THREE

SPIRITUAL INTERPENITRATION (IMPREGNATION) BIRTHING MOTHER-FATHER-MIDWIFE

BIRTH PARENTS: SPIRITUAL INTERPENITRATION

The DOCTRINE OF INTERPENETRATION in scriptures is persons entering into each other, as Paul said of Corinthians and Philippians being in his heart (2 Cor. 7:3; Phil. 1:7); God being in Christ (2 Cor. 5; 19); Christ being in God(John 14:20); God and Christ being in each other(Jn. 14:10-11); men being in both the Father and the son(1 Jn. 2:24); men being in Christ(2 Cor.5:17); Men and the spirit being in each other(Rom.8:9); Christ being in men(Col.1:27; Rom.8:10)men and Christ being in each other(Jn.14:20); all creation being in God(Acts 17:28); and Satan entering into men(Luke 22:3; John 13:27). It means in union with, consecration to the same end – one mind, purpose, and life, not bodily entrance into. It may be best understood by a man and a woman becoming one in life together, to be in each other's plans, life, etc. When people of Like spirits connect, whether in the case of a harlot as Paul describes in the book of Corinthians (1 Cor.6:15-20); or when two people 'connect' in the spirit, we develop INTERPENETRATION. A Discourse or interaction between a Prophet and Prophetess can lead to the unfolding of great revelations and confirmations of the word of God; See

Isaiah chapter eight and Hosea chapter one. Now I understand why my discussions at first with Holly sharp, after I had posted 'the table is prepared', led to such great revelations. She shared through private messages to me what she had gone through and the things God had shown and spoken to her. She and I were like the husband and wife or mid-wives preparing the prophetess to be birthed. '....Shall be in him a well springing up into everlasting life", says Jesus in John 4:14. The woman at the well understanding this to be like a water bag said: "Sir, give me this water...." (John 4:15). Again the disciples on the road to Emmaus, "And they said one to another, did not our heart burn within us, while he talked with us by the way, and while he opened to us the scriptures?"(Luke 24:32)......EMOTIONAL INTERACTION!

BIRTH PARENT-MOTHER: SPIRITUAL CONCEPTION

"Dr. Simmons ~ Thank you for your post, "I've been in the pit...I've known the prison...now to the palace." I wanted to share privately how that does touch my spirit. In 2003 as I lay in a hospital room under close and careful watch (without visitors allowed) because of a white blood count of "nil" the Holy Spirit spoke these words, "I HAVE TAKEN YOU FROM THE PRISON TO THE PALACE."

Your words reminded me of that moment....all alone, and all I could hear was what was happening outside of my door. The Lord spoke, "YOU ARE THE DAUGHTER OF THE KING AND

YOU NEED NOT FEAR, FOR AS THE DAUGHTER OF THE KING ALL THAT YOU NEED IS BEING TAKEN CARE OF. YOU DO NOT HAVE TO SEE IT, FOR IT IS STILL BEING TAKEN CARE OF. A PRINCESS, A DAUGHTER OF THE KING DOES NOT WORRY FOR HER FATHER IS THE KING AND ALL THAT YOU HAVE NEED OF IS IN HIS HAND AND AT HIS COMMAND. REST."

I just wanted to share that with the son of the King this morning. God bless you." -**Prophetess Holly Sharp. July 29th 2010**

BIRTH PARENT-FATHER: SPIRITUAL SEED GIVING

"My dear Prophetess Holly;

God bless you for such a profound and powerful word on this morning. Many times people don't know or understand the adversities that we sometimes face. July for me personally has been a month of testing, transitioning, and stretching but God has stood and has spoken. Some of the greatest whispers to my heart came within this month. I feel today such a shifting.

I was driving along the causeway from St. Simons Island yesterday (July 28th 2010) and a spirit of praise and a shout came upon me. I couldn't stop praising Jesus and declaring victory. Thank you for this word of encouragement and for your friendship. I value it dearly."
-**Dr. Randy E. Simmons July 29th 2010.**

BIRTH PARENT-MOTHER:
SPIRITUAL MORNING SICKNESS

"ALL who questions refocused me to the Lord. It was a beautiful experience. In my times of unrest and uncertainty there was never unrest or uncertainty in Him. Through it all I now understand that it has been a sanctification and consecration process. The alone time and the time of transition and experiencing things others didn't understand pushed me to press in closer to Him. It was the budding of a Prophet and I didn't know it. I just KNEW I was always different. So in all things, we give Praise. God is surrounding you even as you are unaware of His very presence...at times you are not even thinking on Him. He is orchestrating, putting people in place, shifting the atmosphere, causing a taking away and an adding to. He is multiplying by dividing. He is opening by closing. He is walking by teaching you to stand still...Ok...I shall stop for this moment..."-
Prophetess Holly Sharp July 29th 2010

BIRTH PARENT-FATHER:
THE FATHER'S AWAIT THE NEWS

"My dear Sister Holly;

The brilliance and prophetic utterance of a Prophetess of God is so welcomed. I have walk in the realm of the unknown, as you have so noted. People didn't understand, but that is the lot of a Prophet of God. Our mission: "TO SPEAK TRUTH TO POWER!"

Jeremiah understood this. Isaiah understood this. Elijah understood this. Malachi proclaims:

"Behold, I will send you Elijah the prophet before the coming of the great and dreadful day of the Lord: And he shall turn the heart of the fathers to the children, and the heart of the children to their fathers, lest I come and smite the earth with a curse."(Mal.4:5-6). Jesus recognized the spirit of Elijah upon John the Baptist. He came in the spirit and power of Elijah. He spoke of bringing forth fruit to repentance. What fruit are we birthing? Today America needs to understand the Prophetic office. I sense in the Spirit the unction upon you and through your words. My own anointing quickens. I see with eyes of wisdom and understand who you are and that which you carry. Bring forth woman of God. The children's hearts are waiting to be turned to the fathers. The fathers await the unction of the anointed seed yet to be birthed. Bring forth. Speak. Prophesy according to the prophecy of Joel and Peter: "...and on my Hand Maidens I will pour out in those days of my Spirit; and they shall prophesy :"(Acts 2:18). Prophesy...bring to birth. The fathers await!"

Dr. Randy E. Simmons July 29th 2010

BIRTH PARENT-MOTHER: SPIRITUAL BIRTH PAINS

"Holly, you are so intuitive" and I thought, hmmm. Ok, I am intuitive. Now there is a Godly understanding and I am humbled so much, and so relieved to know it has been God all these years. Dr. Simmons, there is much to be birthed and people are waiting. The birth pains are everywhere. It is also evident that some are experiencing a spiritual miscarriage, or even worse, a spiritual abortion. It is those who are in great need of healing. Some have lost all hope because of spiritual abuse; others have simply walked away and said I don't want it. We have to keep praying for them. We have to reveal truth to them. I so appreciate how solid you are in the Word of God. You speak the truth and you make it plain. Praise God! The distractions, the trials, the stretching are merely an opportunity to allow the garment of praise to fit perfectly as the Man of God wears it. You represent the Father and everything about Him is tailored to perfection. Made in His image, we accept the process and the fitting of the cloak He lays upon us."-**Prophetess Holly Sharp July 29th 2010**

BIRTH PARENT-FATHER: 'SEED' THE VISION

"Yes dear Prophetess.

So be it. "God will do nothing except he reveals his secrets to his servants the Prophets", so says Amos. I sense as my bowels of Prophetic instincts begin to turn, that you have been and continually stay within His presence. You know his secrets.

Hezekiah felt as you feel. He sent to Isaiah the Prophet these words: "This day is a day of trouble, and of rebuke, and blasphemy: for the children are come to the birth, and there is not strength to bring forth."(2 Kings 19:3). Wow! Can you imagine woman of God being pregnant but because of the times and trouble upon the land the pregnant women would rather not give birth. Your observation is dead on. As in the days of Hezekiah and Isaiah, so in the days of you and I.

Or woman of God, imagine this, as in your other observation of miscarriage or abortion. In the days of Hosea God saw the same thing. Look what He said: "As for Ephraim, their glory shall fly away like a bird, from the birth, and from the womb, and from conception. Though they bring up their children, yet will I bereave them, that there shall not be a man left: yea, woe also to them when I depart from them! Ephraim, as I saw Tyrus, is planted in a pleasant place: but Ephraim shall bring forth his children to the murderer. Give them, O Lord: what wilt thou give? Give them a miscarrying womb and dry breasts." (Hos.9:11-14).

Woman of God; you see well and speak accurately. This sounds like the church of America. No one is birthing. No one is preparing the nursery. Can't we take a lesson from the earth: "for we know that the whole creation groaneth and travaileth in pain until now"(Rom.8:22). It waits, woman of God, "...for the manifestation of the sons of God". (Rom.8:19). Yes...the Sons of God.

Handmaids wait also for the seed of the anointed; men with a vision. As did the word say: 'men shall see visions'. As I like to expand the word 'see'. Men shall 'seed' the vision. Stand up Sons of God. The daughters of Zion are ready to 'seed' the vision; to prophesy it; to procreate it; to proclaim it. Let me stop, dear sister. I am too high in the Spirit now. But you see correctly." -**Dr. Randy E. Simmons July 30th 2010**

BIRTH PARENT-MOTHER-
THE MAN-CHILD MUST COME FORTH:

"The Lord spoke this concerning my own household, and I praise Him for it...."I begin your training and preparation within your own household for a man/woman who can withstand the pain of the movement of God within her own household can be used to minister to others. This is a vessel filling moment. Do not bring comfort which overrides my Word, but be settled in the truth. Do not allow comfort to compromise what I have told you. Stand for what I love and hate only that which I hate. "Dr. Simmons, there is a world waiting. There is transition, there is travail (hard work and intense pain), and there is dilation and birth. The world is overflowing with all stages of the birthing process. Someone has to push the baby out, someone has to catch the baby and someone must raise the baby.

Recently the Lord began to minister to my heart and reveal that many, many women try to carry a man. I have twin sons, nearly 19 years old. Our Father God revealed this, "Do not carry the weight of a man on the frame of a woman." Secondly He revealed, "There is no room in the womb." It is time for the Godly women to stand up and assume their position as GOD has positioned them....many women carry the weight and responsibility intended for

men and we end up contributing to spiritual immaturity of these men. Our "comfort with compromise" enables men in our lives to remain in the stage of infancy, and then we murmur and complain about them, we are contributing to their delinquency.
Ahhhh....Lord, I pray you will allow this woman to reveal these truths to other women so that spiritual order can be restored and Men of God will not only be birthed, but RELEASED from their mothers and be the men they have been purposed to be.

The past several days the Lord has been speaking to my heart concerning many aspects of birth and the real "change of life" for the women of God in particular. For some the Lord is revealing that a spiritual hysterectomy will be necessary. For some there are scars that have adhered to the vital organs and have caused undue and unnecessary pain and suffering. Once the spiritual hysterectomy takes place "things change"....we can no longer rely on old ways of doing things and even intimacy is changed. We must renew our minds and hearts and not rely simply upon the physical manifestation of intimacy; yet seek the deeper, more true and lasting intimacy which comes only by being in the ever present presence of the Lord. Some will require a spiritual dissection ~ the breaking down, piece by piece and identify the problem areas, how those areas are intended to function and how to recover, rebuild, and restore the broken areas. Only the master, the creator can be called upon for such process, for He alone is worthy of the design and reconciliation of such design for His purpose. Scars....yes, there may be scars; however scars are simply reminders of something which needed to be removed is now gone. Blessed and highly favored are you Man of God. Words cannot begin to express the depth of gratitude for you have enlightened me with scripture to bear witness to what the Lord is and has been speaking to this heart. We praise God for that which we may not yet see with the eye, yet see in the Spirit. I am humbled as God is beginning to select and connect those of like mind and Spirit so that we may encourage one another in the ways of the Kingdom. There is Godly wisdom, structure and accountability as we allow God to establish relationships for us." -**Prophetess Holly Sharp; July 29th 2010**

BIRTH PARENT-FATHER:
"JOSEPH, FEAR NOT TO TAKE..."

In meditation this morning, I heard this word whisper to my spirit:

"TODAY, MY SON, FOR A BRIEF MOMENT CREATION CEASES TO GROAN AND TRAVAIL...FOR A BRIEF MOMENT IT CEASES TO TURN...FOR TODAY A SON OF GOD HAS BEEN BIRTHED...TODAY A SON OF GOD HAS BEEN MANIFESTED. TODAY HAS COME FORTH A MAN-CHILD THAT SHALL CARRY THE WORD OF LIFE TO GENERATIONS. TODAY THE DAUGHTERS OF ZION HAVE COME TO BIRTH".

THE TABLE IS PREPARED:

"I sense that a new season is upon us. It is a season of rest and plenty. It is a season of bounty and glory from the Lord. It is a season where I believe that God will truly bless the works of our hands. I heard in the Spirit this morning: 'THE TABLE IS PREPARED'! Truly God has set the table. The providential care of God is at hand and some things can and will be done only by miracles; the supernatural ability of God to produce something from nothing…THIS IS A MIRACLE! He is the God which calleth those things which be not as though they are (Rom. 4:17).

I rejoice this day. I feel as if for a brief moment that the creation has stopped groaning and travailing. I feel that for a brief moment as if the earth has stopped spinning and instead has stood still just to give birth, today I feel as if a Son of God has been birthed by a thousand daughters of Zion; and today I feel that creation is laughing with joy because a male child has come forth.

THIS IS A MOMENT IN TIME OF GREATNESS. THIS IS A MOMENT IN TIME OF BLESSINGS. THIS IS A MOMENT OF TIME IN VICTORY. THIS IS A MOMENT OF TIME IN THE MANIFESTATION OF ALL THINGS.

At two am this morning, I found myself speaking to the wind; I found myself speaking to the city of Brunswick, Georgia to release its hidden treasures of darkness and its riches of secret places (Isa. 45:3). I walked the floor and spoke to the wind to blow away the dross and reveal the resources. This morning I saw the earth tilt on its axis and pour its resources into the hands of the people of God, that we may establish his covenant upon the earth and to do kingdom business (Deut.8:18). This day I saw, and this day it shall be. I stand on the word and Brunswick, Georgia and the world shall know that there are prophets in their midst. Be blessed today...THE TABLE HAS BEEN PREPARED!"

This I heard. What have you birthed woman of God? I sense your delivery. Then I was reminded of this word which came to me on: 02-18-10 @8:00pm

"My son, when the Holy Spirit came upon the virgin Mary, earthly flesh from the earthly ground received Spiritual, Holy seed to conceive my son Jesus. Who but God could do such a thing? This is the mystery of Immaculate Conception; God in you! Now Spirit meets with spirits for greater impregnation...Spirit to spirit for birthing of my end time sons and daughters into the kingdom. Jesus spoke of greater works...this, my son, is the season of greater works!

Many Hand Maids today will prophesy (produce, give birth) not to the natural word of God, but to the word of God spread abroad within the hearts of men. They shall give birth to new revelation, new vision, and new life within the body of Christ. Truly the children have come to birth but 'there is not strength to bring forth'. But I will strengthen the wombs of the daughters of Zion and they shall give birth to the word of God. Their hearts will burn within them like the disciples on the Emmaus road. And, like the woman at the well, it shall spring up in them a well of water of life. No longer will I curse the wombs of the daughters of Zion. And once again, the true sons of God will look through spiritual eyes at the daughters of men and find them fair. Only this time their seed shall be pure, holy and undefiled."

I've passed through the birth canal of Prophecy as I did through the fires and waters of purification. Today I feel new. Today I feel changed. Today a mother has brought forth a son." -**Dr. Randy E. Simmons. July 30th 2010 @ 7:51am**

BIRTH PARENT-MOTHER: "JOY THAT A.....CHILD IS BORN"

"On this word I am weeping inwardly as well as outwardly. Our God is so intimate, even to allow us to experience not only rebirth but to allow us to grasp an understanding of who is being birthed (for Him) and who He has birthed spiritually to birth others. Spiritual midwives as such. Without conception there is no birth. Praise God for what seed has been planted in the sons and daughters for ooh my Jesus, in the Kingdom of God both men and women conceive and give birth for His seed is in both. It is herein another "foolish thing to confound the wise". From the moment of the birthing the joy and the journey begin. And within only a matter of brief time the body is prepared to conceive again. God is constantly preparing us to conceive again and the beautiful truth is we were conceived in His very heart long before the earthly hearts ever longed for us. Dr. Simmons I declare and I decree that a new man, a new Son of God has been brought forth! You have been DELIVERED. You have pushed through and have left the comfort of the womb only to be birthed into the manhood required and ordained by your Father God. This seed has now been birthed in you and the spiritual womb is being prepared for conception. For a moment all heaven and earth hush and rejoice in the birth and then God calls HIS MAN to go forth. I just had this vision why God won't allow a woman to carry the weight of a man in the womb (beyond season) or on her shoulders, for the weight is far too great for the greater of a man and the responsibility of a Godly man is to carry the weight of a Godly woman. The woman carries the weight of honoring the Man of God which is indeed a heavy burden if He does not walk uprightly before God. Ooooh my sweet, sweet father I do thank you on today.

What has been birthed in me I believe you asked? There has been the birth of a Prophet Sir. Yes it was time to either be birthed or to go past the birthing season only to discover what was carried inside had ceased to be. Surrounded the birth of the prophet came that same hush you speak of where travail has passed, where pushing and even the resistance to push is complete for the birthing was fulfilled...there was a spiritual delivery. This baby prophet wailed at her spiritual birth for she had no idea who she was conceived to be. She is humbled by the beauty and elegance of

first words He has placed in her to speak for this prophet knows the sound of her Fathers voice as He speaks through her. This woman who has been birthed is a new creature. Praise God. There is a sense of great unworthiness to carry the mantle yet the Father selected my birth garment and I shall wear it willingly and in a way as such to please only Him. Dr Simmons, we have both been born as of this past month or past moment. The date doesn't matter but the assignment does. I celebrate who you are in Christ and your fresh anointing. I thank God we have both experienced delivery on today! A brother and sister in Christ celebrate today and thank you Father! Amen!"
-**Prophetess Holly Sharp July 30th 2010 @ 9:14am**

BIRTH PARENT-FATHER:
"JOY THAT A.....CHILD IS BORN"

Sister Holly,

"For she hath joy that a man child has been brought forth". So is the process of delivery. So is the process of the seed. And so you are correct that the seed has no gender. He called one a 'Man'. The next he called 'Wo-man', man with a womb. As in natural conception the life is in both so also in spirit is the life of the seed. It must fall into the 'ground' in order to die that life may come.

In the prophetic to many these are mysteries, but only to those whose eyes are blind and whose ears are deaf. We, as servants of God, are neither. We have looked deep into the heart and intimacy of God. Male and female are meaningless in the spirit. They are of no value. To say that 'I'm pregnant' as a man to the natural ears would be ludicrous, but to the spiritual it makes sense. God made them...he formed them...He put the seed of life within itself to recreate and to rebirth. This is no mystery.

My dear woman of God, You have allowed me to express the depths of my spirit and have looked into my spirit man and have seen with the eye of God his intended purpose. You have shared with me the depth of your own prophetic utterances and birthings. I feel a kindred spirit and for this I am honored. Sister Holly may God continue to enrich your 'eye'….your vision. May you continue to be drawn deeper into the depths of his glory and majesty. May you have laughter like Sarah over the birth of your Isaacs. Bring forth in this season. Rise and, as the woman before the great dragon, may God always protect your seed and prepare a place for it.

I'm honored to have had this dialogue with you. I am richer and blessed for it. You brought me into my new season and have stood as a midwife in the birthing. I therefore call you 'god-mother'. For so shall you be for all future birthings of my seed and spiritual sons and daughters. May God bless the fruit of your womb and may women called you blessed as they did Mary, the mother our precious Saviour and Lord Jesus Christ.

The ministry and the work is confirmed. The ends of the ages await. We go forth to bring to the birth. No more dry seasons. No more

miscarrying. No more still births. No more aborting of visions. We will teach them. We will push them to their purpose. We will walk with them to the 'hospitals' for the wards are full. This generation shall arise. They shall not be a generation of miscarriers. They shall bring forth; and in so doing they shall remember 'god-mother' Holly. Be blessed woman of God!"
-Dr. Randy E. Simmons July 30 @9:33am

CHAPTER FOUR

THE BIRTH: - "AND ADAM KNEW EVE… AND SHE CONCEIVED!"

THE BIRTHING: - The Prophetic birth itself. Birthing is a process. Conception, trimesters, morning sickness; dilation; water bags; and delivery. This is how the process of Spiritual birthing also seems to unfold. As I remember the series of long discussions between myself and Sis Denise Borchers, over the many revelations, prophecies, attacks by Satan and near death, that she had experienced; and after all that she finally realized she was being birthed. I was her father or mid-wife if you please. The angel discussed with Mary her birthing of Jesus the word of God; "And, behold, thou shalt conceive in thy womb, and bring forth a son, and shalt call his name Jesus…..Then said Mary unto the angel, How shall this be, seeing I know not a man?...and she brought forth her firstborn son…."(Luke 1:31, 34; 2:7)

CHAPTER FOUR

THE BIRTH:
"AND ADAM KNEW EVE... AND SHE CONCEIVED!"

THE BIRTHING: The Prophetic Birth itself. Birthing is a process. It begins with the impregnation of a seed; Conception, embryo; morning sickness; incubation period; first trimester, second trimester, third trimester; dilation; water bags; and delivery – THE GIVING OF BIRTH!. This is how the process of Spiritual Birthing also seems to unfold. As I remember the series of long discussions between myself and Sis Denise Borchers, over the many revelations, prophecies, attacks by Satan and near death, that she had experienced; and after all that she finally realized she was being birthed. I was her father or mid-wife if you please. The angel discussed with Mary her birthing of Jesus the word of God; "And, behold, thou shalt conceive in thy womb, and bring forth a son, and shalt call his name Jesus…..Then said Mary unto the angel, How shall this be, seeing I know not a man?...and she brought forth her firstborn son…."(Luke 1:31, 34; 2:7)

TESTIMONY FROM ANOTHER: (07-30-10)

Wow Randy. You still remember well the Connection request, that is amazing....yes in the Land down under.....a Spanish Explorer in the 1600's named Australia **THE GREAT**

SOUTH LAND OF THE HOLY SPIRIT.....
thank you for those words of blessings from God and prayers and comments, have always believed that this was a divinely ordered connection AMEN. I pray for you as a Great Leader doing Kingdom Work....you are an Anointed Man of God....moving in each of the 5 Fold Ascension Ministry Gifting...giving Glory to God.....-**Denise Borchers :(07-30-10)**

A PROPHETIC WORD:
THE IMPREGNATION OF A SEED
(John 12:24)

Then I was reminded of this word which came to me on: 02-18-10 @8:00pm

"My son, when the Holy Spirit came upon the virgin Mary, earthly flesh from the earthly ground received Spiritual, Holy seed to conceive my son Jesus. Who but God could do such a thing? This is the mystery of Immaculate Conception; God in you! Now Spirit meets with spirits for greater impregnation...Spirit to spirit for birthing of my end time sons and daughters into the kingdom. Jesus spoke of greater works...this, my son, is the season of greater works! Many Hand Maids today will prophesy (produce, give birth) not to the natural word of God, but to the word of God spread abroad within the hearts of men. They shall give birth to new revelation, new vision, and new life within the body of Christ. Truly the children have come to birth but 'there is not strength to bring forth'. But I will strengthen the wombs of the daughters of Zion and they shall give birth to the word of God.

Their hearts will burn within them like the disciples on the Emmaus road. And, like the woman at the well, it shall spring up in them a well of water of life. No longer will I curse the wombs of the daughters of Zion. And once again, the true sons of God will look through spiritual eyes at the daughters of men and find them fair. Only this time their seed shall be pure, holy and undefiled."

THE PROCESS OF BIRTHING: CONCEPTION

I SHARED THE ABOVE WORD ALSO WITH THIS OTHER PROPHETESS, DENISE BORCHERS BECAUSE OF HER TESTIMONY OF ME. THIS WAS HER RESPONSE:

"Brother Randy ......Sis Dee is overwhelmed.... A word to "MY SON".........Crying and speechless ....I accept and receive every Blessed Word out of the Mouth of God ....feel led to place in my notes please as I do not want to ever be unable to look and gaze upon with reverential awe and wonderment ....this speaking to me as I read and my Spirit is rejoicing ....words fail me ....this shall come to pass ...so be it AMEN........ ONLY THIS TIME THEIR SEED SHALL BE PURE, HOLY AND UNDERFILED ....whispering Glory Hallelujah.....cannot disturb the Peace and the place that I am in ... this Hand Maiden and Vessel of the Lord is in a new place and it is manifesting .....Have to stay within the still calm voice and listen and feel and........................"-**Denise Borchers (07-30-10)**

THE PROCESS OF BIRTHING: SPIRITUAL EMBRYO

"Sis Dee...I sense your impregnation and the positioning of your birthing. I honor the presence of the Lord upon you and see in the Spirit that the time of your delivery is soon to come. Bring forth. Push when the time is right. The midwives are ready. The nursery has been prepared. Australia and the world shall know of this deliverance. The birth canal of prophecy has been made ready and the Holy seed shall come forth, not to mingle itself with the cares of this world. God has prepared a place for this 'man child'. Fear not...bring forth! -**Bro. Randy July 30th 2010**

THE PROCESS OF BIRTHING: MORNING SICKNESS

"Bro. Randy...

Thank you for explaining what is occurring within me, I did not completely comprehend........so you sense my impregnation...I can actually feel that.....deep within my impregnation...and I am feeling transitional occurrences also.....thank you for Honoring the Presence of the Lord upon me.....this is such a place of refuge and haven that I have never experienced before.......awaiting delivery and giving birth.......oh Bro..... crying again.........shall bring forth and push when the time is right ..... He shall tell me and you may confirm it ....blurry vision with these joyous tears ....think that you may be one of the

midwives in my case ………yes I know that the nursery has been prepared for nearly 9 months would you believe, yes you would !!!!! The birth canal of prophecy has been made ready and the Holy
Seed shall come forth, not to mingle itself with the cares of this world. God has prepared a place for this 'man child'…..no fear… shall bring
forth………..have been bringing prophetic for some time and a Minister of religion also received many personal words through me the other night and he said PUSH FURTHER ……and I did and he received although he does not allow many to pray or prophesy or speak forth over him ……………this is so very different ………was spoken of me 10th June that I would prophesy Internationally and Globally not that you need any confirmation ……..Pro…….you have no idea of my personal life…thus this special Word to me from you…….very cherished, valued and special….. you see I was told in real life aged 17 and newly Engaged that I had serious problems and would probably not give birth, Rex chose me and said adoption …….18 months and many doctors tests I brought forth our only Live Child …..now 46 years of old ……Had to have an Emergency Tubal Litigation aged 28 and Hysterectomy aged 30 no more children ……..I miscarried twins around 4 months….then another around 5 months…… then David lived 3 days and Michael 3 hours ……… so you see how editing and spiritual this has become to me ……I am to give birth with a "man child" which shall live……. this is Holy Seed not touching the cares of this World

alive...........God has prepared His place for this birthing...... and I am delighted to have been impregnated.....a Holy Conception ....Sincerest Spiritual thanks .....You have so blessed me ......tears of joy that I have been chosen.....wonder how many others are experiencing any of this......to be chosen of God ....Love Dee <3

THE PROCESS OF BIRTHING: INCUBATION

"My dear sister Dee;

I'm awestruck yet honored over your testimony. Awestruck, not because of the depth of your situation, but the majesty of our God in his miracles upon your life. Yes I'm honored to have shared this time with you. You have elevated my spirit and confirmed the ministry of purpose this day. A new season indeed has begun.

When women everywhere hear you and know of your testimony, they shall themselves see the wonder and experience the glory of the great God of heaven. You shall be their testimony. You shall be their evidence of the might and power of a great God. Bring to birth...cease not. '...travail in pain again till Christ is formed in them'. For this is our purpose. This is our mission. This generation shall not miscarry. They shall not abort. They shall not have dry breast according to Hosea 9:11-14. No they shall bring forth. You are a witness. You are a sign. You have seen and known the deep and intimate places of God. He

has walked with you and comforted you in your purpose. God has done great and wonderful things. So I bless and confirm you, woman of God. Speak to the nations. Tell them of his wonderful works. Declare his glory and let his majesty reign. Time is now. The glory cloud has appeared. His presence is with you and He shall go forth before you.
See...hear...feel...speak...declare...for the time is now!" -**Bro. Randy July 30th 2010**

THE BIRTHING PROCESS: FIRST TRIMESTER

'My Dear Brother Randy,

Can understand your being awestruck about my testimony...just knew I had to share with you.....YES...THAT IS THE WORD....THE MAJESTY OF OUR GOD IN HIS MIRACLES UPON MY LIFE. So glad your spirit has been elevated and confirmed the ministry of purpose this day, a new season has indeed begun.

Did not realize until you spoke that my testimony would allow other women to see for themselves the wonder and experience the Glory of the great God of heaven......I shall be their testimony.......evidence of the might and power of a great God.........Yes bringing to birth ....shall not cease.....travail in pain again till Christ be formed in them.......for this is our purpose this is our mission AMEN......

Blessed words of assurance Randy...this generation shall not miscarry.....they shall not abort, they shall not have dry breast....... Amen....... We shall bring forth.....speechless again and a little teared up......I am a witness. I am a sign....Yes so blessed to have seen and known the deep and intimate places of God (as have you) God has indeed done great and wonderful things always.

You have Imparted and Commissioned me Man of God Randy......... you bless and confirm me Woman of God ....to Speak to the Nations....tell them of His wonderful works .... Declare His Glory and let His majesty reign ......Time is now. The glory cloud has appeared.
His presence is with me and He shall go forth before me ....Amen.
See......hear....feel...speak.....declare...for the time is now!!!!!!!   Received.......

Have an awesome Testimony of when the enemy tried to kill me on a Birthday outing last month and it was prophesied over me by Prophets Paula Sanford as she interpreted this Testimony......you are another confirmation ....or the other way around...and Robert Blake and others also confirmed it Brother....think I shall place that on the wall again first.......as I see....hear....feel.....speak...declare.....for the time is now....To Him be the Glory, Amen.

Thanks yours in His Service...." -**Sis Dee with love**
LOL <3 July 30th 2010 @ 11:25am

THE BIRTHING PROCESS: SECOND TRIMESTER

My Dear Sis Dee;

Your spirit draws me. In tearful yet joyful melancholy with glee to be named as confirmed of such great prophets of God. But yes I confirm you. Your nation awaits. Indeed the world waits. The hills and mountains declare the glory of God and even the trees clap their hands at the rising of yet another Prophetess of God. The waters are clear and fresh springs appear. The stars align themselves for this day that which has been spoken forth has come. That which has been declared has come to birth. That which has waited for nine months is within its second trimester. Indeed we, the prophets of God are happy.

Prophecy is the seed bed of life...**PRO**; **PRO**duce; **PRO**create; **PRO**claim; **PRO**mote; yes bring forth that which cannot any longer be still. The devil knew what was being birthed; therefore he tried to kill you. He knew what was about to be therefore he prepared the Nile to swallow the babies. But the midwives would not allow it. God would not allow it. There's always a Miriam, waiting to find and bring the true nursing mother for the baby, even at the expense of Pharaoh. God always prepares a table...even in the midst of the enemy. Your life couldn't be touched because you were destined for such a time as this.
Oh to be...Oh to see...

The company of the prophets of God, those who speak forth and decree and declare the truth of a Mighty God. Pharaoh couldn't stop Moses; the red sea couldn't prevent him; the wilderness didn't deter him. He stopped his own purpose by not giving glory to God, whose it is alone. Moses is dead, dear sister. The generation of old is dead...passed on. We see the Joshuas of this day...a new breed of prophet...a new Seer...a new Discerner of the hearts and intents of men and women. Men and women who wouldn't back down or shake under the pressure...we will take the Promised Land. We see Jesus!
So arise...
Awake...
Defend...
Proclaim...
For the time has come!

Soon I will declare you PROPHETESS DENISE BORCHER" **-Dr. Randy E. Simmons July 30th 2010**

THE BIRTHING PROCESS: THIRD TRIMESTER (BIRTHING)

My Dear bro Randy.......

Just read all of these Blessed Holy Words out to my Husband Rex and he CONFIRMS ....what you declare at the end he has wanted me to place PROPHETESS in front of my name for months now Lol.....My Joy draws me also Brother.....as yourself........those words "in tearful yet gleeful melancholy with confirmed of such great prophets of God".........Receiving confirmation my Nation

awaits ....being obedient and donning the garment of humility ... the world waits.... those scriptural words hills and mountains declare the glory of God and even the trees clap their hands at the rising of another Prophetess of God ....have had them in my head for years now ......and always produced a question mark in my heart and mind to God...and the answer was always IT SHALL COME TO PASS.......and it has.......the stars in alignment for this day......YOU are a Prophet
Man of God and have declared that you are happy that 9 months has passed and BIRTH HAS TAKEN PLACE....... I am a joy filled Mother and PROPHETESS ......**PRO**phecy is the seed of life ....PRO.....**PRO**duce, **PRO**create, **PRO**claim, **PRO**mote, yes shall bring forth that which cannot lay still any longer...the Male Child Babe is born and is moving and squirming ....this feels so good and so right...MAJESTIC..... Dignified and Serene.....understand now why the devil tried to kill me which you shall read in the Testimony together with the notes, one lady wanted to mentor me but said I needed a special page etc., and I think my own page is just fine, also another Prophet has confirmed many things on his page, which I no longer visit for over 2 months now....wanted me to pay for his Mentoring!!!!!!!

Yes the devil knew but as you shall read God when I prayed the 23rd Psalm in bed the evening before I got to 'Yea though I walk through the valley of death....' could not go further....spoke in tongues...no......realized needed to listen heard the words YOU SHALL

NOT DIE !!!!!!! Yes the Nile wanted to swallow the babies but the midwives would not allow it. God would not allow it.....those Miriam waiting to find and bring the true nursing mother for the baby, even at the expense of Pharaoh, have often intrigued me. God always prepares a table, even in the midst of the enemy...so agree...many times the enemy has tried to kill me even with Brain Bleeds....God prepared His table and I could not be touched. Aged 33 I died and met 2 eyes and 2 hands in the midst of GLORY......and I was Commissioned and sent back with the words: "YOU SHALL GO FORTH BACK INTO THE WORLD AND BRING YOURSELF AND OTHERS TO ME, YOU SHALL USE YOUR HANDS FOR OUR FATHER'S GLORY....." Unbelievable Testimony..... **PRO** my life cannot be touched Amen...He had destined me for such a time as this.....Praising His Holy Name, Amen.

Oh to be...Oh to see....
The company of the Prophets of God....Those who speak forth and decree and declare the Truth of a Mighty God......reverential awe....
....for such a one as me!!!! Pharaoh couldn't stop Moses, the red sea couldn't prevent him, the wilderness did not deter him, you have so blessed me Randy......Yes he did stop his own purpose by not giving
Glory to God whose it is alone AMEN. Moses is dead.....yes dear Brother Randy ......The old generation of old is dead ...passed on...... Yes we see the Joshuas of this day..... (Thought of Caleb then)....the Joshuas of this day...a new breed of prophet....a new Seer...a new Discerner of the hearts and intents of men.

Men and Women who wouldn't back down or shake under the pressure....we shall take the Promised Land.....WE SEE JESUS......AMEN.....

So arising...Awakening....Defending...Proclaiming...
For the time has come!!!!!!!

YOUR DECLARATION HAS BEEN DECLARED AND SPOKEN FORTH AND I RECEIVE YOUR UTTERANCES AS PROPHETESS DENISE BORCHERS!

CHAPTER FIVE

THE NURSERY:
THE NANNY-'FAMILY'-FRIENDS

THE NURSERY:-THE NANNY-'FAMILY'-FRIENDS: This is the after birthing process. This is like the nursery process. Family comes to visit, friends offer well wishes. Remember Mary went to Elizabeth before the birth for comfort (Luke 1:39-56); the prophet Simeon blesses the birth of Jesus (Luke 2:25-32); the Prophetess Anna gives thanks (Luke 2:36-38). A nanny is essential to the growth of a baby, spiritually or otherwise. Someone should always be prepared to speak into their lives. Miriam the sister of the great prophet Moses recognized this also and said to pharaoh's daughter: "Shall I go and call thee a nurse of the Hebrew women, that she may nurse the child for thee?"(Ex.2:7)

CHAPTER FIVE

THE NURSERY: THE NANNY-'FAMILY'-FRIENDS

This is the after birth process. A lady from Kenya sent a message and told me all that sis Borchers had shared with her. Then she began to speak into my life. This is like the nursery process. Family comes to visit, friends offer well wishes. Remember Mary went to Elizabeth before the birth for comfort (Luke 1:39-56); the prophet Simeon blesses the birth of Jesus (Luke 2:25-32); the Prophetess Anna gives thanks (Luke 2:36-38). A nanny is essential to the growth of a baby, spiritually or otherwise. Someone should always be prepared to speak into their lives. Miriam the sister of the great prophet Moses recognized this also and said to pharaoh's daughter: "Shall I go and call thee a nurse of the Hebrew women, that she may nurse the child for thee?"(Ex.2:7)

ANNA REJOICES "…AND SPAKE OF HIM TO ALL THAT LOOKED FOR REDEMPTION…"

"Greetings MOG!

Blessings TO YOU ON THIS DAY. My spiritual sister and friend, Dee has spoken so much about you with me and how she has been uplifted by you more so, I have read much of the Word you have given to her.
So, I decided to connect with you at her request.

My prayer that we shall connect and share as we stir one another till we reach our goal here....Be His Full MEASURE. Greetings from Kenya!" -**GRACE BECKI: July 31st 2010 @ 10:36am**

"WOG; Greetings.

To God be glory that my name should be so hailed. For the rising of Prophetess Borchers, honor goes to so many before me. God just allowed me to partake in the increase. I value your friend request and gladly accept. In these times we shall see the hand of God so much more. I look forward to interaction with you and bless God for your graciousness." -**DR. RANDY E. SIMMONS**: **July 31st 2010 @ 12:40pm**

"Amen. Thank you. I have been encouraging her to speak out. So glad you are mentoring her now. I too am glad to meet, know and share with one such as you. All we did was give honor to whom it is due, as the word teaches. Shalom." -**GRACE BECKI: July 31st 2010 @ 12:49pm**

"I see the wind at your back....and the oil of Olives beneath your feet, for they are anointed to tread the winepresses of the earth!" -**DR. RANDY E. SIMMONS:** July 31st 2010 @ 2:29pm

"That is Awesome! Glory to God. Thank you MOG! I am speechless!"
-**GRACE BECKI: July 31st 2010 @ 2:53pm**

"Yes. But as I look upon your face, I see the fields of Kenya. They are ripe unto harvest, and the feet of those that would bring the good tidings are becoming weary. Be not weary in well doing. Help is on the way. The purpose of oil is to apply friction and smooth of movement, but it is also to preserve the life of a car or thing and give it longevity. WOG look at the fields of Kenya, they are white. But they are like no other fields. They are fields of glory. See the fields and know that anointing which you carry upon your life." -**DR. RANDY E. SIMMONS: July 31st 2010 @ 3:09pm**

"You are right! To know how right you are, go to my page and read my post which reads; 's'thing is not right....' read also the first comment I made then tell me what you see about it. This is getting very amazing!" -**GRACE BECKI: July 31st 2010 @ 3:17pm**

"I Will do. I will go to your page. May the Spirit of God give me eyes to see. Yes it is getting amazing...you have a Prophetic pull about you!"
-**DR. RANDY E. SIMMONS: July 31st 2010 @ 3:19pm**

"Amen and glory. I am waiting." -**GRACE BECKI: July 31st 2010 @ 3:26pm**

SIMEON PROCLAIMS-
"A LIGHT TO THE GENTILES"
(Luke 2:32)

"You test me also...there is witch craft all around you so therefore it is hard for you to trust. Even as men hold to the doctrine of the Nicolaitanes, which doctrine holds the laity captive through abuse and captivity of the conquerors. Nicholas was a great conqueror and that spirit prevails with the church. Men go where their coffers can be filled...I just shared a word with another minister in the Bahamas a moment ago, and I will share it with you soon. So yes your fields are unique, because the resources given by God to previous men and women of God to fulfill his covenant upon the earth have not been done. As I said to the other minister in the Bahamas, and I now share it with you: Even the wicked do not trust us, that is why the wealth of the wicked is no longer pouring into the hands of the 'righteous'. But God has a remnant and that remnant will restore the truth, as Pilate asked Jesus: 'what is truth'?" -**DR. RANDY E. SIMMONS: July 31st 2010 @ 3:31pm**

"Amen. That is where I am. Ready to take Kenya and the world by storm with this truth. But it is such a task. No money, hard task but still trusting and waiting." -**GRACE BECKI: July 31st 2010 @ 3:39pm**

"The facts are, my dear WOG that truth lies in the bosom of God. He did not forget Kenya, nor did the Killing fields destroy his purpose. In fact it enhanced it. It made it more resilient. They did not stop the will of God and nor will poverty or any such thing. So if you look deep and call upon God to remove and destroy the powers of darkness, because it is that which rules yet in the affairs of men. These spirits are the controlling forces, not the men. The men and women are merely instruments as you already know. I call you to task this day and decree and declare that you soon shall see a change…a shifting! I stood in my living room of my modest apartment the other night, the same night that Prophetess Denise was being birthed. I spoke to the winds to blow and decreed that the earth shift and pour out her

treasures of darkness and hidden places in order that the work of God may go forward. Satan comes to kill, steal and destroy, but the thing he cannot take or touch is life, because Jesus came that we might have life and that we might have it more abundantly. He alone is life."
-**DR. RANDY E. SIMMONS: July 31st 2010 @ 3:40pm**

"I agree with you. Please pray for me now. I urgently need financial help urgently and Father says it is now! Would you pray and release it now?" -**GRACE BECKI: July 31st 2010 @ 3:47pm**

"WOG, let's do more than just pray. Let's decree and declare it to be so. Let's demand that the forces of Darkness release their money into the hands of God's people. But moreso let's pray that God would again open the eyes and understanding of his people that we may be a blessing. Much financial wealth has been declared and decreed upon my life. I look for it now so that we may build our Centers for Christian and Social Development around the world. Global Visions Ministries is poised and ready. Like a lion about to leap upon its pray, so are we ready to leap over a wall. I promise you WOG as God prospers, I will not forget you. I stand in agreement for the blessings and the provisions of money to come so that you may be a blessing to your people. I stand with you!" -**DR. RANDY E. SIMMONS: July 31st 2010 @ 4:40pm**

"Amen. I agree completely. Thanks for the lion heart you have been given. As, Abraham, you are a father to many children of many nations.

His zeal in you is as fire that can't give u peace till u accomplishes his will. I like your spirit." -**GRACE BECKI: July 31st 2010 @ 3:47pm**

"WOG you see with a keen spiritual eye. As the lion chases the gazelle on the prairies of Africa, so chase I the will and purpose of God. I will not give up, or give in. I will not fail, though weak at times. I will not let go, though my grip is weakened because he has called me; he has appointed me; he has chosen me for such a time as this. WOG you see the stars and the sands upon the seashores of my heart. My seed is great because Jesus is great. He has placed within me the seed to produce and multiply. It was because once, I was decreed barren and that there would be no fruit, but in this season the fruit trees are bearing. No more dry season. No more barrenness. No more casting of the fig before its time. God has decreed it in the fullness of time. So yes WOG you see my seed and you see well. Pray for me that as that with which I am pregnant and that with which I am able to impregnate may bring forth soon and blossom unto a great harvest. You too WOG are quite fruitful…the seed of your season is about to spring forth. Your fertility is bound in the grace and divine purpose of God. Know this for certain, you shall give birth soon." -**DR. RANDY E. SIMMONS: July 31st 2010 @ 5:01pm**

"Amen. You are so light spiritually that the tiredness will not pull u down. U belong to mighty eagles! Yours is to soar!" -**GRACE BECKI: July 31st 2010 @ 5:08pm**

"WOG I will speak freely. There is a place in God where only angels tread and the sons of God dance with the Daughters of Zion. You have been there. You have walked the depths of God's intimacy and of His wisdom and have seen the might of his power. You have felt the brush of the wings of the messengers of God Almighty and known their very breath...because you have been in the presence of God. So who am i but a son? Who am I but a man? Who am I but one of those same sons who serve you? Who am I but one that carries glad tidings. Yes the weariness will not distract me; it will only make me push more. I am at the hour of my delivery and my pregnancy is hard...so I must push...and I must push. Souls await and the very sons of God demand that we don't give up. After all they are ministering spirits sent to our beckoning call....I cannot afford to be tire! It is God that allows us to mount up on eagles' wings. He causes us to run and not be weary. I think not of that at all, I think only of the glory and like Moses I requested of Him: "Show me your glory". I won't rest till I see it!"
-DR. RANDY E. SIMMONS: **July 31st 2010 @ 5:17pm**

"MOG, you spoke some deep spiritual things that set me to deep worship. It was passed mid night here and I came out at 2 am! Reason for not responding. Yes, the fire, zeal in and on you is great. Push!"
-GRACE BECKI: August 1, 2010 @ 6:22am

'WOG: There is a powerhouse of the anointing for birthing within you. My spiritual instincts tell me so. I see the internal processes of your heart and spirit woman. I am therefore led, and because Prophetess Borchers thinks so highly of you, to share two words I received of the Lord earlier this year. Look deep WOG...tell me what you see!

WORD: SPIRITUAL IMPREGNATION:
(01-17-10)7:25am

"My son, the church is willing to talk about birthing, but because of their fleshly minds they are afraid to talk about the process of impregnation. The Holy Spirit (which is the word of God-sword of the Spirit) impregnated Mary (a virgin) with Himself and bore Himself (for God is one-Father; Son; and Holy Spirit). Life and creation is a process. Except a grain of wheat fall into the ground and die, it abideth alone. But if it dies, it bringeth forth much fruit. The church is barren, their wombs miscarry and their breast are dry(Hos.9:11-17). Unless the water of life begins to spring up in them for whom I designed it(Handmaids/Wo-man, man with a womb) and their purpose(to bear seed through the process of incubation)then the church will die. I will not let this happen. The very gates of hell will not withstand my purpose. What I need, my son, are men with seed...men with vision. The first three letters of seed is 'see'! See this, my son, without vision the people perish; without seeing they have no vision. I said in Joel that young men shall see vision...they shall 'seed' vision. Therefore, without seed the ground lies dormant...break up the fallow ground! It's time to plant seed!"

WORD: SPIRITUAL CONNECTIONS:
(02-22-10)8:15pm

"My son, the day will come when more will be done through spiritual connections than natural connections. As men become more and more busy and technology increases, social interaction will cease as we know it today. Men will learn to connect with each other through their spirits...through their minds. You have heard of the gifts of premonition well is it real. The ability to know men in the spirit as people know me in the spirit will be increased.

Think it not strange to believe that two people can connect through spiritual intervention. It is done every day. The heart of man(wherein is his soul) is a wonderful thing. Women fall in love and they 'feel connected' to their husbands; children are connected to parents; etc. I will increase the spirits of men in these last days and they shall know even as they are known...IN SPIRIT. I will remove the dark glass and they shall see through a clear glass. They will know the power of SPIRIT...the true realm of existence.

To connect in spirit is to bring two spirits together and to know each other as never before. Like social interaction on the internet, so shall men learn the gift of spiritual interaction or connection. These things ponder and let it not go".

I welcome your input."-**DR. RANDY E. SIMMONS:**
August 1, 2010 @ 9:38am

"The first part as I see it refers to lack of true spiritual relationship with the Father which leads to intimacy and conception and birthing.

As long as the church is too busy to seek Him in Spirit and Truth, it receives no seed. Moreover, since His word stands, there are those who, like Mary shall receive the seed of the word to feed the rest. You are counted and chosen to access the royal bedroom of His chambers and received the holy seed." - **GRACE BECKI: August 1, 2010 @ 12:41pm**

"While the first is about church being carnal. The second is about the transformation that comes as the spirit is poured to make church fruitful. Hence, be spiritual, able to quickly pick up and connect with those of same kind. Just as Mary connected with Elizabeth. Spiritual oneness with no race, color or class barriers."- **GRACE BECKI: August 1, 2010 @ 12:53pm**

"WOG;

You leave me speechless. I sit, not in awe, but at the fruitfulness of your spiritual womb and the pull I feel upon my own spiritual bowels. Connection...conception...birthing...Yes you are right and quite quick to point out that indeed I've accessed the Royal chamber and felt the very intimacy of God. He had to teach me this to understand the 'knowing' of God and not just the knowledge of him. The Royal Seed is great; it is destined to bear fruit. Within you yourself I see the seed of life. Within your belly I perceive the well of water, the bag f life, springing up unto eternal life of which Jesus spoke of to the woman at the well in John chapter four. You leave me in deep spiritual anticipation at what you are about to bear next. I see deep and if permitted by you

WOG, I shall look deeper into your fruit and find indeed that seed of life. With that being said I want to share with you a vision I had around the same time of those words. I have shared it this afternoon with Prophetess Borchers and only one other, so deep was the vision. Look into it and extract for yourself the deep mysteries of God. Observe:

"I was caught up into the spirit and taken into a large facility like a hospital or medical lab. The place was pure white inside and out. As I enter the facility the smells of pure oil olive like frankincense, Myrrh, and lavender. The walls were spotless...clean. As I looked in the facility I saw large rooms as far as the eye could see. And laying in rows were tables, thousands of them. Upon each table was what appeared to be an incubator like device, with a life cord (like an umbilical cord) connected and leading away from it. An angel like being stood at the end of each incubator table and the life cord was connected to each one. As I peered into the incubators I saw a female like essence (but neither male nor female) just an essence about to conceive and bring to life."

My dear Prophetess, think me not strange, but the visions and whispers of my heart have been many and very mysterious and as such could not be shared, nor dare I share them with anyone until a Prophetess came into my life as publicist and friend in May of this year. Now I am emboldened, because of the events of the past few days, to share them with you."
- **DR. RANDY E. SIMMONS: August 1, 2010 @ 4:22pm**

"Thank you for the accolades MOG! You are most welcome to see as much as you can. That is a very deep vision you had of the church receiving the divine seed. In fact this has already happened and the sign of this woman used symbolically is about to be manifested physically here on earth. You have seen end time church that is empowered by the life of God to be fruitful. Wish to share more... Awesome...really!"- **GRACE BECKI: August 1, 2010 @ 4:43pm**

"WOG;

What more can I say? Your wisdom and spiritual intuition leaves me searching for more. It would seem that though we here in America have access to so many resources, yet we are so spiritually inept. Had I shared this vision with many of the church here, they wouldn't have seen its spiritual significance as you have explained. Truly you have walked in God's intimacy. You have nursed and cared for the babies of those unable to give suck. As Miriam said to Pharaoh's daughter: "shall I go and call thee a nurse of the Hebrew women, that she may nurse the child for thee?"(Ex.2:7). I see you nursing many...THEREFORE I CALL YOU NANNY!

Many shall be your children and great shall be the fruit of your own womb. "THE CHILDREN OF THE BARREN ARE MANY"! It may seem for now that your resources are limited and money to do that which you desire is limited; but I speak to the winds to blow...uproot...turn over...reveal the hidden treasures of dark places and to release the funds to you that are necessary. Bring to the birth. Produce the fruit of your need. I decree and declare that it shall soon come forth.

I long to hear more of your interpretation of the vision!" - **DR. RANDY E. SIMMONS: August 1, 2010 @ 5:24pm**

"Amen. I will share more 2morrow....It is 12:30 am now...gud day."
- **GRACE BECKI: August 1, 2010 @ 5:32pm**

"Be blessed dear Nanny!" - **DR. RANDY E. SIMMONS: August 1, 2010 @ 5:33pm**

"Good morning MOG!

How are you today???

You know God has really favored you showing you the end time church and how He is injecting life into her.

For we are moving in to another HOUR of His GRACE and the church must be well positioned to pertain of these blessings....

Share more..." - **GRACE BECKI: August 2, 2010 @ 10:53am**

"WOG, Grace Becki:

Again your wisdom and spiritual insight astounds me. I thank God to be thus favored. I hope to be worthy of His trust. Truly there is a new breed of Christian that he is raising up. We must be ready indeed. I want to share another vision with you that I had in Feb of 2010:

'I saw in a vision in February 2010 two beings. Their essence was male and female, yet they were one. Like Adam and Eve. They stood beside each other in a great light of Glory. I then heard the flutter of wings. Appearing around them were many angels and they formed as it were a tunnel around them like a whirlwind. The angels began to fly around them and upward, forming a powerful whirlwind and creating a white wall of angelic wings. As the angels continued, I saw as the two essences, male and female embraced. As they did so, they were slowly taken up and entered the glory of God. It was a moment of intimacy and ecstasy. It was the purest moment of intimacy I'd ever seen. The purest act of lovemaking I'd ever envisioned. GOD...MALE...FEMALE!'"
- **DR. RANDY E. SIMMONS: August 2, 2010 @ 2:44pm**

"For this one, am shedding tears! O Lord, now you have fully revealed this to your son. If only this would be shown to you as it is in the natural! It is the wedding of the lamb. The oneness of the Man Jesus and His bride woman and the rapture! How I wish I would share some deep mystery of this woman! Ask the father open it for you now."
- **GRACE BECKI: August 2, 2010 @ 3:02pm**

"WOG, Grace;

Your spiritual womb is ripe. You have been among the sons of God and seen the rapture of God's intimacy. You are pregnant with his seed. You pull at me WOG. You desire the

Father to let me look at you. You bare your spirit woman before this son of God. I am Royalty. In you is the seed Royal. Wilt thou come away with me in the Spirit? Will you journey to meet me? Your spirit woman is ready to birth the fruit of Kenya. Procreate. Push, your desire is strong. I see you. Lay before me. Let me discover you daughter of Zion. I release the seed Royal of Kenya to you." - **DR. RANDY E. SIMMONS: August 2, 2010 @ 3:17pm**

"Your words are quite encouraging and your visions amazing! I see you are numbered among the few chosen kings whose thrones have been prepared to judge and rule with the King Jesus here on earth!"
- **GRACE BECKI: August 2, 2010 @ 3:38pm**

"WOG, Grace,

Do me honor. As a king I request of you...lay within the Royal Bedchamber of the Spirit. I see all you asked the father to reveal. I see your essence. You are a queen, like Sheba. You have sought the sanctuary of wisdom from the bosom of Solomon. I see you before me; your bowels of mercy and the spirit yearning for the seed of the anointing. Prepare for the greatest impregnation yet to come. Prepare your chamber...for thy king cometh." - **DR. RANDY E. SIMMONS: August 2, 2010 @ 3:44pm**

"Amen! That is awesome! Yes, the royal bedchamber is my place and position. Thank you so much for the word. You are blessed and favored!" - **GRACE BECKI: August 2, 2010 @ 3:56pm**

"I know. I have been there." - **DR. RANDY E. SIMMONS: August 2, 2010 @ 4:00pm**

SHEPHERDS PRAISE:
"AND THIS SHALL BE A SIGN UNTO YOU"
(Luke 2:12)

"Hi, my name is Byron Shaw... I have adopted Mrs. Dee as a spiritual mother... and I see that you have been a very big help in her life... all I ask is that you help me become a strong man of God.... I have
received Jesus as my savior and I have renounced everything of the world and I want to serve Jesus with all of my heart.... but there are some that just don't understand me.... I need guidance and I am in a bad position because I really don't know who to trust anymore.... since the lord has opened my eyes to a lot that's going on in the world.....please help me along with Mrs. Dee.....my father has been down since my 6th grade year and haven't really had a father figure in my life that would trust me and teach me the ways of God.... but I believe God will do it... I know he will because he has been doing it thus far.....please I am seeking true spiritual help....August 2, 2010"-**BYRON SHAW:**

CHAPTER SIX

THE NURSERY: TRAINING-MENTORING-TUTORING

THE NURSERY:-TRAINING-MENTORING-TUTORING: The nurturing begins here. Wow what a process! Prophetess Nixon said to me one day after this process: "Randy, the baby is born, now all you have to do is feed it and change its diapers". She was correct. Even Jesus the son of God knew that there would be a training, mentoring, tutoring process: "And he went down with them, and came to Nazareth, and was subject unto them….And Jesus increased in wisdom and stature, and in favour with God and man".(Luke 2:51-52). Samuel understood nurturing and training: "And Samuel told him every whit and hid nothing from him…And Samuel grew, and the Lord was with him, and did let none of his words fall to the ground. And all Israel from Dan even to Beersheba knew that Samuel was established to be a Prophet of the Lord". (1 Samuel 3:18-20)

CHAPTER SIX

THE NURSERY: TRAINING-MENTORING-TUTORING

THE NURSERY AND THE CRIB: NURTURING

The nurturing begins here. Wow what a process! A Prophetess said to me one day after this process: "Randy, the baby is born; now all you have to do is feed it and change its diapers". She was correct. Even Jesus the son of God knew that there would be a training, mentoring, tutoring process: "And he went down with them, and came to Nazareth, and was subject unto them….And Jesus increased in wisdom and stature, and in favour with God and man".(Luke 2:51-52). Samuel understood nurturing and training: "And Samuel told him every whit, and hid nothing from him…And Samuel grew, and the Lord was with him, and did let none of his words fall to the ground. And all Israel from Dan even to Beersheba knew that Samuel was established to be a Prophet of the Lord". (1 Samuel 3:18-20)

FIRST MESSAGE OF A PROPHETESS:

"Dr. Randy E. Simmons...Pro...

SMILES!!!!! That is amazing what you share about the Crusade you attending and to know that on that date THE LORD WENT BEFORE YOU...BROKE THROUGH AND PREPARED YOUR WAY....YOUR MINISTRY AND ANNOINTING WERE ELEVATED..... GLORY..... (Hard time of our lives our Only Grandson was 6 weeks old and only Child and 2nd Husband proved very difficult out of no-where.....another story for another time...just the timing was interesting to me) especially with the Scripture you mentioned.

DOUBLE PORTION ANNOINTING....... that was spoken over me yesterday by someone. WOW PASTOR ROD PARSLEY....AND LESTER SUMMRHAL ......carried much weight, such power......upon and into You Randy....THAT IS WHAT I FEEL FROM YOU TO ME...GRATEFUL VERY......WHAT!!!!!! SMITHS WIGGLESWORTH.... that is totally awesome the story in itself.......I am so very glad that you value his writings I have been making some notes of some from 'A Spirit Filled Living' and also have other books of the old Church Fathers.....That means a lot to me that we share even Authors....AND MAX LUCADO.... have quite a lot of his.......Randy this is so good to my ears and heart...Yes have that particular Book.....WHEN THE ANGELS WERE SILENT and a 365 Daily Devotional I have been making notes of for my page also. YOU HAVE SO BLESSED ME THANK YOU.....HAVE A WONDERFUL DAY IN THE LORD......THANK YOU FOR YOUR DECREE AND DECLARATION......AMAZING WORDING ......LIKED THAT YOU MENTIONED THAT YOU ARE MY MENTOR AND MIDWIFE..... PROPHETESS MAGNIFICAT.....SO BE IT... AMEN.....That Title MAGNIFICAT is a treasure to me Randy...truly and the Words that you wrote with them....thank you.....2 short words but the meaning conveyed is deep from my heart for all you have done.

I WROTE A FEW NOTES AND PLACED THEM ON MY PAGE...more shall be forthcoming and I am writing them all down...exciting and amazing journeys await us Friend.....Mysteries await.....Learning from my Mentor.....Bless You Pro. Randy.....You are also my Spiritual Father...." -**Love you, Dee <3 August 1st 2010**

THE NURSERY:DIAPERS & MILK:

"My Dear Prophets Borchers;

Greetings.

IT IS DONE. IT IS FINISHED!

Today Heaven yet rejoices as did many of your friends. I heard from one in Kenya and she told me of your words. They were so kind. I've seen a few comments on your page and I'm sure that you have heard many more. The process is just beginning. Today reminds me of a delivery of a new baby and that baby being brought home from the hospital. Friends and Relatives all come to wish the parents well wishes. But the greatest part of all this is how YOU PREPARE THE
NURSERY!

The nursery is where the baby will spend most of it time within the next few months. There's milk and yes diapers. In the spiritual sense, this is the time when people will test the accuracy of your prophecy:

ALWAYS TRUST THE WORD THAT IS IN YOUR HEART IT IS THERE WHERE GOD WHISPERS AND ONCE YOU TRUST THAT THE WORD IS FROM GOD AND CAN BE BACKED UP BY HIS WORD, THEN
BE NOT AFRAID TO SPEAK. GOD WILL STAND BY HIS WORD TO PERFORM IT HE WILL NOT LET IT FALL TO THE GROUND. AND MEN WILL KNOW THAT THERE WAS A PROPHETESS IN THIS PLACE:

Bear with me, my sister for God is showing me this as I go.
We applaud you for your rise to Prophetic office, but we cannot, no dare not forget the man of God, Rex that stands behind you and in whose shadow you too stand. He is the wind beneath your wings and you couldn't have done it without him. As Peter said: "Likewise, ye wives, be in subjection unto your own husbands…while they behold your chaste conversation coupled with fear"(1 Pet. 3:1-6). This, I know is your estate already.

"Arise, Rex, and lead thy captivity captive, thou son of God.
And the princes of Australia were with Denise…and also Rex…so let all think enemies perish, O Lord: but let him that love him be as the sun when he goeth forth in his might. And the land had rest…"

Yes today, Prophetess Borchers, Australia rests…A PROPHETS AND LEADER IS BORN!

So with that being said, yes it's time to learn of God's great Generals. From the Bible times to our own and of the ways of Jesus Christ, the greatest prophet of all time. Well did Moses say:

"The Lord thy God will raise up unto thee a prophet from the midst of thee, of thy brethren, like unto me; unto him ye shall hearken ;"(Deut. 18:15).

It was this same prophet, Jesus Christ who said:

"Verily, verily, I say unto you, he that believeth on me, the works that I do shall he do also; and greater works than these shall he do; because I go unto my Father."(John 14:12).

BELIEVEST THOU THIS PROPHETESS BORCHERS?"-**Dr. Randy E. Simmons, the Prophet Mentor August 1st 2010**

THE NURSERY: FEEDINGS

"GREETINGS IT IS DONE AND FINISHED, AMEN.

GREETINGS MENTOR RANDY.......Your Words and Scriptures have and shall come to pass and prosper. Thank you, I have placed some notes and messages using God's Word on my page yesterday.....I AM ALWAYS OBEDIENT UNTO OUR LORD GOD...Man shall always submit to His Words through you or myself....Amen.....Those precious Words about Rex and I are a cherished valuable Gift...he was so moved as I read them, as was I Friend.

JESUS CHRIST SAID:

"Verily, verily, I say unto you, he that believeth on me, the works that I do shall he do also; and greater works than these shall he do; because I go unto my Father"(John 14:12)

PROPHETESS BORCHERS BELIEVEST THOU ....Going to place some of this on my Page where Rex wrote his Message to me.......Thank you loved Prophet Mentor......." -**Dee <3 August 1st 2010**

THE NURSERY: COMFORTING

"MY dear Prophetess Borchers;

"Your words are too kind. Our God is teaching me as I go. I heard the Spirit say to me a few minutes ago that the blessing of King Solomon upon the people of God is the heart of the Prophet. For it is the desire of the Prophet of God that the people know that God is with them and that he will give them rest and that they will keep his commandments and statutes as did the fathers; further that the Lord will incline his ear unto their call as they incline their hearts to him. If a Prophet of God so do he/she will remind all peoples of the earth that the Lord he is God.

WITH THIS I THEREFORE BESTOW UPON YOU IN JESUS NAME THIS PROPHETIC BLESSING FROM THE LIPS OF KING SOLOMON HIMSELF:

"Blessed be the Lord, that hath given rest unto his people Israel, according to all that he promised: there hath not failed one word of all his good promise, which he promised by the hand of Moses his servant. The Lord our God be with us, as he was with our fathers: let him not leave us, nor forsake us: That he may incline our hearts unto him, to walk in all his ways, and to keep his commandments, and his statutes, and his judgments, which he commanded our fathers.

And let these my words, wherewith I have made supplication before the Lord, be nigh unto the Lord our God day and night, that he maintain the cause of his servant, and the cause of his people Israel at all times, as the matter shall require: That all the people of the earth may know that the Lord is God, and that there is none else. Let your heart therefore be perfect with the Lord our God, to walk in his statutes and to keep his commandments, as at this day."(1 Kings 8:54-61)" -**Dr. Randy E. Simmons, the Prophets Mentor August 1st 2010**

THE NURSERY:TRAIN UP THE CHILD

MY dear Mentor Brother Randy.....

Firstly I need you to know how your page Global has so blessed me and have taken the liberty of sharing one of your notes on my wall, smiles, thank you ... truly a Blessed page shall send out Invites to my Friends later on. More smiles we are both being taught by God as we go. Also on the Global wall there was a post about RAIN and placed a Prophetic Word given me that supports your words...wow.....

King Solomon happens to be one of my favorite Men of the Bible for very many different reasons.....Spirit told you that the Blessing of King Solomon upon the people of God is the heart of the Prophet...my heart has begun thumping with excitement.

KNEELING BEFORE YOU...AS YOU BESTOW THIS PROPHETIC BLESSING UPON ME FROM THE LIPS OF KING SOLOMON HIMSELF:

....
....
....
....

Ohhhhhhhhh THAT IS AN OVERWHELMING BEAUTIFUL PROPHETIC MANTLE AND WORDS PLACED UPON ME...MY HEART HAS SPIRITUALLY BEEN CHANGED ONCE AGAIN......SPEECHLESS....OH THE BEAUTY OF OUR LORD......WE EXALT, ESTEEM, AND SAITH HOLY OF HOLIES HOW GREAT THOU ART, ALLELLUIA.......SO VERY BLESSED.....Humbly and Spiritually Grateful Brother Randy.......

Notice you are now signing THE PROPHETS MENTOR.....Am I Praying for you as you Mentor others.....SMILING....Know the answer, just wanted to let you know that I had noticed the change here....Love in Christ Jesus," -Dee <3 August 1st 2010

THE NURSERY: CRAWLING

My dear Prophetess Dee;

All that is shared is such a blessing. Allow me to share two powerful words I had from the

Lord earlier this year. They baffled me then, but make sense now. I told a dear friend today in an email that God had begun to show me such great revelation on spiritual impregnation that I did not believe that it was ever possible to teach such things to an American audience. But as I began to look and hear what was happen in places like Africa, Australia and other parts of the world concerning such teachings, I gained hope yet dare not teach them yet. It was Dr Cindy Trimm's teachings that began to open my spirit more to the realities of such teachings. Now, with you I am actually living the experience and am walking it out as we share messages. Thank you so very much. Observe:

WORD: SPIRITUAL IMPREGNATION:
(01-17-10)7:25am

"My son, the church is willing to talk about birthing, but because of their fleshly minds they are afraid to talk about the process of impregnation. The Holy Spirit (which is the word of God-sword of the Spirit) impregnated Mary (a virgin) with Himself and bore Himself (for God is one-Father, Son, and Holy Spirit). Life and creation is a process. Except a grain of wheat fall into the ground and die, it abideth alone. But if it dies, it bringeth forth much fruit. The church is barren, their wombs miscarry and their breasts are dry (Hos.9:11-17). Unless the water of life begins to spring up in them for whom I designed it (Handmaids/Wo-man, man with a womb) and their purpose (to bear seed through the process of incubation) then the church will die.

I will not let this happen. The very gates of hell will not withstand my purpose. What I need, my son, are men with seed...men with vision. The first three letters of seed is 'see'! See this, my son, without vision the people perish; without seeing they have no vision. I said in Joel that young men shall see vision...they shall 'seed' vision. Therefore, without seed the ground lies dormant...break up the fallow ground! It's time to plant seed!"

WORD: SPIRITUAL CONNECTIONS
(02-22-10)8:15pm

"My son, the day will come when more will be done through spiritual connections than natural connections. As men become more and more busy and technology increases, social interaction will cease as we know it today. Men will learn to connect with each other through their spirits...through their minds. You have heard of the gifts of premonition well is it real. The ability to know men in the spirit as people know me in the spirit will be increased. Think it not strange to believe that two people can connect through spiritual intervention. It is done every day. The heart of man (wherein is his soul) is a wonderful thing. Women fall in love and they 'feel connected' to their husbands; children are connected to parents; etc. I will increase the spirits of men in these last days and they shall know even as they are known...IN SPIRIT. I will remove the dark glass and they shall see through a clear glass. They will know the power of SPIRIT...the true realm of existence. To connect in spirit is to bring two spirits together and to know each other as never before. Like social interaction on the internet, so shall men learn the gift of spiritual interaction or connection. These things ponder and let it not go".

Thanks also for the visit to my page. The Lord has been showing me that it is time to begin to expose GLOBAL VISIONS MINISTRIES INTL to the world through my teachings as we gear to establish Centers for Christian and Social Development around the world as well as Faith and Restoration centers. And Yes I believe that time will come when others will be birthed and mentored. Not too long ago, as I wrestled with this gift a Prophetess friend of mine declared that I would indeed be a prophetic guide. I see her words unfolding before my very eyes. Be in much prayer as I believe that God will do a quick work.

Be blessed;" -**Randy, Prophet Mentor August 1st 2010**

THE NURSERY: TEETHING

My Dear Mentor Prophet Randy,

The opening paragraph I am so smiling at Friend, triggers an answer to you PRAYER AVAILETH MUCH ... ANSWERED PRAYER as Holy Spirit showed me a picture of you and over the top was a huge question mark?? And I requested that you be given the answers *smiles*.
Wow you actually walking the path in our sharing....thank you...blesses me.

Word = Spiritual Impregnation YOU ARE SUCH A ONE TO SOW THE SEEDS INTO THE HEARTS AND MINDS OF THE BODY OF CHRIST... THIS IS WHY YOU ARE BEING BIRTHED FURTHER INTO THIS POSITION FOR THE GLORY OF GOD...AMEN.

Word = Spiritual Connection....almost speechless that word PREMONITION have often spoken to Rex that it is NOT Women's Intuition I receive.....PREMONITION...this is music to my ears Bro. WE ARE CONNECTED OUR TWO SPIRITS ARE INTERTWINED AND TOGETHER...known one another just a short time....large smiles, yet twas for this that we were set apart and Consecrated before the Foundations of the Earth, Glory Hallelujah.......Praying on these Randy.... ongoing........

CONFIRMED YES it is time that GLOBAL VISIONS MINISTRIES INTL....to go to the World....your teachings need to be spoken forth to the World........Praying.........GLORY HALLELUJAH...so pleased that you saw that cause I was going to give you a WORD CONFIRMING....and I shall be sharing many things on my walls Dr. Simmons...especially during the 3 months I am to be away beginning mid-September.
Okay glad that you believe that the time shall come when others will be birthed and mentored......... the Prophetess was quite correct you are a PROPHETIC GUIDE...you see her words unfolding before your very eyes, how happy that makes me......I have requested my close Friend Grace Becki whom I

already call Prophetess....and often she lets me know when a new post is on her wall for me to go and PRAY AND PROPHESY OR WHATEVER LED, we spoke of you and I asked her to request your Friendship and to message you and explain, although I also told her that you were a very busy man....She has been reading all that went before, up to, and the Birthing of PROPHETESS BORCHERS and was very thrilled and excited at our Journey...... would not do that with many of my Friends!!!!!!

Shall be in much Prayer....long into the night last evening and woken again early....always refreshed when I do sleep and awaken...GOD SHALL DO A QUICK WORK, CONFIRMED.

Blessed," -**Dee, Prophetess ....August 1st 2010; 3:57am:**

THE NURSERY:TODDLER

Dear Prophetess Borchers;

"How blessed are the feet of them who carry glad tidings"

As I slept...you prophesied and confirmed: IT WOULD SEEM THAT YOU HAVE BECOME PREGNANT WITH GLOBAL VISIONS INTL.

It was just last week that I spoke of using my page of ministry more to get God's message out rather than my personal page. Much of your sayings and actions seem to confirm that.

I FEEL THE CONNECTION AS BIRTH PANGS WITHIN MY OWN SPIRITUAL BOWELS! THANKS FOR CONFIRMING THE WORDS SENT. I can now share with you a vision that I had around that same time in February of 2010, one I've been reluctant to share with none except the Prophetess of whom I recently spake. I now share it with you:

"I was caught up into the spirit and taken into a large facility like a hospital or medical lab. The place was pure white inside and out. As I enter the facility the smells of pure oil olive like frankincense, Myrrh, and lavender. The walls were spotless...clean. As I looked in the facility I saw large rooms as far as the eye could see. And laying in rows were tables, thousands of them. Upon each table was what appeared to be an incubator like device, with a life cord (like an umbilical cord) connected and leading away from it. An angel like being stood at the end of each incubator table and the life cord was connected to each one. As I peered into the incubators I saw a female essence (neither male nor female) just an essence about to conceive and bring to life."

My dear Prophetess, think me not strange, but the visions and whispers of my heart have been many and very mysterious and as such could not be shared, nor dare I share them with anyone until that Prophetess came into my life as publicist and friend in May of this year. Now I am embolden, because of the events of the past few days, to share them with you.

THE HEART OF A PROPHET IS A SACRED PLACE OF LIFE. HE/SHE HOLDS THE POWER OF DEATH OR LIFE. I PRAY GOD THAT I PRODUCE LIFE.

Yes I do believe that many more are coming. I believe that the hope of this world will take the prophetic utterance of men and women of God who fear not to decree and declare the oracles of God. A strange series of words came into my spirit last evening:

PROPHETIC IMPREGNATION CENTERS!

As I worshiped at church this morning, I further heard God speak this to my spirit:

THE MISSION STATEMENT OF THE PROPHET IS FOUND IN ISAIAH 61:1-3:

"The Spirit of the Lord God is upon me; because the Lord hath anointed me to preach good tidings unto the meek; he hath sent me to bind up the brokenhearted, to proclaim liberty to the captives, and the opening of the prison to them that are bound; To proclaim the acceptable year of the Lord, and the day of vengeance of our God; to comfort all that mourn; To appoint unto them that mourn in Zion, to give unto them beauty for ashes, the oil of joy for mourning, the garment of praise for the spirit of heaviness; that they might be called trees of righteousness, the planting of the Lord, that he might be glorified."

THIS WAS JESUS' MISSION STATEMENT:

"And Jesus returned in the power of the Spirit into Galilee...And there was delivered unto him the book of the prophet Esaias. And when he had opened the book, he found the place where it was written, The Spirit of the Lord is upon me, because he hath anointed me to preach the gospel to the poor, he hath sent me to heal the brokenhearted, to preach deliverance to the captives, and recovery of sight to the blind, to set at liberty them that are bruised, To preach the acceptable year of the Lord. And he closed the book, and gave it again to the minister, and sat down...And he began to say unto them, THIS DAY IS THIS SCRIPTURE FULFILLED IN YOUR EARS."(Luke 4:14, 17-21).

THESE DO PROPHETESS BORCHERS AND YOU SHALLL SAVE MANY SOULS AND YOURSELF.

Be blessed;" -**Dr. Randy E. Simmons the Prophet Mentor August 1st 2010;**

THE NURSERY: FIRST STEPS

"Dear Mentor Randy,

Tears of Gladness................YES IT WOULD SEEM I HAVE BECOME PREGNANT WITH GLOBAL VISIONS.....sent out 700 odd Invitations yesterday.....this page is so Anointed with many Blessings, as I traveled up and down, and reading the notes I WAS TOUCHED ANEW, seems as though I am like a piece of blotting paper and soaking up all Knowledge from God.

CONFIRM THAT YOUR OWN SPIRITUAL BIRTH PANGS WITHIN YOUR OWN SPIRITUAL BOWELS.... B.L.E.S.S.E.D......................

YOUR FEBRUARY 2010 VISION ....I do not think ye strange Friend ... quite the opposite ... you are speaking language that I truly understand and not having had anyone to share with such things either until you my Mentor ....grateful for your sharing PROPHETIC IMPREGNATION CENTRE I UNDERSTAND ....How Blessed of God art thee ....U.N.B.E.L.I.E.V.A.B.L.E. You heard God speak to your heart and given THE MISSION STATEMENT OF THE PROPHET ....and JESUS' MISSION STATEMENT.....

Will come as no surprise to you whatsoever CONFIRMED.....These Scriptures plus a few others that Holy Spirit gave me 30 years Born Again Christian Day, when I asked Him what was my Purpose for him sending back into the World for His Glory...SHALL MAKE NOTES AND PLACE THOSE ON MY PAGE TODAY...GRATEFUL THANKS RANDY........

PROPHETESS BORCHERS SHALL ENDEAVOUR WITH ALL HER HEART AND SOUL....TO SAVE MANY SOULS AND MYSELF.....Blessings upon you," -Sis Dee ......<3 A dream follows that I had last Evening...**August 2nd 2010, 1:35am**

THE NURSERY:
DEVELOPING, GROWING, SEEING

DREAM/VISION....Awoken at 6.00 am. Our time 1st August, 2010...
Vigilant, wary, standing ......Praying..... Holy Spirit told me to come and write this down for you to peruse Mentor Randy....Later I found out that there was Circus encamped someone in the area of Australian Bush land and Countryside..... River of Water, very beautiful Landscape, and I was watching a graceful Rothschild Giraffe.... being pregnant it was about to give birth......Then I heard angry shouts as Farmers came with shotguns to kill an animals escaped as interfering with their Farms, Livestock and crops, even threatened myself if I did not leave the Giraffe ......I led it to safety down by the riverside and on returning to the higher banks to look at what was going on I realized that I had no torch to see......moonlit led me as Husbandry people everywhere looking for Giraffe and Elephant.....also Pregnant....I led them to where I thought the Elephant was....later this was found to be dead died giving birth and placenta and much blood around. Whilst near the Elephant I felt it topple over and a mass plummet to the ground, and then something "plopped" into my lap!!!! Could nothing to help the 1st Babe Elephant breathing badly and too large for me to lift!!!!! Heard sirens ringing and the Police and Circus people and Farmers were locking horns in the race to gather and find the animals!!!!!!! I sheltered the 1st Baby Elephant ... it needed suckling, it was very weak and cold, I started nursing it in my lap, wrapping

my skirt and clothing around it to keep it warm. Began talking to it and husing it and consoling Babe as if it was my very own ....Husbandry folk found me and I pointed to where the other Baby Elephant was and they got to it and ministered first aid and hypothermia had set in and it was in shock!!!!! We both survived..............was exhausted........

Randy the Gestation period for an Elephant is 2 years which is the time we had been prayerfully considering leaving our Church Home of 18 years!!!!! Was this dream about the lead up to my IMPREGNATION AND BIRTHING AS A PROPHETESS........? ?????? There is more in this I know, Rex said to just share as is.....

When I went to bed after Praying for us ....I pictured and visualized us hand in hand walking together into the Throne Room of Grace ... as I watched our 2 backs going into the Holy Presence I saw a Golden light encircling us ....we continued on into the Glory of God and His Holy Presence .... and we spoke and we communed and we were taught and we were blessed and Anointed Further for.........Thanks," -**Dee <3 August 2nd 2010, 1:35am**

THE NURSERY: LEARNING, TRAINING- UNDERSTANDING THE PROPHETIC EYE:

My dear Prophetess Borchers;

The vision is huge. Your first answer indicates this and your pregnancy is obvious. I am a deep man. I shared the vision I shared with you with your friend Grace. She told me that the vision indicates that I had entered the Royal chamber of God and he had given me the Royal seed to give to the body of Christ. This is getting deep. Ur dream is powerful and the two animals mentioned are significant to Africa's and perhaps Australia's survival. I am a prince and son of God. You have been chosen to nurse and nurture the Royal seed as indicated in your dream. I hope I can tread deep with you. What I'm about to see in the spirit when I look closer into your dream is not for the ordinary. This is deeply spiritual. Not only were you birthed a Prophetess...but a carrier of the Royal seed. Please I do not wish to offend but your dream is deep. I will contemplate it a few hours. You are chosen. I felt the pull and nausea of your pregnancy all day. Why are we so connected?

I reflected again on the statement you made at the friend request. I never thought we would even communicate again like so many of my friends, nor did I know we would be so connected. God visited you in this dream. I hope you are prepared for what is ahead. The Royal seed is anointed and precious. You are the carrier. My God...I can only hope for help."
-**Randy Prophet mentor August 2nd 2010, 3:00am**

THE NURSERY: CURISOSITY, LEARNING

"My dear Mentor Randy......

The Vision is huge ....Thank you for being a deep man......so glad you shared the

Vision with Grace....I held back.....confirming now that she was correct in saying that the Vision indicates that you had entered the Royal chamber of God and have been given the Royal seed to give the Body of Christ. We need to mentor and disciple Sis Grace, she and I have long been a Spiritual backstop ... on Friday evenings for examples she uses the chat box and tells me there is a new post on her page, and Prays as I go over to Prophesy/Preach/Teach whatever I am led to do....and we go backwards and forwards with others and one another sometimes for over 60 comments.....she is a Powerful and Strong Woman of God.....

GETTING DEEP.....Glory....the Dream is powerful ...Praising God.....the two animals are significant for Africa's and perhaps Australia's Survival.... Have loved African Elephants ever since a little girl and wanted to visit there to see and also Giraffes, have a large framed Print of Mother and Child Rothschild Giraffes in our Study MAKULU Mother reaching down to kiss her new born on the top of her head LOVE IS .....is the message beneath ...... so can understand why our Lord uses these significant endangered species.......You are a Prince and Son of God, I have been chosen to nurse and nurture the Royal seed as indicated in my dream THANK YOU.PLEASE TREAD AS DEEP AS NEEDS BYE AND YOU CAN NEVER EVER OFFEND ME ....that which you are about to see in the Spirit as you look closer is not for the ordinary I THOUGHT NOT.....so strongly was I told to leave my bed and come to the Study and write down immediately what I had seen and forgot to say heard everything and all in real life colour and could smell as well.

Thank you Prophet Mentor that you shall contemplate it for a few hours, I PRAISE GOD THAT I AM CHOSEN as a Birthed Prophetess, but a Carrier of the Royal Seed.......that is so amazing and I am still in Reverential Awe...... Happy also that you can feel the pull and nausea of my pregnancy all day.....WHY ARE WE SO CONNCECTED!!!!! BECAUSE GOD DECREED IT TO BE THIS WAY ... HE GIFTED US TO ONE ANOTHER FOR JUST SUCH A TIME AS THIS ....AND MANY MANY MORE JOURNEYS TO BE TRAVELLED TOGETHER FOR HIM........ Yes I too have often reflected on the statement I made at the Friend request, and thought why did I not say more because it was as if I knew you already, but was not the time nor the place and in public for heard the words to Deborah...BIDE YOUR TIME IT WILL AID YOUR DECISIONS ......Yes God visited me in this dream, please do not forget that it all began as I visualized us hand in hand entering the Throne Room of Grace ....I too Pray that I am prepared for what is ahead, I am presuming that Our Lord has and is doing that even now Randy .....THE ROYAL SEED IS ANNOINTED AND SO VERY PRECIOUS..... THAT I AM THE CARRIER...MY GOD....I PRAY THAT HE GRANTS YOU HIS HELP....would say .THAT THE LORD WILL TAKE DELIGHT IN YOU AND THAT HE IS THE HOLY OF HOLIES OF WHICH YOU ARE HIS
PROPHET GUARDIAN OF THE ROYAL SEED THAT IN THE ROYAL CHAMBER HE AWAITS TO COMMUNE WITH YOU.....AND YOU WILL BE

MUCH SOUGHT AFTER AS YOU PASS THROUGH THE GATES OF PARADISE...THE BRONZE GATES CANNOT STOP YOUR ENTRANCE......"-
Prophetess Borchers.... August 2nd 2010, 3:44am

THE NURSERY: STEPS, WALKING

"Dear Prophetess Borchers;

My cognition left me and my spiritual bowels yearned within me as I contemplated your dream and your pregnancy. They are one. The fields of Australia are ripe unto harvest as is indicated by the rich and fruitful bush lands. THE MAJESTY OF THE GIRAFFE is you. THE STRENGTH AND UNFORGETFULNESS OF THE ELEPHANT is me. That both were pregnant is indicative of that which we have been impregnated with. My gestation period has been long and I have labored of a long season to give birth. When I do it will PLOP out and many will rush and seek the seed of the elephant because it is there where the vision lies and WE WON'T, NOR CAN FORGET. Many have chased me over the years and because of my call and yours likewise, we cannot settle for the usual or mundane. Hence the chasing of the circus people and the police. Elephants and giraffes are not a threat one is simply tall, the other huge and cannot and should not be easily contained. They need the beautiful bush lands and rivers to be happy and fulfill their purpose. Often people...THE CIRCUS...tries to contain them and hamper their purpose. This has been my case...BAD RELATIONSHIPS AND CONNECTIONS. Your gestation has been long. Two years ago I started to seek God in deep prayer and fasting hence the visions, word, and ministry. IT CANNOT BE CONTAINED...IT IS GLOBAL. Two years ago you began to seek God as to whether or not to leave your church of 18 years.

We are connected...we are pregnant...a great move of God is about to begin. I often say that it will not begin in America...IT WILL COME TO AMERICA. You covered and nurtured the seed of the elephant at birth. I have been wounded. My birthing delayed. NURTURE...BREASTING... THE COVERING BY YOUR SKIRT. All forms of mothering and acceptance. You have searched for something to adopt as your own birthing sometimes have been difficult. THE SKIRT...a sign of acceptance and protection...caring...YOU ARE MINE! So have you embraced me and my vision...THE SEED OF THE ELEPHANT!

The beautiful lands await, a place where God will birth a new thing...I HAD NO TORCH...the light of the moon gave guidance and direction. You then gave guidance to the Husbandry people. The people are hungry for wisdom, teaching and guidance- THE ELEPHANT! Some seek to destroy it, thus destroying the vision...THE LIGHT OF THE MOON...the farmers and police. But God has those who will protect the vision...THE HUSBANDRY PEOPLE, and nurture and feed the vision...YOU! All survived...THE VISION IS SECURED! Your birthing means more...NOT JUST A PROPHETESS, BUT A PRINCESS...ROYAL SEED! Now I must take you deeper. You saw us..." I pictured and visualized us hand in hand walking together into the Throne Room of Grace ... as I watched our 2 backs going into the Holy Presence I saw a Golden light encircling us........we continued on into the Glory of God and His Holy Presence....and we spoke and we communed and we were taught and we were Blessed and Anointed Further for.........A SPIRITUAL COVENANT...A MARRIAGE IF YOU WILL FOR LACK OF A BETTER COMPARISON...A UNION INTO HIS GLORY! ROYALTY...THE ROYAL HOLY SEED CARRIERS OF AUSTRALIA...THEN THE WORLD!

The delivery of the giraffe seems to have been delayed as you became the nurturer of the baby elephant...THE ROYAL SEED! For elephants are truly king of beast...' WE ARE CONNECTED OUR TWO SPIRITS ARE INTERTWINED AND TOGETHER.' Your words remind me of a vision I had earlier this year similar to that as you saw us enter the throne room of mercy and Glory of God. I SENSE A DEEP SPIRITUAL INTIMACY...AS IN A SPIRITUAL LOVE AFFAIR...A COURTSHIP...A FLIRTING...FROM MENTOR TO MATE??!! -Dr. Randy E. Simmons

THE NURSERY: TUTORS, TEACHERS:

Interpretation of Prophetess Dee's dream by that Prophetess (08-02-10):

'This can be one of two things. The giraffe is the tallest animal and in
Comparison to the others has a long neck. She describes it as graceful which means she has admiration for it. It is also spotted and can be confusing to look at. She has put her 'neck' out

there reaching high for others and cleared their confusion. Yet the angry faithless farmers did not believe or negatively influenced her visions by interrupting their process and prematurely bringing her prophecies forth. In doing so, as with many premature babies, it died because it was not nursed properly. She does not leave because she stands by her word. They were the ones who threatened the vision and prophecies themselves by being impatient. So instead of a full term baby they either committed abortion or infanticide. I must know the color of her elephant. I sense that this elephant was not the natural color.

Elephants are powerful. Intelligent, revered, wise and even worshiped. They once regarded this woman highly and blamed her for things not coming to pass which is the representation of the dead mother. Yet the proof that she is indeed a true Prophetess came in the birth of twins - double for her trouble. Elephants are the largest land animals so can you imagine the size?
Actually to be correct, the gestational period of an elephant is 18 to 22 months (not two years as is commonly believed). This is something I remembered since 5th grade during a project I did on elephants. Twins, an extremely rare thing in elephants are born close to the 18 month time frame. So she saw twin elephants. 18 does indicate twin births in elephants. Time to do what the elephants do. Leave the birth canal and in a matter of minutes stand on her own two feet and WALK ON. Also, the interesting thing about elephant babies is that lions and tigers watch these births from a

distance but rarely attack for fear of being attacked by the herd. So now, those doubters will try to attack again but her herd of prophets, her new company will not allow it and she can walk confidently.

To add to that.... calves are nursed for five years so with her, all will be done within five years." – **that Prophetess on Mon, Aug 2, 2010 at 9:56am.**

THE NURSERY: AN EAGER STUDENT

"Hello Prince Randy,

Thanks for that Prophetess looking at the dream. Will you please thank her for me?

18 months to 22 month gestation period of Elephants she is correct on and I cannot be exactly of our Prayerful Consideration of leaving our Church of 18 years, so that it is confirmed and you yourself may not be exactly sure of the time of your own gestation, so that is cool ..... YES ELEPHANT WAS NOT A NORMAL COLOUR, not dusty as when they roll in the dust definitely an African with the larger east COLOUR WAS A VERY, VERY PALE GREY.....I HAVE ADMIRED GIRAFFES since a young girl (Giraffes) also and she is correct in saying that the prophetic did not die, but that Prophetess is correct as in the Anglican Church was okay, then the Apostolic Church okay, then the one we have just left on again off again 1st Pastor was fine and very encouraging until his wife interfered and aborted many, many and I nearly made to leave the Church over one ...at an Evening Prayer night I was

the 1st one ever to bring a prophesy which was asked IF ANYONE......They got the Confirmation of the Preaching Person that evening and 2 Elders brought 'LEADERSHIP IS IN DISARRAY AND
THUS THE FLOCK IS SCATTERED' were the words that were focused on and was a long word as is this email I was almost burnt at the stake over that one.....Then I was not recognized.... spasmodically.....until FB which completely opened there arms and received. All the rest seems in order. Thanks for that my Prince, Much Love," -**Princess Dee <3 August 3rd 2010, 1:04am**

THE NURSERY: A TUTOR'S PRAISE

I KNEW IT! It's a white elephant she saw...the most revered of all the species. It's a very, very rare birth and they are honored and a sign of peace, prosperity and kingdom control. In fact, only the royals or kings owned them. They are so sacred, that they aren't allowed to be used for labor or anything. I know from a Buddhist friend that Buda's mother dreamt of the white elephant which signified his birth as you know; he is a symbol of holiness in that culture." –**That Prophetess August 3rd 2010,**

CHAPTER SEVEN

THE ROYAL SEED:
PRINCE AND PRINCESS-SPIRITUAL COURTSHIP

2009 The Holy Spirit called me Princess Warrior Prophet

★**SPIRITUAL COURTSHIP**: - There seems to be a time when Prophets become Princes and Prophetess become Princesses. "But ye are a chosen generation, a royal priesthood, an holy nation, a peculiar people; that ye should show forth the praises of him who hath called you out of darkness into his marvelous light;" so say peter 2:9. The Prophetic office is unique and there is a place in God where I've learnt God's intimacy. Females seem to understand this better and try to teach it to the male. <u>The anointing is attractive and there is a dance that seems to go on between a male and female Prophet</u>...a flirtation in the spirit if you please!

CHAPTER SEVEN

THE ROYAL SEED: PRINCE AND PRINCESS- SPIRITUAL COURTSHIP

There seems to be a time when Prophets become Princes and Prophetess become Princesses. "But ye are a chosen generation, a royal priesthood, an holy nation, a peculiar people; that ye should show forth the praises of him who hath called you out of darkness into his marvelous light;" so say peter 2:9. The Prophetic office is unique and there is a place in God where I've learnt God's intimacy. Females seem to understand this better and try to teach it to the male. The anointing is attractive and there is a dance that seems to go on between a male and female Prophet...a flirtation in the spirit if you please!

THE PRINCESS:

Dear Mentor Randy,

Tears of Gladness.................YES IT WOULD SEEM I HAVE BECOME PREGNANT WITH GLOBAL VISIONS.....sent out 700 odd Invitations yesterday.....this page is so Anointed with many Blessings, as
I traveled up and down, and reading the notes I WAS TOUCHED ANEW, seems as though I am like a piece of blotting paper and soaking up all Knowledge from God. CONFIRM THAT YOUR OWN SPIRITUAL BIRTH PANGS WITHIN YOUR OWN SPIRITUAL BOWELS

....B.L.E.S.S.E.D............YOUR FEBRUARY 2010 VISION....I do not think ye strange Friend...quite the opposite...you are speaking language that I truly understand and not having had anyone to share with such things either until you my Mentor....grateful for your sharing
PROPHETIC IMPREGNATION CENTRE I UNDERSTAND.......How Blessed of God art thee....

U.N.B.E.L.I.E.V.A.B.L.E. You heard God speak to your heart and given THE MISSION STATEMENT OF THE PROPHET....and JESUS' MISSION STATEMENT.....Will come as no surprise to you whatsoever CONFIRMED.....These Scriptures plus a few others that Holy Spirit gave me 30 years Born Again Christian Day, when I asked Him what was my Purpose for him sending back into the World for His Glory ... SHALL MAKE NOTES AND PLACE THOSE ON MY PAGE TODAY... GRATEFUL THANKS RANDY......................

PROPHETESS BORCHERS SHALL ENDEAVOUR WITH ALL HER HEART AND SOUL ....TO SAVE MANY SOULS AND MYSELF.....Blessings upon you, Sis Dee ......<3 A dream follows that I had last Evening..." -**August 2nd 2010, 1:35am**

THE PRINCESS DREAMS:

"DREAM/VISION....Awoken at 6.00 am. Our time 1st August, 2010...
Vigilant, wary, standing......Praying.....Holy Spirit told me to come and write this down for you to peruse Mentor Randy....Later I found

out that there was Circus encamped someone in the area of Australian Bush land and Countryside ..... River of Water, very beautiful Landscape, and I was watching a graceful Rothschild Giraffe.... being pregnant it was about to give birth......Then I heard angry shouts as Farmers came with shotguns to kill an animals escaped as interfering with their Farms, Livestock and crops, even threatened myself if I did not leave the Giraffe......I led it to safety down by the riverside and on returning to the higher banks to look at what was going on I realized that I had no torch to see ......moonlit led me as Husbandry people everywhere looking for Giraffe and Elephant.....also Pregnant ....I led them to where I thought the Elephant was ....later this was found to be dead died giving birth and placenta and much blood around.

Whilst near the Elephant I felt it topple over and a mass plummet to the ground, and then something "plopped" into my lap!!!! Could nothing to help the 1st Babe Elephant breathing badly and too large for me to lift!!!!! Heard sirens ringing and the Police and Circus people and Farmers were locking horns in the race to gather and find the animals!!!!!!! I sheltered the 1st Baby Elephant ... it needed suckling, it was very weak and cold, I started nursing it in my lap, wrapping my skirt and clothing around it to keep it warm. Began talking to it and husing it and consoling Babe as if it was my very own ....Husbandry folk found me and I pointed to where the other Baby Elephant was and they got to it and ministered first aid and hypothermia had set in and it was in shock!!!!!

We both survived............. was exhausted ....Randy the Gestation period for an Elephant is 2 years which is the time we had been Prayer fully considering leaving our Church Home of 18 years!!!!! Was this dream about the lead up to my IMPREGNATION AND BIRTHING AS A PROPHETESS........???????There is more in this I know, Rex said to just share as is.....When I went to bed after Praying for us ....I pictured and visualized us hand in hand walking together into the Throne Room of Grace ... as I watched our 2 backs going into the Holy Presence I saw a Golden light encircling us ....we continued on into the Glory of God and His Holy Presence.... and we spoke and we communed and we were taught and we were Blessed and Anointed Further for.........Thanks," -Dee <3August 2nd 2010, 1:35am

THE PRINCE REPLYS:

"My dear Princess Dee;

The vision is huge. Your first answer indicates this and ur pregnancy is obvious. I am a deep man. I shared the vision I shared with you with your friend Grace. She told me that the vision indicates that I had enter the Royal chamber of God and he had given me the Royal seed to give to the body of Christ. This is getting deep. Ur dream is powerful and the two animals mentioned are significant to Africa's and perhaps Australia's survival. I am a prince and son of God. You have been chosen to nurse and nurture the Royal seed as indicated in your dream. I hope I can tread deep with you. What I'm about to see in the spirit when I look closer into your dream is not for the ordinary. This is deeply spiritual. Not only were u birthed a prophetess...but a carrier of the Royal seed. Please I do not wish to offend but your dream is deep. I will contemplate it a few hours. U r chosen. I felt the pull and nausea of ur pregnancy all day. Why are we so connected?

I reflected again on the statement you made at the friend request. I never thought we would even communicate again like so many of my friends, nor did I know we would be so connected. God visited u in this dream. I hope u r prepared for what is ahead. The Royal seed is anointed and precious. U r the carrier. My God...I can only hope for help." -**Randy Prince/Prophet mentor August 2nd 2010, 3:00am**

PRINCESS DEE:

"My dear Mentor Randy......The Vision is huge....................Thank you for being a deep man......so glad you shared the Vision with Grace....I held back.....confirming now that she was correct in saying that the
Vision indicates that you had entered the Royal chamber of God and have been given the Royal seed to give the Body of Christ. We need to mentor and disciple Sis Grace, she and I have long been a Spiritual backstop ... on Friday evenings for examples she uses the chat box and tells me there is a new post on her page, and Prays as I go over to

Prophesy/Preach/Teach whatever I am led to do.....and we go backwards and forwards with others and one another sometimes for over 60 comments.....she is a Powerful and Strong Woman of God.....
GETTING DEEP.....Glory.....the Dream is powerful...Praising God.....the two animals are significant for Africa's and perhaps Australia's Survival....Have loved African Elephants ever since a little girl and wanted to visit there to see and also Giraffes, have a larger framed Print of Mother and Child Rothschild Giraffes in our Study MAKULU Mother reaching down to kiss her new born on the top of her head LOVE IS.....is the message beneath ...... so can understand why our Lord uses these significant endangered species.......You are a Prince and Son of God, I have been chosen to nurse and nurture the Royal seed as indicated in my dream THANK YOU. PLEASE TREAD AS DEEP AS NEEDS BE AND YOU CAN NEVER EVER OFFEND ME........that which you are about to see in the Spirit as you look closer is not for the ordinary I THOUGHT NOT.....so strongly was I told to leave my bed and come to the Study and write down immediately what I had seen and forgot to say heard everything and all in real life color and could smell as well.

Thank you Prophet Mentor that you shall contemplate it for a few hours, I PRAISE GOD THAT I AM CHOSEN as a Birthed Prophetess, but a Carrier of the Royal Seed.......that is so amazing and I am still in Reverential Awe ...... Happy also that you can feel the pull and nausea of my pregnancy all day.....WHY ARE WE SO CONNCECTED!!!!! BECAUSE GOD

DECREED IT TO BE THIS WAY ... HE GIFTED US TO ONE ANOTHER FOR JUST SUCH A TIME AS THIS ....AND MANY, MANY MORE JOURNIES TO BE TRAVELLED TOGETHER FOR HIM........Yes I too have often reflected on the statement I made at the Friend request, and thought why did I not say more because it was as if I knew you already, but was not the time nor the place and in public for heard the words to Deborah...BIDE YOUR TIME IT WILL AID YOUR DECISIONS ......

Yes God visited me in this dream, please do not forget that it all began as I visualized us hand in hand entering the Throne Room of Grace ....I too Pray that I am prepared for what is ahead, I am presuming that Our Lord has and is doing that even now Randy.....THE ROYAL SEED IS ANNOINTED AND SO VERY PRECIOUS.....THAT I AM THE CARRIER...MY GOD.... I PRAY THAT HE GRANTS YOU HIS HELP.... would say .THAT THE LORD WILL TAKE DELIGHT IN YOU AND THAT HE IS THE HOLY OF HOLIES OF WHICH YOU ARE HIS PROPHET GUARDIAN OF THE ROYAL SEED THAT IN THE ROYAL CHAMBER HE AWAITS TO COMMUNE WITH YOU .....AND YOU WILL BE MUCH SOUGHT AFTER AS YOU PASS THROUGH THE GATES OF PARADISE... THE BRONZE GATES CANNOT STOP YOUR ENTRANCE....................."-**Prophetess Borchers....
2.8.2010, 3:44am**

THE PRINCE:

"Dear Princess Dee;

My cognition left me and my spiritual bowels yearned within me as I contemplated your dream and your pregnancy. They are one. The fields of Australia are ripe unto harvest as is indicated by the rich and fruitful bush lands. THE MAJESTY OF THE GIRAFFE is you. THE STRENGTH AND UNFORGETFULNESS OF THE ELEPHANT is me. That both were pregnant is indicative of that which we have been impregnated with. My gestation period has been long and I have labored of a long season to give birth. When I do it will PLOP out and many will rush and seek the seed of the elephant because it is there where the vision lies and WE WON'T, NOR CAN FORGET.

Many have chased me over the years and because of my call, and yours likewise, we cannot settle for the usual or mundane. Hence the chasing of the circus people and the police. Elephants and giraffes are not a threat one is simply tall, the other huge and cannot and should not be easily contained. They need the beautiful bush lands and rivers to be happy and fulfill their purpose. Often people...THE CIRCUS...tries to contain them and hamper their purpose. This has been my case...BAD RELATIONSHIPS AND CONNECTIONS. Your gestation has been long. Two years ago I started to seek God in deep prayer and fasting hence the visions, word, and ministry. IT CANNOT BE CONTAINED...IT IS GLOBL. Two years ago you began to seek God as to whether or not to leave your church of 18 years.

We are connected...we are pregnant...a great move of God is about to begin. I often say that it will not begin in America...IT WILL COME TO AMERICA. You covered and nurtured the seed of the elephant at birth. I have been wounded. My birthing delayed. NURTURE...BREASTING... THE COVERING BY YOUR SKIRT. All forms of mothering and acceptance. You have searched for something to adopt as your own birthing sometimes have been difficult. THE SKIRT...a sign of acceptance and protection...caring...YOU ARE MINE! So have you embraced me and my vision...THE SEED OF THE ELEPHANT!

The beautiful lands await, a place where God will birth a new thing...'I HAD NO TORCH...' the light of the moon gave guidance and direction. You then gave guidance to the Husbandry people. The people are hungry for wisdom, teaching and guidance- THE ELEPHANT! Some seek to destroy it, thus destroying the vision...THE LIGHT OF THE MOON...the farmers and police. But God has those who will protect the vision...THE HUSBANDRY PEOPLE, and nurture and feed the vision...YOU! All survived...THE VISION IS SECURED! Your birthing means more...NOT JUST A PROPHETESS, BUT A PRINCESS...ROYAL SEED! Now I must take you deeper. You saw us..." I pictured and visualized us hand in hand walking together into the Throne Room of Grace ... as I watched our 2 backs going into the Holy Presence I saw a Golden light encircling us........we continued on into the Glory of God and His Holy Presence....and we spoke and we communed and we were taught and we were Blessed and Anointed Further for ....A SPIRITUAL COVENANT...A MARRIAGE IF YOU WILL FOR LACK OF A BETTER COMPARISON...A UNION INTO HIS GLORY! ROYALTY...THE ROYAL HOLY SEED CARRIERS OF AUSTRALIA...THEN THE WORLD!" -**August 2nd 2010, 9:32am**

PRINCESS DEE:

"Dear Mentor Randy,

Your First Portion of and interpretation was amazing......understand that cognition departed from you, as it did to me also explain further later please. We are so intertwined IN LOVE BELOVED MAN OF GOD ....TRULY AMAZING...TEARS OF JOY......The fields of Australia ripe unto harvest (I was born in the Country in Victoria and roamed the river and lagoons and the bush land seeing many beautiful things, even real tiger snakes did not bother me, I used to ride fresh Water Turtles down the river falls)....... GLORY HALLELUJAH.... I am the Graceful Giraffe in MAJESTY....YOU ARE THE ELEPHANT REPRESENTING THE STRENGTH AND UNFORGETFULNESS...GLORY... WOW....okay so both impregnated but you have labored long and hard and shall PLOP OUT (that is the noise I heard) MANY SEEK BUT NOT ALL SHALL BE ALLOWED TO FIND....WE SHALL NOT AND CANNOT FORGET....So agree Randy we cannot settle

nor should we for the mundane or normal CANNOT BE CONTAINED ...TIS GLOBAL....ALWAYS KNEW THAT IN MY SPIRIT....Both have been in bad relationships and many have sought us for the wrong reasons and have been hurt and endured through thick and thin.....same gestation period AMAZING .... YES WE ARE CONNECTED AND PREGNANT THIS MOVE OF GOD IS AWAITING AND BEGINNING (Someone said today on my wall shall start in Queens land Australia and then Ian Bunyan of The Power Station saw my request to pray for the PM of Australia think I explained about her and he is going to place something on their discussion board from some of the words on my wall today under the Australian Flag...some of the words came FROM YOU)
THE SEED OF THE ELEPHANT IS COVERED ... YES I AM YOURS I HAVE EMBRACED YOU AND YOUR VISION COMPLETELY AMEN.

NEXT THE BEAUTIFUL LANDS AWAIT....... THE LIGHT OF THE MOON... I think you spoke of that in earlier notes also..... Hungry for Wisdom, Teaching and Guidance AMEN, AMEN, AMEN WORDS OF WISDOM AND TRUTH ......THE ELEPHANT SHALL NOT BE DESTROYED....EVER......
YES GOD HAS THOSE WHO SHALL PROTECT THE VISION.....GOOD GRIEF I AM THE HUSBANDRY PEOPLE who nurture and feed the vision THANK YOU.....THE VISION IS SECURED ... SINGING IN MY SPIRIT.....COMMUNING...... B.E.A.U.T.I.F.U.L. GRACE FILLED GIRAFFE....MAJESTY..... HE REIGNS.......ON HIS THRONE..... SPEECHLESS...MY BIRTHING

MEANS MORE....NOT JUST A PROPHETESS....BUT A PRINCESS...ROYAL SEED........CAN HARDLY TYPE.....THAT I HAVE BEEN SO CHOSEN ....THAT I HAVE BEEN SO HONOURED AS HIS HAND MAIDEN AND VESSEL ......SO SPIRITUALLY BEAUTIFUL AND TO BE PRIZED AND IN REVERENTIAL AWE.......

YOU ARE GOING TO TAKE ME DEEPER EVEN THAN.....YES I SAW US VERY CLEARLY ......AS THOUGH WE WERE IN LOVE.....IN THE SPIRITUAL SENSE AND BELONGED TOGETHER .. BEFORE I READ FURTHER PERHAPS THE ELEPHANT AND THE GIRAFFE ARE PRINCE AND PRINCESS.....A SPIRITUAL COVENANT....YES, YES A MARRIAGE IS WHAT I THOUGHT I SAW AS THOUGH WE WERE APPROACHING TOGETHER FOR THE HOLY UNCTION......A UNION INTO HIS GLORY.... YES, YES, YES, YES......THE FURTHER WE WALKED THE SMALLER WE GOT OUR FIGURES IN THE DISTANCE AND WE JUST JOURNEYED FURTHER INTO HIS MAJESTY, GLORY AND GRACE.....A UNION OF GLORY....ROYALTY...WE ARE THE ROYAL HOLY SEED CARRIERS OF AUSTRALIA...THEN THE WORLD !!!!!!!

SORRY my bowels are being wrenched with a type of happiness for want of a better word than I have ever known before....... EXTRAORDINARY HOLINESS WITHIN ME ... SHALL TOUCH YOU IF IT HAS NOT ALREADY.....** more to come** THANK YOU BELOVED ELEPHANT FROM YOUR BELOVED GIRAFFE...THE ROYALTY OF THE ROYAL HOLY

SEED CARRIERS OF AUSTRALIA, THEN THE WORLD......

Thank you Beloved Man.......Much Love......" -
Dee <3 August 2nd 2010, 10:06am

THE PRINCE:

"Dear Princess Dee;

The delivery of the giraffe seems to have been delayed as you became the nurturer of the baby elephant...THE ROYAL SEED! For elephants are truly king of beast...' WE ARE CONNECTED OUR TWO SPIRITS ARE INTERTWINED AND TOGETHER.' Your words remind me of a vision I had earlier this year similar to that as you saw us enter the throne room of mercy and Glory of God. I SENSE A DEEP SPIRITUAL INTIMACY...AS IN A SPIRITUAL LOVE AFFAIR...A COURTSHIP...A FLIRTING...FROM MENTOR TO MATE??!!

I saw in a vision in February 2010 two beings. Their essence was male and female, yet they were one. Like Adam and Eve. They stood beside each other in a great light of Glory. I then heard the flutter of wings. Appearing around them were many angels and the formed as it were a tunnel around them like a whirlwind. The angels began to fly around them and upward, forming a powerful whirl wind and creating a white wall of angelic wings. As the angels continued, I saw as the two essences, male and female embrace. As they did so, they were slowly taken up and entered the glory of God. It was a moment of intimacy and ecstasy. It was the purest moment of intimacy I'd ever seen. The purest act of lovemaking I'd ever envisioned. GOD...MALE...FEMALE!

Now I see it all clearly. I CALL YOU PRINCESS...ROYAL SEED CARRIER...SPIRITUAL WIFE...SPIRIT MATE! This is deep. I feel it...I see you. I see the fruit of your womb...HOLY BIRTHINGS...the end time harvest. It will get deeper. God what are you saying?" -**August 2nd 2010, 11:44am**

PRINCESS DEE:

"Dear Prince Randy,

Yes the Delivery of the Giraffe was delayed as I became the nurturer of the baby elephant needed me more at that particular moment and my Motherly Womb activated as you described earlier. ELEPHANTS ARE TRULY KING OF BEAST ....YES, YES, YES ......WE ARE CONNECTED OUR TWO SPIRITS ARE INTERTWINED AND TOGETHER ....REALLY FELT THAT DEEP WITHIN THE ESSENCE OF MY BEING, YES DARLING THERE IS A DEEP SPIRITUAL INTIMACY...AS IN A SPIRITUAL LOVE AFFAIR ... A COURTSHIP ....A FLIRTING ... FROM MENTOR TO MATE....YES, YES, YES......ACCEPTED....COME BELOVED ....Your Vision is so very beautiful and I can visualize it very, very, well...... MALE AND FEMALE...ESSENCE BEING ONE......
THAT WALL OF WHITE ANGELIC WINGS PROTECTING.....AS THE SLOWLY TAKEN UPWARDS AND ENTERED THE GLORY OF

GOD..... TRULY A MOMENT OF PUREST INTIMACY...THE PUREST ACT OF LOVEMAKING YOU HAD EVER ENVISIONED........GOD...MALE.... FEMALE..........B.E.A.U.T.I.F.U.L.!ECSTASY AND INTIMACY OF THE ROYAL ORDER......SEEING MORE CLEARLY......... I AM YOUR PRINCESS ... ROYAL SEED.... CARRIER ... SPIRITUAL WIFE ... SPIRIT MATE........ This is profoundly deep, deep, deep...... I feel you....I feel it....the fruit of my womb...HOLY BIRTHINGS.... YESSSSSSSSSSSSSSSSSSSSS THE END TIME HARVEST....... GETTING DEEPER.....WAITING BELOVED.........Lord God please answer my Spiritual Husband's Prayer...Amen <3 Goodnight................Speechless, unbelievably beautiful <3" -**August 2nd 2010, 11:58am**

THE PRINCE SPEAKS:

"Dearest Princess;

The balm in Gilead Greet thee. The moon and stars and sun rise to meet thee, and may all thy mothers children call thee blessed... The birth of the giraffe will come. The majestic strength of its neck waits to raise high above the tallest trees...even Lebanon! As lions graze and the majestic elephants roam...this day a PRINCESS IS DECLARED AND A PRINCE IS FORMED. ENTHRONED ARE THEY IN MAJESTY...GRAVEN IN THE BRONZE GLORY OF GOD'S OWN FIRE...PURGED PURE AND WHITE...SENT FORTH TO BIRTH THE PRECIOUS FRUIT OF THE EARTH!

JOINED ARE THEY IN SPIRITS...SEALED IN PURPOSE...REARED IN DESTINY! TWO AS ONE....YET ONE AS TWO...GOD, YET MAN...DIVINE, YET FLESH...GOD MAN...GOD WOMAN! PRINCE AND PRINCESS ARE THEY BEFORE GOD. THIS IS YOU DEAR PRINCESS OF AUSTRALIA...TODAY THE DAUGHTERS OF JERUSALEM ENVY YOU!
TODAY...I DECLARE YOU PRINCESS DEE!

Behold, thou art fair, my love; behold, thou art fair; thou hast doves' eyes within thy locks: thy hair is as a flock of goats that appear from mount Gilead. Thy teeth are like a flock of sheep that are even shorn, which came up from the washing; whereof every one bear twins, and none is barren among them. Thy lips are like a thread of scarlet, and thy speech is comely: thy temples are like a piece of a pomegranate within thy locks. Thy neck is like the tower of David builded for an armory, whereon there hang a thousand bucklers, all shields of mighty men. Thy two breasts are like two young roes that are twins, which feed among the lilies. Until the day break and the shadows flee away, I will get me to the mountain of myrrh, and to the hill of frankincense. Thou art all fair, my love; there is no spot in thee. Come with me from Lebanon, my spouse, with me from Lebanon: look from the top of Amana, from the top of Shenir and Hermon, from the lions' dens, from the mountains of the leopards. Thou hast ravished my heart, my sister, my spouse; thou hast ravished my heart with one of thine eyes, with one chain of thy neck. How fair is thy love, my sister, my spouse! How much better is thy love than wine! and the smell of thine ointments than all spices! Thy lips, O my spouse, drop as the honeycomb: honey and milk are under thy tongue; and the smell of thy garments is like the smell of Lebanon. A garden enclosed is my sister, my spouse; a spring shut up, a fountain sealed. Thy plants are an orchard of pomegranates, with pleasant fruits; camphire, with spikenard, Spikenard and saffron; calamus and cinnamon, with all trees of frankincense; myrrh and aloes, with all the chief spices: A fountain of gardens, a well of living waters, and streams from Lebanon. Awake, O north wind; and come, thou south; blow upon my garden, that the spices thereof may flow out. Let my beloved come into his garden, and eat his pleasant fruits." -**Prince and Prophet Mentor; Randy August 2nd 2010**

THE PRINCESS:

"Beloved Prince,

The Balm of Gilead greeted me; yes your Graceful Giraffe awaits... THIS DAY A PRINCESS IS DECLARED....AND A PRINCE IS FORMED... ENTHRONED ARE THEY IN MAJESTY...GRAVEN IN THE BRONZE GLORY OF GOD'S OWN FIRE.....PURGED PURE AND WHITE...SENT FORTH TO BIRTH THE PRECIOUS FRUIT OF THE EARTH........Precious ....YES JOINED IN SPIRITS....SEALED IN PURPOSE...REARED IN DESTINY... BEFORE THE FOUNDATIONS OF THE EARTH...TWO AS ONE...YET ONE AS TWO...GOD YET MAN...DIVINE, YET FLESH ....GOD MAN., GOD

WOMAN!!! PRINCE AND PRINCESS WE ARE BEFORE GOD....THIS IS YOUR BELOVED PRINCESS OF AUSTRALIA AND TODAY THE DAUGHTERS OF JERUSALEM ENVY ME......Cherished..................
PRINCESS DEE HAS COME FORTH TO HER PRINCE.....Behold, thou are handsome my love, behold thou eyes shine with love within for me... my locks are spun around your hands ...my lips await your placement of thine upon.....,thy speech of love to me is comely and my neck is built for intercessory warfare....my breasts are twins....come suckle. Until the day break and the shadows flee away...you shall go to the mountain of myrrh and to the hill of frankincense and come fragrance my breasts and body. Coming away with you to wherever you wish....always with you and by your side hands held and hearts intertwined. Thou hast ravished my heart my brother, my spouse, thou hast ravished my heart also with both of my eyes for I look into thine sweet eyes from my does eyes....Our love is better than wine, though we shall sup and drink together, thine ointments of mine are fragrantly beautiful, nothing can compare, yes honey and milk are under my tongue come find........A garden enclosed is within your Sister your Spouse, my Beloved Brother, my Spouse. The spring shut up and fountain sealed ... please let the tinkling waters fall lingerly beside us in the garden of love.......The orchard's fruit we shall partake of together, a fountain of gardens await, a well of living waters await...The north wind has woken, thy south has come ...blowing upon our garden...the spices thereof are flowing

out.....together my Beloved Spouse we are entering into his garden......

How handsome you are my lover!!!! Oh, how charming, and our bed is verdant. I am faint with love, Your left arm is under my fair tressed locks and your right arm embraces your Beloved, listen my lover ....flowers appear on the earth, the season of singing has come, the cooing of doves is heard in our land, arise, come my darling, come with me, show me your face, let me hear your voice against my throat and breasts, for your voice is sweet and you are Handsome dear one,
My lover is mine, and I am his, oh how handsome are my Beloved,
there is no flaw in you....come into my garden Brother and Husband, my head is drenched with dew, my hair with the dampness of the night and moonlight overhead, I have taken off my robe, must I put it on again?? My love thrust his hand through the opening....my heart is pounding for him...I AM FAINT FOR LOVE OF THE ... COME AWAY MY DARLING...PARTAKE OF THY SPOUSE...LOVER I AWAIT THE......" -**Princess Dee; August 2nd 2010;**

CHAPTER EIGHT

THE ROYAL PRIESTHOOD: THE SEED AND THE CALL

THE ROYAL PRIESTHOOD: - THE SEED AND THE CALL: Every Prophet or Prophetess is called for a time and a season, for this is how God operates. When Earth demands a change, God will send a prophet. It would seem that every Prophet with a great calling came from a Royal family or were taken care of by royalty until their appointed time. Moses, the future heir of Egypt chose "rather to suffer affliction with the people of God, than to enjoy the pleasures of sin for a season; esteeming the reproach of Christ greater riches than the treasures in Egypt: for he had respect unto the recompense of the reward." (Heb.11:25-26).

CHAPTER EIGHT

THE ROYAL PRIESTHOOD: THE SEED AND THE CALL

Every Prophet or Prophetess is called for a time and a season, for this is how God operates. When Earth demands a change, God will send a prophet. Abraham came to his generation and God called him friend; Moses came and God's presence went with him; Isaiah came and said: "woe is me..."; Elijah came declaring the righteousness of God, and will yet come to 'turn the hearts of the fathers unto the children and the hearts of the children unto the fathers'; Jeremiah came weeping for the nation Israel; Daniel came speaking forth prophecy; Ezekiel came declaring the restoration of Israel; John the Baptist came saying: 'Repent, for the kingdom of heaven is at hand'; Jesus came and went about doing good and healing all that were oppressed of the devil, for God was with him; Paul came, seeing the mysteries of God and declaring the rapture; you and I came to do the works of God... "And greater works than these shall he do; because I go unto my father."(John 14:12), said Jesus. It would seem that every Prophet with a great calling came from a Royal family or were taken care of by royalty until their appointed time. Moses, the future heir of Egypt chose "rather to suffer affliction with the people of God, than to enjoy the pleasures of sin for a season; esteeming the reproach of Christ greater riches than the treasures in Egypt: for he had respect

unto the recompense of the reward."
(Heb.11:25-26).

THE COURTSHIP OF A PROPHETESS AND A PRINCESS:

"Dearest Prophetess/Princess Dee;

I AM FAINT FOR LOVE OF THEE...COME AWAY MY DARLING...PARTAKE OF THY SPOUSE...LOVER I AWAIT THEE...words of such deep beauty and inviting passion. My spirit man within yearns to know what doth God beckon him to?

THE CALL...THE APPOINTMENT...THE ANOINTING...THE FOREKNOWING....THE ORDAINING....THE CHOSENNESS....all so deep...for yet within my bosom lies the desire to rest. Beloved Princess...REST IS SWEET...COMELY...BEAUTIFUL...NURTURING... and under your skirt I rest, as did young baby elephant; too weak to move, yet alive and now nurtured!
The spirit Beckons...there is an anointing given only to the sons of God...FOR HE HATH ANOINTED ME.... (ISA.61:1)...THE ANOINTING UPON THEE DESTROYS THE YOKE... (ISA.10:27)...THE YOKE, SUCH A BURDEN...THE WORK OF MINISTRY SUCH A BURDEN...THE BIRTHING OF SOULS SUCH A BURDEN! Yet dear Princess, God has called thee to the birth...give of thyself, look to the stars, see the moon and the sun bow before thee. Thy Prince awaits...THE ROYAL SEED IS AT HAND...RAPTURE AWAITS...LOVES AWAIT...PASSION OF SPIRITS

AWAIT...ANOINTING AWAITS...GO NOW SEE THY PRINCE...BIRTH! FOR THOU ART CALLED TO THE BIRTH...ONLY BIRTH THOU WELL! So says thy PRINCE...PROPHET...MENTOR...KING; Prince Randy" -**Dr. Randy E. Simmons-August 3rd 2010, 6:33am**

"Dearest Prince/Prophet/Mentor/King,

I AM FAINT FOR LOVE OF THEE..... COMING AWAY WITH YOU BELOVED... TO PARTAKE OF MY SPOUSE....LOVER I AWAIT THEE...yes words of such deep beauty and inviting passion....your spirit man within yearns to know what doth God beckon him to?????

THE CALL ...THE APPOINTMENT....THE ANOINTING...THE FOREKNOWING... THE ORDAINING...THE CHOSENESS....all very very deep.......for yet within your bosom lies the desire to rest......
BELOVED PRINCE....REST....COMELY... BEAUTIFULLY...I shall
NURTURE you.....and under my skirt you are resting as did the young baby elephant...too weak to move, yet alive and now nurtured and suckled and sweet endearments as I covered your body with Love.

The spirit Beckons...there is an anointing given only to the sons of God FOR HE HATH ANOINTED YOU...... THE ANOINTING UPON THEE DESTROYS THE YOKE....SUCH A BURDEN...THE WORK OF MINISTRY SUCH A BURDEN...THE BIRTHING OF SOULS SUCH A BIRDEN.....

Yes my Dear Prince...yes we shall be together at the Birth.....giving of myself in every way possible ALL OF THE ESSENCE OF MY BEING........my Prince awaits.....THE ROYAL SEED IS AT HAND...RAPTURE AWAITS...LOVE AWAITS...PASSION OF SPIRITS AWAIT...ANOINTING AWAITS..... COMING TO SEE MY PRINCE....BIRTH FOR I AM CALLED TO BIRTH...SHALL BIRTH WELL ......GLORY......SO SAYS MY PRINCE...PROPHET...MENTOR....KING....BELOVED...I RECEIVE....DEE <3" -**Prophetess Denise Borchers - August 3rd 2010, 4:34am**

THE SEARCH OF A PRINCE FOR GUIDANCE:

"God has spoken and decreed. I fell on my face in the last hour and poured out my heart to my God. I said to God: 'Lord, you said that you would take care of everything'. I poured to God my heart as a man, an ordinary man. I said to God,' they call me great man of God, they call me Prince, they call me king, they call me anointed, but I'm just a man, an ordinary man'.

As I continued to pray and pour out my heart to God I said to God: 'send me to the world, send me to the fields, send me to the ministry or send me to my career...I'm just a man.' I poured out my heart, not in despair or in depression, not entertaining the cares of the world, but as a man, an ordinary man who trust in God and leans not to my own understanding, who frets not but has committed his ways unto God, one who has renounced the hidden and dark things, one who cast all cares on him, an ordinary man. One who hears, 'come unto me, all ye that are heavy laden and I will give you rest'. Just a man.

But then I heard the Spirit speak to me: 'plow the fields...prepare for the harvest'. Then I heard: 'break up the fallow ground'. Then I heard, 'look upon the fields...they are ripe unto harvest'. Then I heard, 'the husbandman waiteth for the fruit of the earth and hath patience for it until the latter rain'. This I heard. Then I listened...and I heard rain. I couldn't believe it so I got up from my knees and surely it was raining outside. Heavy...and only for five minutes then stopped. Then I heard the Spirit say, 'you are not just an ordinary man'.

The significance of the word and timing of the rain, only for five minutes and no more has to be significant. There were three scriptures mentioned with this event this morning: Hosea.10:12-13; Luke 10:2; and James 5:7. All significant to my ministry in the past. Hosea. 10:12-13 was my favorite text for sermons as a young Evangelist; Luke 10:2 is the banner for Global Visions Minis Intl: 'INTO THE HARVEST'; and James 5:7 was used under my logo, the shower of rain falling under the umbrella of the anointing.

Also I believe that the symbol and sign of the last days move will be the elephant and the giraffe. The elephant for its strength, unforgetfulness and long gestation period. The giraffe because it reaches so high to heaven and for its gracefulness. Remember I told you first. Prince Randy" -**Dr. Randy E. Simmons -August 3rd 2010, 12:32 pm**

THE PRINCESS ANSWERS:

"Dear Prophet,

As I read of your prayerful journey as you poured your beloved heart out unto God.....then you were given those words after you had renounced the hidden and dark things......you were given the prophetic about breaking up the fallow ground.....patience for it until the latter rain......you heard that the husbandman waiteth for the fruit of the earth... you listened ...... and heard the beautiful heavy downpour of rain....heavy...YOU ARE NOT JUST AN ORDINARY MAN....
YOU ARE NOT JUST AN ORDINARY MAN ...YOU ARE AN EXTRA ORDINARY MAN ...UNIQUE AND LIKE NO OTHER.

YES THE SIGNIFICANCE OF THE 3 MINUTES OF RAIN TO ME with the Words I placed on my wall yesterday and again today WERE BECAUSE OF Y.O.U....... WATERS OF LIFE ...WATERS OF DEPTH ...WATERS OF SPIRITUAL SIGNIFACANCE
..........YESSSSSSSSSSSSS

Thank you for sharing the Scriptures and their meanings....
HOSEA is a favorite book of mine.

YES agree that the symbol and sign of the last days move ...will be the elephant and the

giraffe. The elephant being yourself for its strength, unforgetfulness and long gestation period AGREED.... the giraffe because it reaches so high to heaven and for its gracefulness AGREED...... REMEMBER I TOLD YOU FIRST??????? CURIOUS STATEMENT....Thanking my Prince/Prophet Mentor/Father ....with love from your Princess Prophetess Lover......" -
Princess/Prophetess Denise Borchers -August 4th 2010 12:52 am

THE NANNY SPEAKS:

"Good morning MOG. My hope that you had a restful night.

This is truly awesome word you received. It is time............ you have been given all the signs that re-confirm what you already have. Quite incredible! So what do you do next?" -
Grace Becki -August 4th 2010, 9:37am

THE PRINCE ANSWERS:

"Thank you WOG...as usual your spiritual perception is always on target...I will continue to watch the road signs and see where they lead. I will share a dream I had with you later today...Be blessed." -**Dr. Randy E. Simmons -August 4th 2010 4:31pm**

THE NANNY ANSWERS:

"Amen. Waiting!" -**Grace Becki -August 4th 2010 4:39pm**

THE MIDWIFE SPEAKS:

"Allowing the Lord to speak....I am listening. The rain is indeed significant." -**Holly Sharp** - **August 4th 2010 2:55pm**

THE PRINCE ANSWERS:

"Thank you...I will share with you a dream I had this morning a little latter..." -**Dr. Randy E. Simmons -August 4th 2010 4:30pm**

THE MIDWIFE SPEAKS -Prophetess Holly Sharp:

"Realizing now the difference between a prophetic anointing and functioning as a prophetess I desire to be in complete and total submission to God and to they over me in the Lord. Perhaps I am hesitant of the power of God within. Our discussion about ordinary man/woman vs. extraordinary man/woman has lingered in my heart. Made in His image, we are indeed extraordinary. When the Word comes forth it is with such strength even though it may be delivered softly. Here is a question....is a Prophet soft spoken? I am so very, very grateful for the time you invest in teaching me and imparting wisdom and understanding into me. -**August 5 2010 at 6:34pm**

"How may I pour into you on this day sir?" - **August 5 2010 at 6:35pm**

THE PRINCE ANSWERS:

"Woman of God. You already see my spirit. I feel that you have asked God to show me to you. I feel open before you. Prophetess I feel your presence...I feel your pull. I submit, do as God is showing you. Take all spiritual liberties. I feel your connection. I wait for you. **Dr. Randy E. Simmons - August 5 2010 at 6:41pm**

THE MIDWIFE SPEAKS YET AGAIN:

"Thank you Man of God....Just today I was thanking God to be alive. Just today I was thanking God for the extra years and weeping before Him over the years I wasted not serving Him and seeking His generous forgiveness. I have not time for mere "chatter" with friends for it nourishes not. I do love many friends dearly, however am beginning to sense the increased loneliness and separation a prophetess experiences. It seems as if none want to travel the road, although I am certain many are called. We have walked untrained and untamed and they are content to operate as such....carrying the garment but unwilling to wear it. I seek to learn, to grow, to be changed....stripped down and humbled before our God. None of the old friendships go with me. So be it and be it so for God doth reveal new friendship truly connected in Him. Thank you. You also may take all spiritual liberties and disclose the depth of the spirit within as the Father allows. ~" - **Prophetess Holly Sharp August 5 2010 at 6:54pm**

THE PRINCE DECLARES AND DECREES:

"Woman of God you stir me. You cause my spiritual bowels to quicken; transparency from one Prophet to another is the deepest interaction of all. I was reading some of your previous notes today and your words were quite transparent. What you have caused to be birthed only time will tell; but I sense a royal seed arising and the pregnancy you carry is deep and profound and your fruit not many can touch. God has seen fit to protect you from even some of the greatest of his prophets that carry the 'male gene' mostly...Again think me not strange but I can only speak on this level.

Yes the life of a prophet is indeed a lonely one. I have been away in my apartment now for almost two weeks with no real interacting with human beings except for going to the store and church; what I am seeking is deep. I AM AFTER THE INTIMACY OF GOD. You dear prophetess increased that desire within me to search when I had my first exchange with you; I reread your notes just to be sure; and yes you spoke of pregnancy, aborting, miscarrying, so I know that you live on a level that God gives to so few; I see it greatly. You have made me hunger, thirst, and reach for the very intimacy of God. FOR LACK OF A BETTER TERM IN SPIRIT, AND ONLY AN EARTHLY TERM CAN DESCRIBE IT, MY FIRST CONVERSATION WITH YOU FELT LIKE A LOVE AFFAIR IN THE SPIRIT; AN INTERCOURSING INTO THE DEEPER THINGS OF GOD IF YOU WILL. FORGIVE PLEASE MY FRANKNESS AND TRANSPARENCY, BUT YOU PULL ME. God bless you for you have opened up the spiritual curiosity and interest of a prophet of God to 'know' and to understand...SPIRITUAL LOVE UNHINDERED! STOP MAN OF GOD, STOP!" —**Dr. Randy E. Simmons August 5 at 9:49pm**

THE ANOINTING OF JOSEPH- CALL OF THE DREAMER:

THE PRINCE AND PROPHET SPEAKS:

"Dear Princess/Prophetess;

Greetings.

The Spirit of God continues to do profound things. You are right. I am not ordinary. God has spoken...He has decreed...He will do. The water of life has come. I heard the Spirit speak to my spirit about 10:00pm eastern time these words: "My son, if 100 people will stand behind you in support...then you could take my message to the world."

I wish to share a dream with you I had this afternoon:
I dreamed a dream this morning. In the dream I was a young boy living at home with my siblings. There was quarrelling and confusion and fighting among us. My brother Glen dominated. I watched as soon he disconnected the air condition and soon it became so hot that it was unbearable. In the sweltering heat of the house we fainted no air was even coming in. I heard my sister Maryann speak of dying.

I watched in the dream as my brother pranced around in his domineering manner. As I looked I saw him coming out of the bathroom with a horse as if he had given the horse a bath in the tub.

At this point the dream shifted and we were on Harbour Island. But it was only my sister Maryann and I (this was our custom every summer to get away from the other children). She was at my aunt Mamon's house where she often stayed during the summer months. I saw her very faint and I was working frantically to restore the air condition. I watched as a long vent appeared from the ceiling and began to blow cool air. I quickly put her under it.

The dream shifted and I found myself walking about Harbour Island and everywhere there were the biggest and ripest mangoes you could imagine. They were everywhere. I gathered many and took them to my aunt. Again I walked and this time I visited homes of people. In the dream every home I visited had shredded newspaper on the floors and among the newspaper was the freshest fish you ever saw. At every house it was so.

I then came to an open field up the Alley from my grandparents' house and as I walked across the field Raymond Bowleg met me and asked me to come say hi to his mom; (Funny thing I never remembered them having a mother growing up, their father raised them). As we crossed the field I said to Raymond as I gestured with my arms: "boy this field is large, I don't remember it being so big when we were kids". He smiled. We came to the front door of their home and he opened the door and yelled out: "mommy come meet Randy". I glanced at the floor...shredded newspaper and fresh fish. This time I saw snappers, yellow tails, grouper, grunts, jack fish; porgies, all kinds. I said to

Raymond: "what is the reason everyone's floor is covered in shredded newspaper and fresh fish...what does it mean?"
I never heard his answer. I woke up." -
**Prince/Prophet Mentor Dr. Randy E. Simmons –
August 4 2010 at 11:28pm**

THE PRINCESS AND PROPHETESS SEES THE CALL:

"Dear Prince/Prophet,

Greetings..............

Confirm if 100 people stand behind you in support then you can take my message to the World Amen Let it be so ......10.00 am Eastern Standard Time = 8.00 pm. Western Australia........Was Praying !!!!!!!

DREAM.......shall have to ponder and Pray upon, shall just right Spirit Led for the moment Prince............REX said have always between downtrodden and going to be release and fortune awaits Spiritual and in the natural ..... Ministry and Book? We spoke and I agree with both of those Randy.

You were a young boy Randy and your brother Glen had bathed and came out prancing and domineering as if he had bathed the horse..... Authority Figures on their High Horses think they can do whatever, whenever, especially to those they see as absolutely no threat as he acted to all of you.....

Sweltering heat and fainted when he turned the air conditioning off.....Your Sister spoke of dying....... Glen had a death wish and was jealous of the Siblings.... He wanted complete dominance over all.....YOU shall shortly have or are having people in your Life and Business who wish to dominate you and trying to cut off your air stream ......to cease your Ministry now and that to come ....Interesting no a Parental authority or backup!!!! Also Glen had bathed but he was not allowing anyone else to.... meaning he was clean and you and siblings dirty and unclean and he meant you to stay that way... Many shall attack you in Ministry as they already have ......you shall brush any on Horses and any switching A/C on off and bathing before YOU AWAY WITH A FLICK OF YOUR WRIST ....

Harbour Island ... place of Holiday, rest, fun, happiness... family together.....in summer.....this season is important for some reason.....Maryann was at your Aunt Mamon's house ......you saw her faint as in the dream ....once again the air condition i.e. no air available .... indicating death again ....death of something in your ministry or mine or ours .....shall not happen no weapon formed can prosper. The long vent appeared from the ceiling I believe means Heaven and God's assistance as he saw you frantically trying to get air to your Sister, the cool air blowing represents you will always be saved by our Lord God from anything that threatens you or yours and Holy Spirit entered the room with cool air .....

Walking freely about Harbour Island ....by the way you need to Holiday ....a rest from Work and Ministry.....Sabbatical for refreshing, etc, Those big and ripe mangoes you could imagine are your MINISTRY ......NOW...AND TO COME.....ready to burst forth........and for people everywhere to partake of......okay your Aunt received the many you gathered...your mercy and compassion for others......The shredded newspapers is a little......unusual in the midst of all the other....a sudden twist a sudden change on Harbour Island could indicate just that in your life Randy. You visited homes of people as you do now and shall do with your Global Ministries and Books and your Notes........ each house was so.... could mean untidiness could mean needs to be Spiritually cleaned up and that shredded newspaper could also have a double meaning in that you may have to put some matters out of your life to concentrate on more important matters, thus the shredded newspaper getting rid of that you no longer require in your life.

You came to the open filed LARGER MINISTRY AWAITS.......up the Alley it is going to be a tight squeeze to your Kingdom work..........
.....meeting Raymond Bowleg....he wanted you in his home to meet Mom........your memory no Mom in his life may indicate a Woman needed in your life ....to help nurture your dreams and visions in life Spiritually and Supernaturally and in reality ......You gesturing with your arms ... you shall be speaking and teaching at Seminars and you use these movements to demonstrate that which you speak of........ .....means a lot more...very significant ....also Prayer.........
.....Worship......the large field as kids seemed smaller...often that is the way when we revisit a childhood place ....larger or smaller

..........but in this case believe that it means harvest a plenty in your enlarged field of expertise and Ministry.....his smile means that our Lord God is pleased and wants you to continue ....a confirmation if you like.

Front door of their home.....a place of haven and safety as you wanted to go with Raymond...incidentally BOWLEG has a place....not sure where or why......he called out to Mommy whom you do not remember him having suggesting that you shall be with someone by your side calling out to our Lord God for assistance and help to bring others to meet PRINCE RANDY........again the shredded newspaper....means lots of people need to clean up their acts and Prophets/Prophetess/Teachers shall lead them the path to follow.....all the many and varieties of fish.....very fresh....means to me FRESH DOORS OPEN ... FRESH PEOPLE AWAIT...FRESH NATIONS AWAIT...FRESH MINISTRY AWAITS as the Holy Spirit Rush wind blows through your life and works clearing all the debris and bringing forth fresh new things...the sea is also represented here....WATERS OF LIFE SPRINGING UP AFRESH!!!!!! By the Mangoes have seed IMPREGNATION...biggest and ripest mangoes...READY TO BURST FORTH AND OPEN UP UNTO THEE ....WHEN YOU CHOOSE OR ARE LED AND the colour of the mangoes also indicates something ...... Mmmmmmmmmmmmmmmmm more to come.....Love from your Princess/Prophetess/Giraffe.....and Beloved..."

-**Prophetess Denise Borchers: August 5 2010 at 12:10am**

THE MIDWIFE SEES THE CALL:

Hmmmm.....wonder if there were many Fishers of Men trying to bring forth the Good News. Many fish of many colors, shapes, sizes and kinds were freshly caught and laid out on the newspaper. It's Just a thought....not saying it's a prophetic word....You are seeing now how HUGE the field is....which is very opposite for it would generally be the youth who would see the field as large. At one time a boy desires to play in the field....as he matures; he desires to harvest the field. .

Everything you are sharing about the dream is representative of life, of restoration of life, of fields of fruit ripe for the picking, of fish...as in fish which have been caught or even representative of the fish that were divided among the people and everyone ate and was satisfied, with even bread and fish remaining......God IS speaking to you even through this dream....even as you recognize the dominance of one who has called you 'brother'...." -**Prophetess Holly Sharp: August 4th 2010 @11:34pm**

THE NANNY SEES THE CALL:

"Quite interesting! Would the Lord be warning you of your brothers (spiritual) conspiracy against you and the rest of your family?? Sounds to me as the Joseph case!

Your "brother" is trying to kill you and the rest of the family spiritually..... He would be nay of the many spiritual brothers... Is he the elder?? Then he has his powers; strength and is very proud...pride spirit.....

Your sister, is suffocating(spiritually) from the spiritual activities going on and you are trying to REVIVE her back to life...so it is work you need to do...GIVE LIFE EVEN WHEN YOURS IS ON LINE!

The fresh fish at every house...may refer to new believers, those who have just been fished out of the sea...but they need to be prepared before they rot.....would that be your work? To teach......these new comers about the kingdom; prepare the fish....to be eatable...they are everywhere you are...the apostles were fishers of men...evangelism.... but you are shown those already caught...so your job is to prepare and cook them...to be fit, eatable by king....The harvest is done....TEACH. This is as much as I am led to share with you MOG. Hope it is what you had in mind...you are a great dreamer really! ~
-**Grace Becki: August 5 2010 at 11:12am**

THE CALL CONFIRMED: "IT IS FINISHED...IT IS DONE!"

THE PRIINCESS SPEAKS:

"My Prince after our messaging today....things here take on quite a perspective ...
Mmmmmmm *muah*...-**Prophetess Dee; August 5 2010 at 10:34am**

THE PRINCE: IT IS DONE..IT IS FINISHED!

"My princess;

I agree with you. God just woke me he spoke to me that "it is done". He showed me your efforts. The work in Australia is huge, not just for new souls, but for many already in the church. The fish is caught but must be prepared. The fruit is ripe and cannot spoil on the vine.

America awaits, Australia awaits, Kenya awaits, Ethiopia awaits, Albania awaits. Countries of the world await. This is a new season for birthing, God has brought the church to the third trimester; Hezekiah said it well: 'for the children are come to the birth, but there is not strength to bring forth'(2 Kings 19:3). But we must bring forth, we must find strength. We have come to this season of birthing. Prophets await to be birthed. Evangelist await to be birthed. Apostles await to be birthed. Teachers and Pastors await to be birthed. "It is done...it is finished". According to Hos 6:2, God has brought us to the third day...we must arise. The clarion call of the church must be that of Isaiah the Prophet: 'here am I Lord, send me'. We must look again at the fields...they are ripe unto harvest, white as cotton and ready to be picked. We must listen for the sound of the mighty wind of the Holy Spirit for he comes just before the latter rain. The husbandman indeed waits...he has patience...the latter rain is coming we must get in the shower.

Before we can plow the fields, they must be broken up again. The ground of the church has become fallow. There can be no harvest without plowing or planting. The seed must go into the ground (John 12:23). 'Break up the fallow ground'. It's time to sow in righteousness. It's time to seek the Lord. The ground is hard...the hearts of the people are hard.

How can they go except they are sent? How can they preach except they are called? The world awaits...the souls are dying. 'In the third day the lord will raise us up'. This is the third day...'Awake thou that sleepest, arise from the dead and Christ shall give thee life'. I hear the fields calling; I see the harvest is ready; yes the ground is fallow, but as the Spirit of God moved upon the face of the deep in Genesis... beginnings; so now His Spirit moves upon this ground...the earth. He will reap the harvest...IT IS DONE...IT IS FINISHED!" -**Dr. Randy E. Simmons -Prophet Mentor/Prince/Priest; August 5 2010 at 12:35pm**

LOVE LETTER FROM PAKISTAN:
August 9th 2010

Dear Brother in Christ-
Greetings in the mighty name of our Lord Jesus!

I am Pastor Shahzad Ansar from Lahore; Pakistan. I am really blessed by your ministry calling and would like to work with you in networking. Also do let me know how we can work in partnership (if God's will). Because I would like you to come in Pakistan and bless our nation as we need such kind of God's Generals.

Kindly do ask me if you have any question and comment.......

With love,

Pastor Shahzad Ansar
Founder & President
The Vision Ministries, Churches and Bible Schools
+923014629116
Email: shahzadansar@yahoo.com

"…..ahhhhh….your vision has been sent to Pakistan…..God is your passport….the formality is merely a photo session! We must speak on this Man of God.

I am just speechless because I just posted pictures from Pakistan ten minutes ago. Hmm what was that question you posed about the prophet and the prophetess dance?" -**Prophetess Holly Sharp August 9th 2010**

CHAPTER NINE
REBIRTH: - THE PROCESS REPEATS ITSELF!

We conceive, we travail, we give birth, we rest, we conceive again, and the process repeats itself. The intimacy with the Lord is first that…….intimate! We are excited about what is to be birthed. Even in our zeal, some spiritual pregnancies do not see fruition and there is deep sadness, even a sense of unworthiness or embarrassment. However, even the loss, the miscarriage does not eliminate the desire to conceive, so we try again and again and again, until the time is upon us. "My little children, of whom I travail in **BIRTH AGAIN** until Christ be formed in you, I desire to be present with you now and to change my voice; for I stand in doubt of you" (Gal.4:19-20)

CHAPTER NINE

REBIRTH:
THE PROCESS REPEATS ITSELF!

Remember, we conceive, we travail, we give birth, we rest, we conceive again, and...

.........THE PROCESS REPEATS ITSELF!

The intimacy with the Lord is first that.......intimate! For true intimacy to take place there must be desire. As our desire grows for the Lord we allow intimacy with him. We allow the conception to take place, not against our wills. God does not rape us, Satan does. We are intimate with God and we desire conception to take place. Once we have conceived, we hold great anticipation of what is to come forth.

We are excited about what is to be birthed. Even in our zeal, some spiritual pregnancies do not see fruition and there is deep sadness, even a sense of unworthiness or embarrassment. However, even the loss, the miscarriage does not eliminate the desire to conceive, so we try again and again and again, until the time is upon us.

Anticipate a spiritual conception, man of God. But do not think that every spiritual movement will be one of conception. Part of intimacy with God is simply enjoying the intimacy of being with him, near him, in his presence, hearing his voice, being so intimate that you hear and recognize his voice even in the dark. You smell him; you have your nostrils turned up; and your ear tuned; and your heart tuned for your time with him. Intimacy with God is beautiful in that it can and does not be reserved for private, but can be experienced publicly.

NO STRENGTH TO BRING FORTH: (2 Kings 19:3)

"Dear Dr. Simmons ~ The Spirit of the Lord speaks through you. I am always challenged to grasp the understanding of the Word and He uses you to bring clarity. As you have referenced 2 Kings 19:3 "....there is no strength to bring them forth..." I am reminded of the birth of my daughter. As I labored and was complete for delivery I could not deliver her unassisted. The nurse literally laid her body crosswise over my body to assist in the pushing out of the baby. It was uncomfortable, perhaps even a bit awkward, yet I welcomed her presence for we had the purpose....DELIVER! Without her assistance; her willingness; and knowledge of precisely when to help me bear down and push together there would have been "no strength to bring forth" what needed to be delivered.

The more we invest time reasoning together of the deep things of God the clarity comes. It is indeed VERY humbling for I know not nor have I studied the Word of God as you have; yet the Spirit of the Lord continues to reveal and allows us to bring together what each has been given and share. Thank you so much for investing time with me for His Glory. As the five-fold is birthed, each comes forth with a purpose. We cannot continue to wail that initial birth cry but rather grow quickly and accept our spiritual birth and walk in it. If we remain in the wailing condition we have not strength, power or God given confidence to assist in the birth of the next Apostle, Prophet, Evangelist, Pastor or Teacher. We are not birthed before our time if we wait upon God. Premature birth is often a result of "self" desiring to come forth. God says, "No! That is not my way!" You have brought to light several issues that have touched my heart on today. I have never had a heart for other countries...perhaps because I have hardly ever been away from home so to speak. Only minimal travel and have always lived within 10 miles of my original hometown. I had no concept. When the Lord began to allow "friend requests" through FB I allowed Him to select and connect. Suddenly the requests have come from Australia, Nairobi, Pakistan, Tanzania...Suddenly eyes of my heart have been opened and the Spirit has shown people all over the world need Jesus, not just those within my hometown. In the natural, I knew it, but now in the supernatural it has taken on life. Your hand is set to the plow. You do not look over your shoulder other than to glance where you have been. You stir up the hardened ground, you turn it and till it and cultivate it. Ground breaking is significant for ground is broken when there is a vision of something to come. Someone has to press in the first shovel and then the celebration begins....ground has been broken....then the REAL work begins and people are positioned and postured to transform the vision into reality. You are a ground breaker. You go into

the "hard hat" areas where people are hard headed and even covered by more hardness....hard hats, steel toes, protective gear...yet you remove that and break ground so that one day they may break bread with The Father.... Whew! A man after God's own heart. Conceived to be born and birth others!"
- **Prophet Holly Sharp: August 5 2010 at 2:50pm**

CONVERSATIONS BETWEEN PROPHETS: THE PROCESS OF REBIRTH

"LOL...Well I am a married woman and have been pregnant a few times. I have also experienced four miscarriages and three miracle births....soooo....just saying! I believe that one reason the Lord reunited me with my husband is because he understands and covers me like none other. We met when I was fifteen and he was seventeen. We married each other twenty three years later.

Test the Prophet?????

Oooppsss.....testing the Prophet>????

This woman of God will not release the word unless God allows. Premature is unsatisfying. Patience!" - **Prophet Holly Sharp:**

"Well. Trying a spirit is more like it....he will tell you more....." - **Dr. Randy E. Simmons:**

"Is the Lord telling me there is a plan I know not of at this time? Is it to press me to cause me to speak out clearly and not to hold back? What man of God....do tell me!" - **Prophet Holly Sharp:**

"Well it is to always trust the word in your spirit. Many will not speak directly 'thus says the Lord...' they speak in riddles of little importance to the body of Christ...I JUST HEARD HIM SAY THAT!' - **Dr. Randy E. Simmons:**

"Do I speak clearly Man of God?" - **Prophet Holly Sharp:**

"Woman of God....your word is good...it bears fruit...it is impregnating that to which it was sent!" - **Dr. Randy E. Simmons:**

"Then his word accomplishes what it is sent to do...that is good. That brings pleasure to our God!" - **Prophet Holly Sharp:**

"Yes...truly...now he will let your eye see what it has seen!" - **Dr. Randy E. Simmons:**

"The Spirit of God woos you to Himself Dr. Simmons. He is calling you with intensity, the intensity that only can be found in the Spirit. There is no man, woman, friend, lover, coworker, alter worker, staff member, brother, sister, mother, father, child who can woo you and touch you like the Spirit of the Lord. The Spirit will enlighten you, equip, enable you (even disable you from yourself) and then He will entrust others into your care and your leadership." - **Prophet Holly Sharp:**

"Does God hold me in such esteem?" - **Dr. Randy E. Simmons:**

"Why did the Spirit of the Lord mention Alter Worker just now? Yes." - **Prophet Holly Sharp:**

"Hmmm….the sanctity of the altar I guess…a place that is intimate…hmmmm!" - **Dr. Randy E. Simmons:**

"You must be cautious. You are a man who still carries brokenness. You still grieve. You still have the longings of a man even though you carry yourself as a gentleman. You must be cautious of the cougars. You must be cautious of those who seek to "find a man" and find your "availability" attractive." - **Prophet Holly Sharp:**

"WOMAN OF GOD…HOW PERCEPTIVE…YOU READ MY VERY SPIRIT…MANY SPEAK AND SAY THAT THEY ARE MY WIFE…GOD SAID:'I DID NOT SEND THEM'! WHO ARE YOU WOMAN OF GOD?" - **Dr. Randy E. Simmons:**

"You must be keenly aware that the Holy Spirit is attractive and some may be drawn to you because the Holy Spirit draws them, yet they will not be sincere in their intentions toward or with you. Some will want to spiritually and physically (oh Jesus help me….)…some will want to spiritually and physically rape you and take you to places that will cost you much and leave you emotionally, physically and spiritually unsatisfied….for MAN OF GOD…it is GOD who has set you apart for Himself. He has not released you otherwise as of yet. Hear me clearly sayeth the Lord, "It is I who have placed you in this position so that you would cease any thought or activity that is not of me. I have set you apart and apart I shall keep you to teach and train to prepare and to send forth. Do not despise the time of separation sayeth the Lord."

The Lord says, "Randy, die out to the flesh. Randy, become so tender in me that the flesh literally falls from the bone. I am doing something in you Randy. Do not rush me sayeth the Lord." - **Prophet Holly Sharp:**

"LORD...I HEAR....LORD...I KNOW...LORD I OBEY...LORD I REST!" - **Dr. Randy E. Simmons:**

"Ahhhhh....finally. j \" - **Prophet Holly Sharp:**

"YES...FINALLY...LOL...LOL...LOL..." - **Dr. Randy E. Simmons:**

"MOG, you have pressed in on tonight!" - **Prophet Holly Sharp:**

"LOL...LOL...LOL...LOL..." - **Dr. Randy E. Simmons:**

"You have stretched the prophet of God!" - **Prophet Holly Sharp:**

"Woman of God...YES I HAVE IT'S ABOUT TIME SOMEBODY DID." - **Dr. Randy E. Simmons:**

"God has delivered both. LOL!" - **Prophet Holly Sharp:**

"YES...NO ONE HAS PUSHED YOU SO!" - **Dr. Randy E. Simmons:**

"Obviously> lol!" - **Prophet Holly Sharp:**

"WOG...DO YOU KNOW ME?" - **Dr. Randy E. Simmons:**

"Only in the spirit." - **Prophet Holly Sharp:**

"TRULY...DO YOU KNOW ME? YES...THAT IS WHAT I MEAN

YOU ARE A PROPHETESS OF GOD...I WILL ALWAYS HAIL YOU THUS." - **Dr. Randy E. Simmons:**

"There is a difference between a man and a Man of God. This Prophet of the Lord is committed to helping you see and understand which you are." - **Prophet Holly Sharp:**

"YES...I AM AWARE OF THAT...LOL...LOL...BUT NOT MANY ARE...ISA.61:1-4 TELLS US THE MISSION STATEMENT OF THE PROPHET. IT WAS ALSO Jesus MISSION STATEMENT...HE FULFILLED IT IN LUKE CHAP.4. HOLLY...YOU ARE DIFFERENT...TELL ME IS THERE A COURTSHIP BETWEEN PROPHTETS OF GOD?!" - **Dr. Randy E. Simmons:**

"I hear the Lord say, "Rise up Man of God and be a real man for me. In time, in due season, I will restore and bring to you a wife of my choosing....one I select for you who will be worthy to share the platform and the responsibility of ministry with you.

I do not know that for I have never inquired of God." - **Prophet Holly Sharp:**

"YES...SHE IS BEING BORN NOW...I KNOW...IT IS NOT MY DESIRE TO SEEK A WIFE NOW... LOL...LOL...LOL...SHE IS BEING PREPARED AND WOULD NOT YET HAVE BEEN CONTAMINATED BY RELIGION." - **Dr. Randy E. Simmons:**

"I know that. You do not need a wife, or a "mistress" now for that would be untimely and detrimental to what God is doing in you." Amen!" - **Prophet Holly Sharp:**

"SHE IS DIFFERENT AND HER GIFTS ARE HIDDEN." - **Dr. Randy E. Simmons:**

"Yes....in time your God shall reveal her to you, but for now, you are HIS bride and He is your bridegroom." - **Prophet Holly Sharp:**

"YES...I KNOW...HER TIME IS YET A FEW YEARS AWAY...I AM AWARE...THOUGH I AM CHASED DAILY..." - **Dr. Randy E. Simmons:**

"Remember this as a warning....I am urged and unctioned by the Spirit of the Lord to remind you that the Holy Spirit is attractive. Do not allow anyone to confuse or compromise the pureness of the Spirit. Do not allow anyone to profess "love" when then recognize not who they are attracted to. The Holy Spirit will reveal to you when and how to shut these pursuits down. Continue to hide yourself and seek not the counsel of many women for your movement is being watched....

I should hush now." - **Prophet Holly Sharp:**

"HAVE YOU SPOKEN ALL THAT GOD WOULD SAY IN THIS SEASON?" - **Dr. Randy E. Simmons:**

"I believe for tonight. Yes. And you?" - **Prophet Holly Sharp:**

"MY SPIRIT IS TIRED...YOU HAVE PULLED MUCH UNCTION FROM ME..." - **Dr. Randy E. Simmons:**

"Yes....and you asked for it! LOL!" - **Prophet Holly Sharp:**

"WOMAN OF GOD...I THANK YOU...PERHAPS WE WILL SPEAK AGAIN...HOW CAN I POUR INTO YOU?" - **Dr. Randy E. Simmons:**

"Good night sir. May the Lord clear your thoughts, your mind and your spirit on tonight. May you rest in peace and understanding tonight. You have. I am drenched. Now the Lord calls for your intimate time with Him. Rest." - **Prophet Holly Sharp:**

"THANK YOU WOMAN OF GOD...GOOD NIGHT!"
- **Dr. Randy E. Simmons:**

"You are quite welcome MAN OF GOD." - **Prophet Holly Sharp:**

"BE BLESSED!" - **Dr. Randy E. Simmons:**

"...and highly favored." - **Prophet Holly Sharp:**

August 6, 2010; 1:14am-2:05am

THE PREGNANCY OF HOLLY SHARP:

"Teach me to pray. It is in me yet not released verbally with power and authority. Teach me to be free please.

Few would understand unless they see conception truly through spiritual eyes. In the natural the womb has seen its purpose and has been removed. In the spiritual the womb is ripe. I desire for God to impregnate me as He selects. Mary was a simple virgin girl but God chose her to birth our King. I am a simple woman who God has called extraordinary. I embrace the simplicity for He sets me apart with it. Difficult to express in writing however

I know that the simplicity of the spoken word allows the word to reach many hearts and I am grateful. I long and long and long for what He desires to conceive and birth in me. I do not desire an empty womb for the empty tomb changed everything about me. What is my prophetic calling? I know I am quiet and perhaps reserved in public situations. I must get over that somehow. Again being totally transparent I honestly sense I do not recognize my worth or value to the King or the Kingdom. Speak to me about this if you will Man of God. You are of great spiritual depth and I pull on that. Neither to drain or deplete you nor to have your seed spilled on the ground. I want to grow, flourish, and produce spiritual fruit to feed the hungry people. Only God. Only God!"
–**August 13th 2010**

THE PREGNANCY OF EMILY MOOBI:

"I've been pregnant for long, I can feel the pangs of birth this morning, I feel the urge to push out a miracle and touch somebody, ohh my my my, the baby inside me is leaping, my water is about to break, nobody can stop me from screaming this morning, Halleluyah"
-**August 5 2010 @ 11:31pm**

"Yeah! P.U. S. H. Tht miracle ma sister. Without that PUSH, the baby might delay. Pray. Until Something Happens. PUSH IT. Morn ma sister." -**Mbulelo Moobi: August 5 2010 @11:57pm**

"Yes, yes, yes, that's what it is all about, standing in the gap for my country, my brothers and my sister. Now that baby is about to come out. Amen...Good Morning Mbu!" - **Emily Moobi: August 6 2010 @ 12:25am**

"Oh boy, my, my, my, the devil is liar, ma sister can I preach?" When the blind was pregnant with blindness, he heard that there was a doctor coming his way, he started pushing, and he pushed and pushed. Oh ma God! They, they tried to stop him but he refused to listen to them, he kept pushing and pushing to give birth to his sight. Emily don't stop pushing, continue, until the Doctor hears you. Don't listen to those stopping you...NO KEEP PUSHNG; YOUR MIRACLE is almost there. The bible says the blind man continued pushing until the Doctor heard him. Push ma sister, push ma brother! My goodness!" - **Mbulelo Moobi: August 6 2010 @1:08am**

"Ohh, Glory, preach Mbulelo in The Name of Jesus. I am pushing all the way. Amen!" -**Emily Moobi: August 6 2010 @1:14am**

"Oh thank you. I feel the fire burning this morn. Oh glory to God. Ma sister the bible says "the blind man never stop pushing for his precious baby. He ran like a mad man because of the joy he had after giving birth to his sight. Push for that car, money, job, family and success. Push for that profitable living. Push for that promo. Push for the Best doctor JESUS IS HEARING YOU. Amen somebody." -**Mbulelo Moobi: August 6 2010 @1:27am**

"And the church of Christ says Amen! Yes Lord, it's a Yes day. Thank You Jesus." -**Emily Moobi: August 6 2010 @ 1:24am**

"The best gift we can give back 2 God is a soul, can we PUSH 4 souls this am. Can we start by addressing God's need, seek ye 1st the kingdom of God... When we take care of His needs He izili tyks care of our needs, wants n desires. Each 1 reach 1 n bless God with @ least 1 soul 2day, the harvest is plenty we are few coz many of us are running after benefits without doing da will of God, let's gird up n PUSH 4 souls n bring joy 2 da heavenlies." - **Babalwa Mkutukana August 6 2010 @1:48am**

"Ohhh yes, Amen n Amen, again Amen. This is the time for our colleaques, our family members, and our friends to come into The Kingdom. Increase our territory Lord Jesus. I declare that Africa is saved in Jesus Name. Lord use us to make disciples of many nations. I am giving birth today; I might not know the time all I know is that it is today. Thank You Jesus." -**Emily Moobi: August 6 2010 @ 1:24am**

"@ZUKI, Thank u sisi, He has heard you pushing. Glory to him. Amen."
-**Mbulelo Moobi: August 6 2010 @2:55am**

"Isaiah prophesied about this day saying, "The children have come to birth but there is no strength to bring forth." @Emily, is the pregnancy from the Holy Ghost or from man-made doctrines? Because the principle in God is:" Like begat like". Boom Salute!" - **Dazang Ranking Deezed Gwom: August 6 2010 @ 9:31am**

"@Dazang, when Mary was pregnant people were asking the same question you asking but she went on to give birth beside all the questions. That's where I am right now, nobody will stop my baby from coming out. I am pushing even when the critics are shouting it's man-made. God bless you now and forevermore" -**Emily Moobi: August 6 2010 @ 11:31am**

"Good morning from South Africa, I just happen to read your post and Boom you wrote about birthing, that's a confirmation for me. Praise God. God richly bless you. Hallelujah!"- **Emily Moobi: August 6 2010 @ 12:27am**

"Well praise God. I tried to tag you in it because I saw in my spirit that you were pregnant. But it would only let me tag thirty people...well I wanted to comment on your post but what could I say so I liked it..." - **Dr. Randy E, Simmons: August 6 2010 @12:43am**

"We truly serve an Awesome God. Its ok, the Lord had His way of tagging me. God richly bless you. The time is now. Praise God. It's pay day. Wow!" -**Emily Moobi: August 6 2010 @ 1:24am**

"Yes it is. I sensed your pregnancy the first time you contacted me. Your fruit is great and of the royal seed. Your labor shall be shortened and contractions few. Now Push. Push. Push." - **Dr. Randy E, Simmons: August 6 2010 at 4:26am**

"Thank you Jesus. Delivery time is now; the labor room is ready.oh Jesus, Jesus, Jesus Emily Moobi." -**Emily Moobi: August 6 2010 @ 6:35am**

"Woman of God Push. This is the third trimester and the world doesn't want you to give birth...Push! Push! Push! The world doesn't want to see miracles; and sadly many in the church don't either.

But this is a time of rebirth. This is a time of renewal. The sun clothed woman is about to give birth but the dragon stands ready to devour the male child. Don't be afraid, God has prepared a place in the wilderness for the child. A place of safety, a place of power, a place of protection. So bring your miracle forth. I connect with you as mid-wife in your rebirthing; others stand with you.

You are a woman of much fruit; your womb is ready; the labor and dilation has begun; the contractions are closer. Your birthing will be a blessing to South Africa and many areas...BIRTH THIS BABY! The world us waiting. And birth again. And birth again. And birth again. I stand with you; the dragon shall not devour your man child." -**Dr. Randy E, Simmons: August 6 2010 @1:21pm**

"Dr Simmons on behalf of Africans I say yes and Amen to that confirmation. This is the hour of birthing, our families, our colleagues, my brothers and sisters are coming out of the chains of darkness, its Delivery time, Hallelujah, Hallelujah, Hallelujah. Amen and Amen and Amen. Yes Lord, this is Africa's season, this is Africa's season. Thank You Jesus.Ohhh my Jesus, I say yes I am pushing Lord, and no demon in hell will stop me in the Name of Jesus." -**Emily Moobi: August 6 2010 @ 2:33pm**

"WOMAN OF GOD, EMILY;

"For the earnest expectation of the creature waiteth for the manifestation of the sons of God. For we know that the whole creation groaneth and travaileth in pain together until now". So says Paul in Romans 8:19, 22. I am... a son of God. I have been manifested. I have returned to the glory and as such I am seed royal, a Royal Priesthood (1 Peter 2:9). You are a princess of the seed royal. Therefore you have the right to bear the royal birth children. As an heir and joint heir you have rights to the royal bed chamber. COME; SPEND A NIGHT WITH THE KING!

As a son of God I offer you my royal seed for the continued rebirthing of South Africa. I stand as intercessor; seed (or vision giver); provider of all that the royal house can give. You are fertile...bring to the birth.... Do not be afraid like the women in Hezekiah's day who were afraid to bring to the birth because of the time of trouble(2 Kings 19:3); which one of your commentators alluded to but he forget to mention the reason...IT WAS A TIME OF TROUBLE! Therefore, the motherly instincts of a woman are to protect her baby at any cost and if it means prolonging the trimester, she will do so. BUT NOT SO NOW! The children will be delivered. You are of a different breed, a different seed-SEED ROYAL-You know how to birth.

I offer the seed of my anointing. The impregnation of the anointing goes deep within your belly as Jesus told the woman at the well in John chapter four. Its living water, springing up inside of you. Women understand these things, for nine months they carry a water bag within their bellies; Hallelujah! So Push! Birth! And get ready to REBIRTH AGAIN! I offer you my SEED ROYAL!" -**Dr. Randy E, Simmons: August 6 2010 @3:42pm**

"Amen. Oh yes, Dr. Simmons I receive, my body soul and mind what The Lord has ordained you to deposit into my spirit. Ohh I have a preview, of my baby and yes the pains are getting stronger. Lord I am ready, Dr. Simmons I am ready, I see The Lord... has leveled all the mountains and broke all the barriers and removed all the obstacles that delayed the birth of my baby, right now I can't help it, the water is broken, thank You Dr. Simmons for taking the position of a midwife to help me in this process. I bless The Lord for your obedience. The time is now. Jesus, Jesus, Jesus, thank My God, thank. My Everything.

Dr. Simmons I feel you in this journey, may The Lord multiply your anointing and richly bless you and your family." -**Emily Moobi: August 6 2010 @ 5:33pm**

"The nursery is prepared...the nanny stands by...joy has come over the fact a baby is being delivered...NOW PUSH! DELIVER! BIRTH FORTH! AND PREPARE FOR YOUR NEXT CONCEPTION!" -**Dr. Randy E, Simmons: August 7 2010 @1:36pm**

"Dr. Simmons, God is good. The enemy is too late; Our Awesome God is in the midst of the delivery, Thank you Jesus for leading the birthing process. God is great, my baby is alive, no weapon formed against me and my baby will prosper, the medical team is armed, Thank You Jesus." -**Emily Moobi: August 6 2010 @1:39pm**

"I stand with you as Father...Covering...Protector!" -**Dr. Randy E, Simmons: August 7 2010 @1:36pm**

"Hallelujah, hallelujah!!! Thank You Jesus!!! Lord I thank you for Dr. Simmons; I thank you for the anointing power over His life!!! I thank you Lord for Dr. Simmons obedience and I pray more fruitfulness in his life in Jesus Name!!! Thank you Jesus! You are great and you do miracles so great. Bless Your Name. Amen!!!

Thank you Dr. Simmons and I know The Lord is using you for the ministry assign to me." -**Emily Moobi: August 7 2010 @2:44pm**

"Look deep into the Spirit. Search out the crawl spaces; be sure to take the light. The baby shall not be harmed, for a place has been prepared for it in the land of Moab and Ammon. Your fruit is precious...your place important for the restoring of South Africa. It is not by chance. Now nurse the baby...for you are a healthy Hebrew woman, unlike the daughter of Pharaoh. In the nursery mentor the baby, prepare it for its season of growth. This is what the Lord will say to you woman of God." -**Dr. Randy E, Simmons: August 7 2010 @2:49pm**

"Sjoo, Thank You Jesus, now I feel like jumping on my bed Dr. Simmons you have to excuse me coz when The Lord opens His mouth Dr. Simmons I take long before I stop rejoicing." -**Emily Moobi: August 7 2010 @2:44pm**

"Ha.ha.ha.ha.ha.ha.ha.ha.ha.ha!!!!!!!!

"Sing, O barren, thou that didst not bear; break forth into singing, and cry aloud, thou that didst not travail with child: for more are the children of the desolate than the children of the married wife, saith the LORD. Enlarge the place of thy tent, and let them stretch forth the curtains of thine habitations: spare not, lengthen thy cords, and strengthen thy stakes; for thou shalt break forth on the right hand and on the left; and thy seed shall inherit the Gentiles, and make the desolate cities to be inhabited. Fear not; for thou shalt not be ashamed: neither be thou confounded; for thou shalt not be put to shame: for thou shalt forget the shame of thy youth, and shalt not remember the reproach of thy widowhood any more. For thy Maker is thine husband; the LORD of hosts is his name; and thy Redeemer the Holy One of Israel; The God of the whole earth shall he be called. For the LORD hath called thee as a woman forsaken and grieved in spirit, and a wife of youth, when thou wast refused, saith thy God. For a small moment have I forsaken thee; but with great mercies will I gather thee. In a little wrath I hid my face from thee for a moment; but with everlasting kindness will I have mercy on thee, saith the LORD thy Redeemer. O thou afflicted, tossed with tempest, and not comforted, behold, I will lay thy stones with fair colours, and lay thy foundations with sapphires. And I will make thy windows of agates, and thy gates of carbuncles, and all thy borders of pleasant stones.

And all thy children shall be taught of the LORD; and great shall be the peace of thy children. In righteousness shalt thou be established: thou shalt be far from oppression; for thou shalt not fear: and from terror; for it shall not come near thee. Behold, they shall surely gather together, but not by me:

whosoever shall gather together against thee shall fall for thy sake. No weapon that is formed against thee shall prosper; and every tongue that shall rise against thee in judgment thou shalt condemn. This is the heritage of the servants of the LORD, and their righteousness is of me, saith the LORD."(Isaiah 54:1-14)-**Dr. Randy E, Simmons: August 7 2010 @3:56pm**

"Amen, Amen, again Amen. Lord I bless You, Lord with all my heart and my being I know it's all because of your mercies that are new every morning. Thank You for Your favor, You saw it fitting that I give birth to Your child and right now I dedicate...this child to you and I say "here is Your child Lord,Thy Will be done and not my will". I Thank You for I will always give you back what you first gave me. Thank You for Your word that You spoke over my life "that in blessing I will bless thee, and in multiplying I will multiply thy seed as the stars of the heaven, and as the sand which is upon the sea shore; and thy seed shall possess the gate of his enemies; and in thy seed shall all the nations of the earth be blessed; because thou hast obeyed my voice" Thank You Lord for Your Word that is Yes and Amen.

Dr. Simmons, the Lord is speaking through you to confirm over and over what He said over my life. You are a blessing and I know The Lord has chosen you for a purpose. May The Lord abide more and more in you as you abide in Him, may He anoint you more and bless you more in Jesus Name. Blessed is you Dr Simmons in Jesus Name. Amen! -**Emily Moobi: August 8 2010 @5:17am**

THE PREGNANCY OF GRACE BECKI:

"WOG:

I sense your spirit woman therefore I will speak as unto her. Much is being birthed within you this day and I feel the spiritual morning sickness. The call and burden of the travail of the harvest is indeed great. I feel your birth pangs.

"For we know that the whole creation groaneth and travaileth in pain together until now. (Rom.8:22). "For the earnest expectation of the creature waiteth for the manifestation of the sons of God"(Rom.8:19). Will the sons of God please stand up!

But we know "Likewise the Spirit also helpeth our infirmities: for we know not what we should pray for as we ought: but the Spirit itself maketh intercession for us with groanings which cannot be uttered."(Rom.8:26). So groan and travail Woman of God. I hear them though you utter them not. God has seen and heard. Birth forth. The nations await. I too, a son of God wait: "For I long to see you, that I may impart unto you some spiritual gift, to the end ye may be established; that is, that I may be comforted together with you by the mutual comfort together with you by the mutual faith both of you and me."(Rom.1:11-12). Be blessed;" -**Dr. Randy E, Simmons: August 5 2010 @ 5:39pm**

"Amen!! Sincerely, I am groaning and pushing …it has to be now… The pain is sooooo intense…..too intense…..it has to be NOW MOG!

It is now; another day…… I am in pain… to see this child.
I have waited and agonized MOG in ways you do not know…
I have been here, waiting….waiting…waiting. Each day believing t is the day……. I am really in terrible pain. It has to be now… this cannot be false labor…..I really don't know what to say to let you see my pain in every area. It is difficulty even to relate with anyone right now….. I have to concentrate…Bless you. Thank you for the encouragements. Just lift my hand up as you do…." -**Grace Becki: August 6 2010 @11:13am**

THE PREGNANCY OF LIANDHA MADONDO:

"I may not understand physical Birthing but one thing I know is that there is a process and procedure to be followed. Before the birthing occurs the "Church" must be ready for a 'sperm' for impregnated. Not be in a state of turmoil as is now. The…whole 9 months of going through hormones, changes, late night binges or purging of impurities….until finally the Birthing. During Birthing a midwife must prepare for the birth of a baby….it's a slow process that cannot be aborted. Sometimes we want to rush things and yet the baby is not ready and Abort the fetus before time. God's timing and our timing are different…..until we begin to think like Him then we shall Birth healthy babies....SELAH!!!" -Liandha Madondo: August 9 2010 @6:03am

"Woman of God;

I address you personally and am so thankful for your beautiful comment on the piece on spiritual impregnation. May I say that you are pregnant indeed. Pregnant with your healing; pregnant with souls and interceding for the lives of people; pregnant with purpose and pregnant with your destiny...to walk again!

On July 7th of this year was my birthday. I remember feeling led to bestow upon you my birthday gift. It was the gift of healing. Now I see far more. It is as if that was a time when the Spirit of God impressed upon me to impregnate (impart) and distribute to you as you have so brilliantly called it spiritual 'sperm'. All truth is parallel, as in the natural so is the spiritual. And even though you may not have had the natural experience, you certainly have had the spiritual.

Imagine this if you will, a young hand maid named Mary, a virgin, suddenly is told that she will have a son. She never knew a man, so how can these things be? One day she feels a presence come upon her and in her belly she begins to feel a life begin to conceive. Insightful isn't it? Well it happened and our Lord Jesus Christ was born.

Today I speak to you, Liahnda; you are pregnant with your healing. On July 7th 2010 you're impregnated. The anointing came upon you and you conceived it; you feel the morning sickness and the day your two nieces helped you walk, you were at the beginning of your first trimester. Nine months you said, nine months. Carry this baby in your belly. Feel it growing every day. Endure the morning sickness. Get the cravings. For you will not abort this baby. As the angel told Mary, his name shall be called Jesus. I tell you today handmaid. His name shall be called healing walk. Watch for the signs and in the third trimester you will see it. Contractions will come, labor pains will start, then dilation. Then get ready to PUSH!" -**Dr. Randy E. Simmons: August 10 2010 @1:42pm**

"Dr. Randy...Wow I just felt my spirit not leap but listening and taking in every word spoken from the mouth of God. I'm in awe of the word of God knowing that it will come to pass. Your Gift of Healing bestowed upon me by you on your birthday the 7th July is...was...Awesome. I couldn't have asked for more. Thank you for your obedience to the Holy Spirit. Your prayers mean a lot to me. God bless you man of God!!!" -**Liandha Madondo: August 10 2010 @5:09pm**

"Woman of God...There is much going on within you. As you transition without, you transition within. The spirit woman that you are is flexing her womb and therefore the outer woman must respond. That which you are pregnant with will far supersede anything that the outer woman can feel, sense, or see. The flesh must become subject to the spirit because of what the spirit is carrying. YOU ARE

PREGNANT WITH PUEPOSE!" -Dr. Randy E. Simmons: August 13 2010 @12:28am

"I hear you Dr. Randy....what am I missing...is my flesh not in line with the spirit man???" -
Liandha Madondo: August 13 2010 @5:55am

"Liandha; God created man and then breathed in him the breath of life and man became a living soul. Imagine if you will, a lump of red clay lying on the ground in the form of a man. It was a perfectly formed image but with no life. Then the spirit of God hovered over this clay figure just the way he hovered over the face of the deep. Then God himself, like a vapor, entered the nostrils of this figure and suddenly the clay figure began to stand up. Let's supposed it happened slowly as if it had to adjust to just being alive or it jumped up and ran up and down. Either way this figure knew one thing...it now possessed the very breath of God within it.

Liandha, we know you have the faith. It's quite evident. Faith comes by hearing and by hearing the word of God (Rom.10:17). A man was lame for years and couldn't walk until Jesus said to him: "rise up, take up thy bed and walk". Your faith is the key to your victory and healing and you have the grain of seed faith. So be it unto you accordingly.

Now let's activate a point of contact in your spirit woman and I want you to become pregnant with this process. You spoke of spiritual birthing verses natural. Now see it. See the 'sperm' of God which we will call his spirit entering you at this moment. Feel in your body conception taking place. Now sense an embryo being formed. Now feel the life and spirit of God being formed in your body. Now feel your body being recreated, formed anew. Now carry your healing through the first trimester, morning sickness, and nausea because what you are now pregnant with is your healing. And you shall walk again if you can conceive this thing. In the second trimester watch for the signs of life and begin to walk them out. In the third trimester get ready...get up...walk!" -Dr. Randy E. Simmons: August 13 2010 @11:38am

"Hi Dr. Randy. How are you doing? Today I started healing School.
I think I'm ready to give birth now!!!!! -Liandha Madondo: Sept. 3, 2010 @1:01pm

"Praise God. Today I begin the shout of victory with you. See it, birth it, and recreate it in Jesus name." -Dr. Randy E. Simmons: Sept. 3, 2010 @1:06pm

"Amen! Will do so...just a bit tired from a hectic day...I would need to have an early night. I want and need to be healed before 18 days of healing is done. I'm ready and God knows it and will perfect what he has begun in me!!!!!"
-Liandha Madondo: Sept. 3, 2010 @1:25pm

Yessss! I stand in agreement with you. Get ready to dance! -Dr. Randy E. Simmons: Sept. 3, 2010 @1:36pm

"Amen...Amen...I am soooooo Ready. Thank you for standing in agreement with me Dr. Randy....About to explode with excitement!!" - **Liandha Madondo: Sept. 3, 2010 @2:12pm**

"I stand in agreement to the end....till you are healed." -**Dr. Randy E. Simmons: Sept. 3, 2010 @3:06pm**

CHAPTER TEN

SPIRITUAL INTIMACY:
GOD DESIRES TO KNOW YOU!

SPIRITUAL INTIMACY: - GOD DESIRES TO KNOW YOU. God is indeed calling me to a greater intimacy with him and he has been slowly teaching me how to be intimate with him. Intimacy is precious...sacred! The cougars come looking for seed, they claim to be able to birth, but they rape away the anointing for their own pleasure. OH HOW I SEEK DAILY THE INTIMACY OF GOD!!! Paul said it this way: "That I may know him, and the power of his resurrection, and the fellowship of his sufferings, being made conformable unto his death..." (Phil 3:10)

CHAPTER TEN

SPIRITUAL INTIMACY: GOD DESIRES TO KNOW YOU!

God desires to **'KNOW'** you. God is indeed calling you and me to a greater intimacy with him and he has been slowly teaching us how to be intimate with him. The intimacy with the Lord is first that……. Intimate!. Intimacy is precious…sacred! The cougars come looking for seed, they claim to be able to birth, but they rape away the anointing for their own pleasure. **OH HOW I SEEK DAILY THE INTIMACY OF GOD!!!** Paul said it this way: "That I may know him, and the power of his resurrection, and the fellowship of his sufferings, being made conformable unto his death…" (Phil 3:10).

THE INTIIMACY OF PROPHETESS HOLLY SHARP:

"I was weeping inside for it was as if I were truly His bride and He truly knew and knows my very heart and the inner most workings….we were in comm**UNION** together. The Lord and I, in unison, in union, coupled together, fitly and rightly joined. OHHHHHH I wanted to weep and be still and be stirred all at the same moment. I am tenderized nearly to falling off the bone. My heart is cut with a single whisper from Him. Wow. What a day. It has been like 48 hours of intimacy with God. Spiritual intimacy…God desires to **KNOW** you." -**August 6 2010 at 3:00pm**

"Oh my, oh my, God filled His **WOG** this morning. Attended a Leadership Summit and the Word given through the anointed Men of God was so prophetic and so sound I could barely keep from weeping. As I entered the sanctuary (filled with probably 200 leaders from local and surrounding churches) I sensed such a dry spirit. This was a church where I had attended for nearly 20 years. It was so incredibly dry. Worship was dry, the people were dry, the praises were dry....there was no rain....My heart was heavy burdened as I thought, "these are the leaders Oh God....they are without so they cannot adequately minister to others for they have little to give." It was as if the clapping was dulled as we sang. Only some was lifting their voices. It was **ONLY** after the Men of God imparted to the people that **LIFE** came. It was literally a **BIRTH** in process. I could watch it. The words He shared were much like those of our recent conversations, only different. They were delivered by a different spiritual midwife and the pressing was different, yet wonderful. He addressed the intimacy with God and I said, "Lord you have had me and held me in this place of intimacy with you and I am here not against my will, but in line with your will father. You hold me Lord not as one held against her will, but willing to be held. For you know my intimate nature and my intimate thoughts toward you Oh Lord." -**August 6 2010 @2:56pm**

CALL TO INTIMACY OF A MAN OF GOD.... RANDY E. SIMMONS:

"Woman of God...Prophet Holly;

You have spoken profound and true things into my life. God said indeed: "Beware of the cougars". And I have been chased by cougars since I began to seek his intimacy. They claim to bring birth, but have left me stripped and unfulfilled. It's as if they were spiritual vampires, sucking the life out me. You spoke truth and for these past hours I could only reflect. God is indeed calling me to a greater intimacy with him and he has been slowly teaching me how to be intimate with him. Intimacy is precious...sacred! The cougars come looking for seed, they claim to be able to birth, but they rape away the anointing for their own pleasure. **OH HOW I SEEK DAILY THE INTIMACY OF GOD!!!**

He speaks daily to me, I hear his voice but in my hurts and pain I fail to hear his healing. So much hurt and yes healing has come but there is a place of intimacy. How I long for it. The other day when I told you about rain it had not rained here since. But after that day I hear God speak: "after the strong rain, you shall see the miracles and break thru". This morning about two am it rained, thundered, lightening. It smelled so good. I heard the spirit say: "stand in the rain". I went out and got drenched. For an hour I stood in the rain confessing my sins and the sins of the people; I stood declaring the break through and decreeing God's order upon this earth. When it was over I felt a new cleanliness; new anointing; new intimacy with God! Thank you woman of God" - **August 7 2010 @1:04pm**

THE INTIMACY OF RAIN:

"Allowing the Lord to speak....I am listening. The rain is indeed significant." -**Prophetess Holly sharp- August 7 2010@ 2:55pm**

"Thank you...I will share with you a dream I had this morning a little latter..." -**Dr. Simmons- August 7 2010 @ 4:30pm**

"When lightning strikes close, we hear the loud thunder. You will see the light before you hear the thunder and when one hears the thunder he is close enough to be struck by the lightening. Light and sound travel at different speeds, in the natural and in the supernatural.

Dr. Simmons, this is what I have heard the Lord say today. I do trust that you will weigh it carefully ~

The Lord says, "Do not seek cover from the rain when I desire for you to get wet. For not only do I desire you get wet, I desire you be drenched for when one is drenched, they surrender to the rain ~ and can even enjoy the walk in it. When one is but damp they continue to seek cover, concerned and consumed by the outward appearance. I say this day, I am desirous to **POUR** out upon you~to **DRENCH** you, **SOAK** you, **SATURATE** you for the purpose of harvesting the field~You are a vessel, even with earthly holes and minor leaks, you are useable, for even the smallest of cracks is still found useful to water the path from here to there and bring forth life. I say to you, even as you desire a perfect vessel, I use you even as I am turning and shaping you. Do not think I do not see the flaws, but know son, that even the flaws have had purpose. For **YOU** are unsatisfied and desire to be made whole, and healed so you can deliver all I have for you to deliver. You have become a willing vessel. You seek perfection ~ I seek precision, for they are closely related, yet different. **Only I AM** perfect, yet I call you to precision ~ precision in delivering **MY WORD** and precision in harvesting the field, even one plant at a time. To do so, you must **GET WET** ~ you must be as a soaking sponge, eager to be saturated, only to be squeezed and pressed and twisted and rung out ~ yet I, Your Father, return you to your intended shape, for your intended purpose, only to fill you, saturate you, squeeze you, press, twist and wring you out again, and again and again and again. If you have no filling, you cannot fill. Listen for the rain. Look for the lightening. Hear the thunder and **KNOW** I am close. At my command, not step, but JUMP in and be drenched....thus sayeth the Lord." -**Prophetess Holly sharp- August 7 2010 @11:09pm**

"Good Evening Dr. Simmons ~ It has rained off and on here all day and into the evening. There have been quick cloud burst and some mighty rushing winds. As I stepped out as the winds began, I could literally smell the smell of rain in the air. Ohhhhh I love that smell. The next thing I knew, our glass table, with an umbrella in it was completely knocked over.

The glass didn't break, but the umbrella did. My first thought was "get in the rain"...... the Word inside. We often stay under the "umbrella" of safety. We believe we are being covered and protected, and yet while that is true, there are times we must experience the soaking, drenching, down pouring of the rain. Even as I am writing this, the rain, the thunder and the lightening have begun again. It is a **BEAUTIFUL** sound. There is a famine in the land, pray for rain!" -Prophetess Holly sharp- August 7 2010 @11:23pm

"The Lord has touched! To stand in the rain...to be drenched...not only to be washed but to be cleansed. It is part of the delivery process for even at birth the water breaks and birth is the one time of the presence of both water and of blood! Amazing huh? I can picture the drenching process as the Father's rain intermingled with even your own salty tears. Salt. Necessary to the body. Hmmm. I will seek the Lord on that for I did sense a lingering upon that one word. The cougars are out there and like a hungry lioness they slink and display sleek beauty yet many yes sir hear me, many display this based on their own hunger. Even if one hungers for righteousness she must find that through intimacy with God before she will be released to find that with man. Turn your face. Bring your own desire into subjection and do not get out of season. What is happening in you is God. Again you are being sanctified and even circumcised again. The very skin must be lifted in all areas of your life for it is one thing to be washed and another to be cleansed. Dr. Simmons, sir, press in, endure the scrubbing. God has you in a remarkable position of being alone yet so far from being alone. You cannot possibly yet see where you are going or who will be part of your life in the future. God is all over you and you are experiencing temple maintenance! Not always pretty but always necessary! Do not attempt to salvage what God says must be destroyed. Go to the crawl space again for something remains waaaaayyyy back in the darkest corner. Small...so you better bring His light with you when you go looking to drag it out. Praise God and Hallelujah." – **Prophetess Holly sharp**: **August 7 2010 @1:43pm**

LET'S TALK INTIMACY: "THAT I MAY KNOW HIM!" (Phil.3:10)-August 7th 2010

"Hello Man of God. I sent you a message." - **Prophetess Holly Sharp-4:07pm**

"Yes woman of God...I read an earlier one...but not recently.
How are you today Woman of God?" -**Dr. Randy E.Simmons-4:09pm**

'Sooo full." - **Prophetess Holly Sharp-4:12pm**

"Yes...you are Woman of God...yes you are." - **Dr. Randy E. Simmons:-4:15pm**

"I am still delighting in your drenching experience with the Lord." - **Prophetess Holly Sharp-4:17pm**

"How precious is that?!" - **Dr. Randy E. Simmons-4:20pm**

"I sent the message an hour or two ago via BB. You have most likely received it. I drench every single day in the shower. Seriously, like thirty minutes. Bless my husband for not minding the water bill. He knows it is my soaking time." - **Prophetess Holly Sharp-4:23pm**

"Thank you...the rain is still pouring even as we speak." - **Dr. Randy E. Simmons-4:25pm**

"Shall I allow you to continue soaking and share thoughts later?" - **Prophetess Holly Sharp-4:26pm**

"No...I am ready. God spoke to me as I was mopping the floor earlier that it will rain again." - **Dr. Randy E. Simmons-4:28pm**

"And?" - **Prophetess Holly Sharp-4:29pmHolly**

"Meaning 'double portion' of his blessings and anointing" - **Dr. Randy E. Simmons-4:30pm**

"Remember the Lord spoke after the **STRONG** rain....Sometimes the rain stings. Sometimes the rain is gentle; Sometimes the rain is quick." - **Prophetess Holly Sharp-4:31pm**

"But always refreshing...lol...lol..." - **Dr. Randy E. Simmons-4:31pm**

"Sometimes it rains and rains and rains. Yes indeed." - **Prophetess Holly Sharp-4:31pm**

"But never again for destruction as promised to Noah." - **Dr. Randy E. Simmons-4:32pm**

"So true. See what God is reminding and restoring and refreshing by the rain. Even the

smell of it...makes you keenly aware it is coming.
We are on a 7 day fast...six am to six pm for. I have been praying for you today. I sense you are going deeper into intimacy with Him." - **Prophetess Holly Sharp-4:32pm**

"Yes. I awoke today and that is all I could think of...THE INTIMACY OF GOD!" - **Dr. Randy E. Simmons-4:35pm**

"Amen. One must learn to make passion with Christ a priority." - **Prophetess Holly Sharp-4:37pm**

"Wow...it's like the passion of Christ. Can you teach me?" - **Dr. Randy E. Simmons-4:39pm**

"I can only teach that which has been revealed to me and will be revealed to me." - **Prophetess Holly Sharp-4:40pm**

"Well woman of God my spirit is open...he shall reveal that that you are to know..." - **Dr. Randy E. Simmons-4:41pm**

"Intimacy brings comfort;
Intimacy with God brings comfort;
Intimacy with God brings pleasure;
Intimacy with God is a defense against temptation;
Intimacy with God declares oneness;
Intimacy with God conceives Life;
Intimacy with God brings forth knowledge.
How's that for starters?" - **Prophetess Holly Sharp-4:43pm**

"Wow...Woman of God...INTIMACY...INTIMACY! Woman of God...what is Intimacy to a man of God?" - **Dr. Randy E. Simmons-4:48pm**

"More challenging than it is to a woman sir." - **Prophetess Holly Sharp-4:54pm**

"Yes...I so discern...for a woman it is easy." - **Dr. Randy E. Simmons-4:56pm**

"Yes, just like in the natural, if I may humbly and cautiously go there for a moment. If a man never becomes intimate with God, He will never truly understand the heart of a woman." - **Prophetess Holly Sharp-4:56pm**

"Yes. It is the only way that a man or woman of God can know him...and I truly mean know him intimately! What is the heart of a woman?" - **Dr. Randy E. Simmons-4:57pm**

"I could write a book on that on one." - **Prophetess Holly Sharp-4:59pm**

"Maybe you should...lol...lol..." - **Dr. Randy E. Simmons-5:01pm**

"I have many books in the makings in my mind. Can't go there just yet..." - **Prophetess Holly Sharp-5:02pm**

"Take me into the heart of God and a woman Holly if he so permits... for How else can I minister to them?" - **Dr. Randy E. Simmons-5:03pm**

"Lots of people think I should write a book about breast cancer and surviving....I just am not called to do that at this time...or perhaps ever. I will however minister one on one any time any place any hour of the day. First I will say this with a word of caution to you if I may....about ministering to women. Your heart, your mind, your physical and emotional self must be **TOTALLY SOLD OUT** to God before you can effectively minister to a woman….." - **Prophetess Holly Sharp-5:05pm**

"Yes. I know…and am learning! Holly take me deeper if the Spirit allows…teach me about women." - **Dr. Randy E. Simmons-5:06pm**

"Only the spiritually and emotionally mature woman could receive counsel from a single pastor….as it pertains to intimate issues. Issues of the heart. What is one of the top questions you have?" - **Prophetess Holly Sharp-5:08pm**

"No questions…I am a novice…but you spoke of spiritually and emotionally mature women and issues of the heart." - **Dr. Randy E. Simmons-5:10pm**

"Women are nurturers….not all, but I will speak of the ones who are. They nurture and nurture and nurture. They enjoy that. But then BAM! They need to be nurtured and a man doesn't even see it coming! LOL
They long to go to God, but it is extremely difficult to get past the need for the natural and be satisfied in the supernatural. Does that make any sense yet?" - **Prophetess Holly Sharp-5:12pm**

"Nurturers. Is this the desire of most Women of God?" - **Dr. Randy E. Simmons-5:13pm**

"I would say some. Not all. Here's a starting point, think for a moment of the fivefold ministry and how each position functions differently. Women are the same. Based on her God given gifts and talents and on the experiences of her life she will be shaped and formed." - **Prophetess Holly Sharp-5:14pm**

"What about the heart and intimacy of Holly...will you share?" - **Dr. Randy E.Simmons-5:16pm**

"The heart of the precious, priceless gift God has been placed in a woman. She sees with her heart, she hears with her heart, she feels with her heart. She is confused by her own heart. She has a desire to serve. Her heart pulls her to serve others. Often her heart gets in the way and she will serve in ways that are carnal rather than spiritual.
Women, particularly Christian women, struggle in some areas. One main area is how they can be Godly and sensuous at the same time.' - **Prophetess Holly Sharp-5:18pm**

"Wow...extraordinary. Is that why Solomon said: 'the ways of a woman are past finding out'?" - **Dr. Randy E. Simmons-5:19pm**

"Probably so. LOL. Even women can't figure it out half the time." - **Prophetess Holly Sharp-5:20pm**

"Sensuality is a woman's greatest gift. Given to her by God." - **Dr. Randy E. Simmons-5:21pm**

"Yes it is, but we have been confused by the voices of radio, TV, adds, books, magazines, friends, foes, oh yes, lets don't forgot churches!
You would be surprised how, if surveyed, the variety of answers you would receive if you asked a woman to describe a Godly Woman." - **Prophetess Holly Sharp-5:23pm**

"Then speak as a Godly...sensual women to my spirit." - **Dr. Randy E. Simmons-5:23pm**

"Oh now that would be transparent indeed....for training and understanding purposes I will proceed as the Lord allows. I will only have about five more minutes until later....ok with that." - **Prophetess Holly Sharp-5:24pm**

"Yes. Shall I call you teacher?" - **Dr. Randy E. Simmons-5:25pm**

"We are often confused by the word sensuous and think of it as a negative rather than a positive. Go back to the five or six points I gave you in the beginning of this chat....about intimacy with God. Those are the same points about intimacy as it pertains to the heart of a Godly woman. Notice I stress **GODLY** woman. If women deny the gifts God has placed in them then there is atrophy...a decline, a decrease in size and a wasting away." - **Prophetess Holly Sharp-5:26pm**

"Yes. I know but we make it sexual...dirty...ungodly, because of the flesh. Therefore men are afraid to be sensual." - **Dr. Randy E. Simmons-5:28pm**

"Because it has been so widely misunderstood, and a man knows not how to approach a woman properly...in the physical or the spiritual.
Shulamith is one to study." - **Prophetess Holly Sharp-5:29pm**

"Allow me the approach if God so decides...will you? Shulamith...hmmmm pretty deep!?" - **Dr. Randy E. Simmons-5:30pm**

"Well.....you did want to know about a woman right....it's in the Bible....what can I say?" - **Prophetess Holly Sharp-5:31pm**

"..Lol...lol...lol....your spirit is so perceptive!" - **Dr. Randy E. Simmons-5:33pm**

"Two years ago I wanted to teach married women in a small setting in my home. You know, they were scared to death....and, to this day they have made excuses as to why **NOT** to attend. Even to the point of saying, "oh, you probably don't feel like teaching tonight." LOL. Will be back later...." - **Prophetess Holly Sharp-5:33pm**

"Yes...I am with you...rise up daughter...I will wait here for you?" - **Dr. Randy E. Simmons-5:35pm**

"Back...Have you marinated?" - **Prophetess Holly Sharp-9:36pm**

"HMMMMMMMMMMM. Yes" - **Dr. Randy E. Simmons-9:38pm**

"Excellent!" - **Prophetess Holly Sharp-9:39pm**

"AND NOW TEACHER?" - **Dr. Randy E. Simmons-9:41pm**

"Where shall we begin?" - **Prophetess Holly Sharp-9:43pm**

"Well, at the beginning...lol...lol..." - **Dr. Randy E. Simmons-9:44pm**

"Intimacy with God is a gift. A gift is something voluntarily given without compensation. He desires to give us a gift and we in turn desire to give Him the gift of ourselves.....and....He certainly woos us much more than we even think to woo Him. For we need not woo our Savior....He already demonstrated His love at the cross. When Bathsheba's son died, how did David comfort her? He lay with her. Yes, she bore then a son....so, sir, as we lay with God in moments of deep intimacy something is conceived within us which we are to birth. Strictly speaking in the spiritual now, please understand that God penetrates our hearts and that is part of the intimacy. You aren't writing a book about all this are you? Lol. When we allow intimacy to take place we are allowing comfort, assistance, support, encouragement, solace....All these things are at the heart of a woman." - **Prophetess Holly Sharp-9:46pm**

"Should I write a book? I want to learn...you are teaching me" - **Dr. Randy E. Simmons-9:52pm**

"It's up to you." I am not really certain what it is you desire to learn so I am just maintaining the subject we have begun. Is this making sense thus far? The Man of God is quiet on tonight." - **Prophetess Holly Sharp-9:53pm**

"Tell me something. I ask you this once you did not answer. Is there a dance of intimacy between prophetess and prophets?" - **Dr. Randy E. Simmons-9:54pm**

"I have not that answer.....I really do not know. Like spirits delight in one another; however the dance of intimacy belongs to God I do believe." - **Prophetess Holly Sharp-9:56pm**

"Do you wish to know why I am so quiet?" - **Dr. Randy E. Simmons-9:57pm**

"If you are lead to reveal." - **Prophetess Holly Sharp-9:58pm**

"You have intrigue me...from the very first conversation back on July 29th 2010" - **Dr. Randy E. Simmons-9:59pm**

"Awwww....it is not I, but the Holy Spirit for the Spirit speaks loudly to you." - **Prophetess Holly Sharp-10:00pm**

"Yes...but deeply and now even deeper..." - **Dr. Randy E. Simmons-10:00pm**

"...Because you seek truth." You seek to know more. You seek to learn answers and have not had one to ask the type of questions to." - **Prophetess Holly Sharp-10:02pm**

"Yes...you are correct...nor trusted their answers...your spirit seems pure." - **Dr. Randy E. Simmons-10:03pm**

"As a prophet, you know that part of the function is to reconcile people to the promise (God). You are a broken man in some areas and you seek spiritual and emotional restoration." - **Prophetess Holly Sharp-10:05pm**

"Yes...and I find that you are allowing me to pour myself into you...I felt that in our very first conversation...yet I tread carefully!" - **Dr. Randy E. Simmons-10:06pm**

"There is **MUCH** God has placed in the WOG, in His Prophet and it is now coming to the surface because you may be one of the first to whom the Spirit has revealed such words, however I believe God is simply helping this Prophet speak **LIFE** and truth. Even in the most difficult, or tender issues.

It is always wise to tread carefully when dealing with such issues as are on your heart.

For you see Man of God, remember I shared the **HOLY SPIRIT** is attractive. Do not allow the carnal man to supersede the spirit man. This will be the challenge for you and you shall pass for I declare and decree it to be so. Your questions are real. My answers will be truthful." - **Prophetess Holly Sharp-10:08pm**

"Yes, but I feel such intimacy....woman of God...you walk close and you know it...your purpose is clear and I understand it! And now...woman of God...?" - **Dr. Randy E. Simmons-10:09pm**

"Now, do you wish to continue....lol?

Diversion.....We divert our passion for Christ into other areas....jobs, children, television, work and even "working for the Kingdom" and in doing so, our lover (the Lord) is left unattended. We rob the very one who desires intimacy and we in essence rob ourselves as well. Are we experiencing computer problems or simply quietness on tonight?" - **Prophetess Holly Sharp-10:11pm**

"We are being tentative...take me into the depths...I have opened my spirit to you." - **Dr. Randy E. Simmons-10:15pm**

"Please help me out here...being tentative?" - **Prophetess Holly Sharp-10:14pm**

"This is a deep area and new for me...women understand intimacy...I don't." - **Dr. Randy E. Simmons10:16pm**

"Oh, actually, I believe you do, more than you realize. I say that because you are willing to listen and to be taught. That is a step in intimacy...with God and in life." - **Prophetess Holly Sharp-10:17pm**

"Hmmm...so intimacy is real...you can feel it!?" - **Dr. Randy E. Simmons-10:18pm**

"Absolutely intimacy is real and can be felt." - **Prophetess Holly Sharp-10:20pm**

"I have felt your intimacy...is that a correct thing to say?" - **Dr. Randy E. Simmons-10:21pm**

"I am an extremely passionate person. One cannot speak of intimate issues without sensing intimacy. I am passionate about life, about people, about Jesus. If you have sensed that, it is most likely because I have allowed there to be a transparency." - **Prophetess Holly Sharp-10:22pm**

"I felt you Holly...even the first time you communicated through the private messages." - **Dr. Randy E. Simmons-10:23pm**

"I am passionate about my husband, my children, and my friends, those who God hand selects and connects. We are here to learn and to be taught so that we can advance people in the Kingdom. Do you know how many people struggle with intimacy with God...let alone with people? I am not sure what you sensed in July however it must have been significant. Much has spilled out and I do believe God is doing a work in you like you did not anticipate. Keeping you from the cougars! Lol." - **Prophetess Holly Sharp-10:25pm**

"Tell me more about these cougars...why do you call them that?" - **Dr. Randy E. Simmons-10:27pm**

"Because they are the women who will seek you out just because of your status, both Godly and availability. There will be women who will flock to get close to you because they want something and see you as a Man Of God who they would either:

1) Wish to conquer
2) Persuade
3) Marry

Do not think that the suit you wear or the Bible you carry will send them looking in another direction, no, Man of God, they will seek to be with you. They sense your passion, and they desire to be the object of your passion. Few, perhaps only one in your lifetime will understand your passion for Christ comes first and will walk with you in that Biblical order......and when that time comes, she will be a TRUE Woman of God....for Christ will be her object of passion as well....and she will understand. And at that time, the three strand cord will be easily established and not easily broken. Is this speaking to your heart on tonight sire? Ooops...lol sir?" - **Prophetess Holly Sharp-10:28**

"Wow! This is deep...you have such wealth...lol...lol..." - **Dr. Randy E. Simmons-10:30pm**

"Hey...you asked for it! Lol!" - **Prophetess Holly Sharp-10:32pm**

"You scare me...am I a target?" - **Dr. Randy E. Simmons-10:33pm**

"I am not the one to scare you....the cougars are! I am an old married lady with five children, 3 grandchildren, a husband I have loved since age 15, three dogs and a cat....and a small house with love packed in! My family has to put up with me all the time too. LOL!" - **Prophetess Holly Sharp-10:34pm**

"Lol...whew! Then tell me more...You are teaching me so much...Why is God doing this now?" - **Dr. Randy E. Simmons-10:35pm**

"Sanctification process. When you are complete you will be so in love with God that you will just simply be transformed. Not that you aren't but you are coming into a new place at this time in life." - **Prophetess Holly Sharp-10:36pm**

"The work is great...the pains and hurts even greater...Someone told me that on my 52 birthday which was exactly one month before now that I would be reborn...is this rebirth for me?" - **Dr. Randy E. Simmons-10:37**

"It hurts to be born. Lots of pushing and pulling and cutting of the cord, being removed from the safety of the womb. We come out wrinkly, covered with "yuck" and screaming our lil heads off! Yup sounds like rebirth to me. LOL!" - **Prophetess Holly Sharp-10:39pm**

"Is God taking me thru a rebirth? What has the end time to declare? How do we find the truth of his will?" - **Dr. Randy E. Simmons-10:41**

"Ok, now you really have to help **ME** out with that one....remember, you are the one who understands the scriptures. I so wish I did." - **Prophetess Holly Sharp-10:44pm**

"Holly I am a theologian...like Nicodemus, what do I know about rebirth and intimacy? Knowing the scriptures doesn't make one an expert on the deeper things of God." - **Dr. Randy E. Simmons-10:46**

"I do wish I knew scripture. I know some, but do not have a deep understanding or the historical reference. It's tough because as a prophet called of God, I am often like **"WHAT IN THE WORLD ARE YOU SAYING GOD? I DON"T SEEM TO GET IT."** Though He has allowed me to speak His heart." - **Prophetess Holly Sharp-10:48pm**

"Holly...you have the heart of God...that is the best. I am hard, dry cold, anointed yes...but lack the deeper intimate things of God. I'm like a Moses, but so desire to know him but afraid to be transparent, even before God...so all we do is ask to see his glory!" - **Dr. Randy E. Simmons-10:50pm**

"Ok. So, that said, 'Lord, we come before you in all humility and ask that you will allow us to work together side by side in ministry. Learning from one another and teaching one another. Lord, place your hand over ours, protect us as we move forward, and speak to us and through us for your Glory. Amen'. I already know there are things you want to say to me." - **Prophetess Holly Sharp-10:52pm**

"Is that your desire Holly; to work beside me in ministry? You are a Martha spirit; I am a Mary spirit...what need we more? Yes...there are things, but what and why? Do you wish us to build a ministry in your town or area...travel the world...what?" - **Dr. Randy E. Simmons-10:54pm**

"God will reveal how we are to work together in time. I have had to allow Him to open my ears and eyes and heart to whatever He desires me to do and who He desires me to work with. Sometimes I am Mary and sometimes I am Martha. Don't you think we all are? There is a sweet book entitled, having a Mary Heart in a Martha World." - **Prophetess Holly Sharp-10:56pm**

"Some of us are learning just how to sit at the master's feet. Isn't that the better thing?" - **Dr. Randy E. Simmons-10:58pm**

"Yes it is 'the better of the two'! May I shift gears for just a moment. I have wanted to share something of a personal nature...perhaps you will better understand my formality at times. - **Prophetess Holly Sharp-10:59pm**

"I have walked the hard halls of corporate America; stood in board rooms of Wendy's and Red Lobster; heard the foul language of Car Dealership managers, and as a Joseph in Egypt, God has kept me...now he must deal with my heart as he has with my head. Yes by all means shift gears..." - **Dr. Randy E. Simmons-11:02pm**

"I was a business professional as well til the twins were born. I gave up panty hose for jeans and tennis shoes and had a ball. Traded in MY ENTIRE 401K and said, "I am raising the children God gave us." Hubby (ex now) flipped and I stood my ground. Have been with them 19 years....no regrets. I was a single mother for two + years and that is when Steve and I reconnected. We dated, married after two years, blended his two and my two and then I became pregnant 3 times in 13 months. Lost all the babies. One year later, pregnant again. Miscarried. About five weeks later I really didn't feel well. Went to the doctor, but before I did I said to a friend, "wouldn't it be just like God for me to go and find out I am expecting?" Well....that's EXACTLY what happened. Only I didn't realize how pregnant I was....13 weeks. I had been carrying twins and miscarried one and not the other! Now that survivor is my precious daughter Jessie.

That isn't even what I wanted to share, but I will share more...." - **Prophetess Holly Sharp-11:04pm**

"If you would like, by all means share...as I said my spirit man is open to you." - **Dr. Randy E. Simmons-11:06pm**

"I was married at 22....my husband went to my parents and I didn't know and told them I wanted to have space from them and they shouldn't contact me....I would contact them. He controlled my
Comings and goings and I didn't realize it. He was Greek and has his own ideas and sexual preferences....We went to church together until the first week after marriage. He stopped going. Three months into marriage he wanted a vasectomy for he was "satisfied" with the one daughter age three he already had. I declined. His response was no relationship for nearly a year unless it pleased him. One year later I submitted to the vasectomy. Three years later I was a single woman. I failed to say he told me AT THE ALTER while lighting

the unity candle and I said I love you....he said, "You'll get over it." He was correct. I did! About a minute and a half after we were married.

Do you want to know more>

I started college. He told me to quit because he wanted me home.
I quit. We divorced. I moved on with $300 and a washer and dryer for which I was grateful..."
- **Prophetess Holly Sharp-1109pm**

"Why do you share this with me?" - **Dr. Randy E. Simmons-11:14pm**

"Because I want to be transparent so you will better understand me....if we are to be in ministry I want you to know me.

Two years later I met my second husband, a businessman. When we planned our wedding at six weeks prior he had not given me a guest list or asked his best man. I suggested we call it off. He was ripe and ready to agree. He said. Six more months. We entered counseling. We married. We were married seven years and had sex 27 times total in seven years!

What do you think that did to the heart and mind of a passionate woman?

Do I understand women? Yes I do. I am one and I know what the abuse of a man can do to the heart of a woman.

It is by the grace of God when I did conceive it was one of those twenty seven times....when he wasn't treating me like a total whore.

Sad but true.

Can you handle hearing this?

Do you see now that I too have been through the rebirth process? I too have injury and deep scars, but I am HEALED.

I do want to walk you through healing.

To this day I believe he was gay." - **Prophetess Holly Sharp-11:18pm**

"I have a friend who runs an online magazine…perhaps you should consider writing your story in her magazine. It would really bless women." - **Dr. Randy E. Simmons-11:20pm**

"I know that his lack of love opened the gate wide for sin. I had an affair…within the church." - **Prophetess Holly Sharp-11:22pm**

"You are so full of passion and life…wow such a pity and your heart now?" - **Dr. Randy E. Simmons-11:24pm**

"God has forgiven me. There was no intercourse, but it was an affair none the less. I was destroyed and the "men", my husband and the other man were the ones who acted wounded. One didn't protect me and one didn't respect me. How about that? Oh, but GOD, my Lord, my Savior saw something worth saving…something worth restoring, something to be used for His purpose." - **Prophetess Holly Sharp-11:25pm**

"I am a strong man and understand much of the issues you speak of. In 2001 I formed GWAP (Global Woman's Advocate Program) to lobby and support women in these same areas. I have a strong heart." - **Dr. Randy E. Simmons-11:26pm**

"He (God) captured my very heart and showed me HE was my husband and He desired me. HE loved me and I was not his whore, I was HIS WOMAN." - **Prophetess Holly Sharp-11:28pm**

"Wow, I did not know that." - **Dr. Randy E. Simmons-11:33**

"Dr. Simmons, I had to get the passion under control because after all the hurt, I just wanted to run, and run and run....I wanted a man in my life. A real man to love me and nurture me and respect the woman I am. I wanted to spill out such abandoned passion on him....and be LOVED in return. I had to learn to bridle that spirit within me and destroy the unclean spirit." - **Prophetess Holly Sharp-11:35**

"So, like me, you are also being rebirthed..." - **Dr. Randy E. Simmons-11:38**

"And....in learning to do so change has come and I have begun to understand intimacy with God.

Yes.

Of course when cancer appeared seven years after we married, people blamed that on my past sin. Then not only did I have cancer, I had people with religious ideas and opinions. Lots of casting stones my direction from a couple of select few.

Again, God had another plan.

I am still here! And strong and healthy and the beauty people say they see is Him in me.

Ok....I'll quit for a minute. I know I have given you "book" material for sure now. LOL!" - **Prophetess Holly Sharp-11:39pm**

"Holly...so why don't you write your story?" - **Dr. Randy E. Simmons-11:41pm**

"Have I exhausted my welcome with the Man of God?

No need at this time. I share one on one as the Spirit leads. Perhaps sometime. Not at this time." - **Prophetess Holly Sharp-11:43pm**

"Holly. What is Love?" - **Dr. Randy E. Simmons-11:45pm**

"I can email you a couple little things, very brief that I have written for someday. Just little snippets that I have considered intermingling with God's response to my life.

THIS!

Because God is love and God has opened doors of truth.
Love is responsive, adventurous, yielding, expressive, and sensuous.

Does that answer your question?" - **Prophetess Holly Sharp-11:46pm**

"You are always welcome with me...but there is such a ministry and testimony within you...how may I help?" - **Dr. Randy E. Simmons-11-51pm**

"I honestly have no earthly idea. Have I been too transparent?" - **Prophetess Holly Sharp-11:53pm**

"If you email these things...are you asking me to write for you? Lol..." - **Dr. Randy E. Simmons-11:55pm**

"Our intimacy with God should not be a chore, but rather a choice...I submit to Him...Naw...just for your interest. So you can see some writings that have just been for my own heart at the moment.

So, have I been too transparent. You are very quiet." - **Prophetess Holly Sharp-11:57pm**

"Now I understand why I feel you so deeply...have you read my biography and testimony?" - **Dr. Randy E. Simmons-11:59pm**

"No." - **Prophetess Holly Sharp-12:01am**

"You have touched me deeply and left me speechless...I've seen much but this passes many. Someday I will post my testimony on fb "Negotiating at the Council of Hell" - **Dr. Randy E. Simmons-12:03am**

"I will look for it." - **Prophetess Holly Sharp-12:05am**

"It tells of my journey to build my corporation Deshan Intl Inc. and the need to find sixty Million dollars and I go to Hell and negotiate with Satan for the money...he calls all his hoards...but bottom line he sees the mark of Jesus on me and becomes disgusted and gives me an ultimatum...a journey if you wish..." - **Dr. Randy E. Simmons-12:07am**

"Oh Lord Jesus....well, as the saying goes, we can negotiate with Satan, but not with Jesus for we have nothing to negotiate with...it all belongs to him. Even we belong to Him." - **Prophetess Holly Sharp-12:10am**

"Its deep and dark...the body is not ready for it...you Holly will understand...you have walked deep. Now you understand why God is taking me thru this...I've walked where many preacher fear to even think of treading. Touched what they will never touch and turned to Satan after I felt God had denied me." - **Dr. Randy E. Simmons-12:13am**

"May I share one more thing, what I intended to share about an hour ago. I am soooo sorry to keep you so long. Please say if you must go. Ugly ain't pretty is it! However, that is what makes you REAL. Others lie and say they haven't been there. Others hide and are so dysfunctional that they allow the dysfunction to continue in their churches because they lead the pack of dysfunction." - **Prophetess Holly Sharp-12:16am**

"Satan loves to negotiate. Remember the temptation of Jesus in the wilderness was nothing more than a negotiation..." - **Dr. Randy E. Simmons-12:19am**

"However he did not prevail..." - **Prophetess Holly Sharp-12:21am**

"I am at your disposal..." - **Dr. Randy E. Simmons-12:23am**

"Yes or no question....have you negotiated with him since July 29th?" - **Prophetess Holly Sharp-12:25am**

Well I don't lie...I can tell you where I've walked Holly...very dark and very deep...my heart has seen and felt the edge of darkness as a Christian...I always tested the limits of my God...BAD IDEA! I've stopped negotiating...I've surrendered only to Jesus. But on July 29th I saw him, Satan walk thru this apartment in the form of a white serpent dragon. His aim to destroy me that is when you and I began to exchange messages and then the prophetess Dee was birthed thereafter." - **Dr. Randy E. Simmons-12:26am**

"God's timing is perfect." - **Prophetess Holly Sharp-12:31am**

"Now I am free and moving deeply towards the intimacy of God." - **Dr. Randy E. Simmons-12:32am**

"And ALL of heaven and earth rejoice. Even Columbus OHO!" - **Prophetess Holly Sharp-12:33am**

"OHIO?" - **Dr. Randy E. Simmons-12:34am**

"Remember the crawl space. Keep going there. I am just reminded over and over to tell you that. And I tell myself as well. Are you tired yet this evening?

How about a few more minutes then we shall pause...." - **Prophetess Holly Sharp-12:35am**

"What do you see Prophet of God...what do you see?" Awww, the crawl spaces...tell me what your desire is?" I feel like a student in a karate movie...lol...lol...lol...I am better however at voicing my thoughts in long emails or messages...these little boxes though friendly seem to limit my thought capacity." - **Dr. Randy E. Simmons-12:37am**

"Movies, books, letters, memories, thoughts, fantasy, imaginations, pictures, articles ...this is what I see in the crawl space... I am sooo sorry. Something still hinders you. Those are just the words that have come into my spirit, not meaning all and perhaps none, but they come in the spirit. Right brain/left brain....lol...lol. Remember I asked you if you had seen Karate Kid? Take the jacket off, hang it up, put the jacket on. Take the jacket off, hang it up, put the jacket on. LOL .Mix the tuna, stomp the grapes. Did you see that one? Ha...ha...ha...ha!
Do you recall how you pressed me the other night....well I press you tonight." - **Prophetess Holly Sharp-12:41am**

"I am not much on movies. TV or vile imaginations I am a thinker...a planner...a family man...without a family and yes many memories. I hardly turn on the TV. So will I pass the intimacy test?

Lol...lol...lol...lol...pressed like a grape!" - **Dr. Randy E. Simmons-12:44am**

"I rarely watch TV or go to movies either. I too am a thinker and a planner. A family woman, with blended family." - **Prophetess Holly Sharp-12:47am**

"And did you get that for which you pressed me?" - **Dr. Randy E. Simmons-12:49am**

"Maybe....My feet are not quiet purple yet. Lol!" - **Prophetess Holly Sharp-12:50am**

"More to come then...lol...lol...lol?!" - **Dr. Randy E. Simmons-12:52am**

"Yes. You do not know my nickname do you?" - **Prophetess Holly Sharp-12:53am**

"Let's see Colombo?!! Lol...lol...lol..." - **Dr. Randy E.Simmons-12:54am**

"Lord have mercy, you otta be moosh (mush sp?) by now...all the pressing. NOPE. Warrior Princess!" - **Prophetess Holly Sharp-12:56am**

"Hmmmm. I am very familiar with both names...quite!" - **Dr. Randy E. Simmons-12:58am**

"A warrior does not quit and a princess is the daughter of the King.
Wonder if I could be a Mary Warrior Princess...or maybe a Merry Warrior Princess? LOL!" - **Prophetess Holly Sharp-12:59am**

"Holly...you pull on my seed if I could use such an expression. As a prince and son of God!' - **Dr. Randy E. Simmons-1:01am**

"Well...ummm...so I guess I will just take that as a good thing. It is good to have some humor. For Life is so full and we must have time to laugh." - **Prophetess Holly Sharp-1:03am**

"Do you? Do you know me...who I am? lol...lol...lol...yes humor...good ole humor! My goal is to open Centers for Christian and Social Development around America and the world. We must rebuild, not as it once was, but the church must take the forefront...the world is looking for leaders and doesn't care where they come from so we, as men and women of God, must lead the charge. This is my purpose and this is my vision." - **Dr. Randy E. Simmons-1:06am**

"I am getting to know you day by day. Sometimes I think you have been sent to train me and mentor me…" - **Prophetess Holly Sharp-1:09am**

"It is that with which I am pregnant!" - **Dr. Randy E. Simmons-1:11am**

"You must get acquainted with my Apostle, my mentor, my friend. Her heart is much the same yet different. We are a church without walls. Well sir, with a vision such as that, you are about to be VERY Pregnant! Is that why you asked me about ministry, travel, etc.?" - **Prophet Holly Sharp-1:13am**

"I have felt the heart of the homeless in the eighties, I have seen the kids on the streets in the nineties, and now I see the economic collapse of an entire financial structure the world over…" - **Dr. Randy E. Simmons-1:17am**

"Your vision is great, your vision is deep and your vision is from God for no man on his own power, thinking or ability to attempt such." - **Prophetess Holly Sharp-1:20am**

"Not just the inner cities of America, not just the slums of the world, but main street, poor middle class…I will raise up an army of people who have the heart of God and the heart of the people…" - **Dr. Randy E. Simmons-1:21am**

"You hear from God." - **Prophetess Holly Sharp-1:24am**

"Not rock star Christians, not celebrities. Men and women of God!

I've seen and I have heard...yes I have felt. THIS IS MY INTIMACY!" - **Dr. Randy E. Simmons-1:25am**

"Dr. Simmons, my family knows my heart. My husband just gives me "that look" when he knows it is time to wait on me because I have to stop to minister to someone, cry with someone, give someone a leaning post. You know, one cannot lean on something of no substance. Then you have found it, you have experienced it and NOW you must continue to develop it. Each intimate encounter is different. I am that middle class world. I understand." - **Prophetess Holly Sharp-1:27am**

"Someday I will share my vision with you...it's already written in a four hundred page book...which few have seen...prepared for this end time. It will operate under four divisions G.W.A.P., F.O.C.U.S., R.E.R.U.N., and P.O.P...."
- **Dr. Randy E.Simmons-1:31am**

"I am not talking upper middle class either. Just your everyday family...God has been preparing you and preparing you and preparing you. Your function and responsibility is great. You MUST have this time to be intimate with God for He has given you an assignment specific to you for He trusts you.

I know I asked already, but may I share one more personal thing and I will make it brief, it is still a fresh wound." - **Prophetess Holly Sharp-1:34am**

"Now you see why your prophecy that the woman to stand beside me is special? I believe that she is in training right now...not to be yet named or revealed to the world...Never an engagement announcement, so that Satan cannot touch her...she too is a warrior and a princes. I have seen her!" - **Dr. Randy E. Simmons-1:37am**

"For thirty years I have been friends with a man. We began by meeting on an airplane in 1979. I could have loved this man for a lifetime. We dated from afar couple months and I soon learned he was to be married. I was shocked. His bride to be was with child. She was about 15 years older than he was. They kept the child who is now about 30 years old. At the time I didn't' understand, now that I am a mother I totally understand. Our relationship was on and off but somehow we were able to train ourselves into friendship only.
....in response to what you just wrote, Yes you have seen her....in spirit only.

Soooo, anyway, he has often, often, often told me that I hear from God, that I move him, that there is something so very special about me. He is a very educated man. All this he has spoken. He travels the world and I have seen the world through his stories. I have been to the Holy Land, Australia, Poland, Germany, and China with him...only though what he tells. I have ministered to the spiritually poor and held the broken hearted. I have been to the orphanage and held the children. I have been to the Wailing Wall and walked where Jesus walked. He has said, "Someday I want to take you there." I have remained disciplined...."

Disciplined and respectful of God. Just recently as the Lord began to move upon me that I should travel at least once and month within the states, I was led to speak to him. I waited as directed by the Lord. I waited one week as the Lord directed. No response. I spoke in third person, as God directed, saying, "this WOG has an assignment, yet fragile resources." I did not ask for money from him. He became uncomfortable because "it doesn't even sound like you Holly....I am not sure it even sounds like God." I was sooo crushed. For this man spoke often of wanting to "take" me but could not see to "send" me....it wasn't ever really that....It was that years he said I heard from God like none other and now I don't hear from God and he doesn't like what he is hearing. I wrestled and struggled and hissed inside. Then I surrendered.

I sent one final message praying for him and his family and said, "God knows my heart" I pressed DELETE.

All communication gone. No reserve number, no email, no address, no work address. Nothing! I had to go to the crawl space. What did I have left of him? Nothing! What was I left with? GOD!

Sanctification process and I am ok with that.

How much more transparent could I possibly be. You know me well now. I understand the heart of a woman to a deep degree.

I met a real man....at the well.

I will hush now and allow you to have the final words on tonight." - **Prophetess Holly Sharp-1:40am**

"Holly you have shared much as I have...my crawl space is deep and has been opened up. I don't fear flesh or sin. This flesh that I live in is corrupt. I am a son of God, I really believe that. I walk by faith and if I told you my situation tonight you won't believe it, so there. But God speaks...he said "after a strong rain...I will bless you"

There was a strong rain early this morning!

This afternoon he spoke..."it shall rain again to show you I will give you a double portion"; it rained two minutes later! I went to the barber and just before that he spoke that "on tomorrow you will meet the man that will change your destiny and the purpose of GVMI"
- **Dr. Randy E. Simmons-1:54am**

"In time you will meet the woman as well." - **Prophetess Holly Sharp-1:58am**

"I attend St Simons Island Community Church since being back in Brunswick, Ga. It is one of the riches zip codes around. I have been lead to go nowhere else so I believe that tomorrow...God will change my destiny...he has never lied to me..." - **Dr. Randy E. Simmons-1:59am**

"Hallelujah!" - **Prophetess Holly Sharp-2:01am**

"BECAUSE THAT IS THE INTIMACY WE SHARE, he will chastise me as fast as bless me, and I never complain!" - **Dr. Randy E. Simmons-2:02am**

"He heals and restores, He tears down only to build up. Your vision is great. Our God is greater. Go where He sends you.

Thank you so very much for allowing me to cleanse tonight.

I shared more in one night than I have in many moons. I generally keep things to myself for I don't want to distract others from the promises of God. I open when God says open....

I will be praying for you tomorrow. I am sure you need to rest tonight. Can't have the Man Of God dragging' into church. LOL!" - **Prophetess Holly Sharp-2:04am**

"Yes...I have poured out much...what do you want from me...will you tell me next time?" - **Dr. Randy E. Simmons-2:07am**

"Thank you for allowing me to share the last portion of the story with you about the friend who I had to let go....that was HUGE!" - **Prophetess Holly Sharp-2:09am**

"Yes. To God be glory!" - **Dr. Randy E.Simmons-2:11am**

"I truly don't know. Teach me; mentor me in that which you believe in your heart the Lord is saying to you. Grow me up so I can go forth. Encourage me as a Prophetess. Convince me that scripture will come and that it's ok if I don't know it yet." - **Prophetess Holly Sharp-2:12am**

"I will go before him...we will bring it about...listen to the spirit!" - **Dr. Randy E.Simmons-2:14am**

"This well is deep. Let us say good night, God bless you, thank you Father for the birth of a friendship." - **Prophetess Holly Sharp-2:16am**

"Yes. Thank you Holly for allowing me in and entering my spirit as well, Good night Prophetess of God and God bless…" - **Dr. Randy E. Simmons-2:18am**

"Good night Gentleman of God." - **Prophetess Holly Sharp-2:20am**

A CONVERSATION BETWEEN Dr. RANDY E. SIMMONS AND PROPHETESS HOLLY SHARP AUG 8TH 2010

CHAPTER ELEVEN
THE COVERING AND COVENANT OF INTIMACY

THE COVERING AND COVENANT OF INTIMACY: - "God is the greatest covenant maker of all and the greatest warrior. He made a covenant with another warrior Abraham; and because he could swear by no other he swore by himself. That is an ultimate covenant. He made a covenant with Adam; one given to subdue the earth and when he was defeated by Satan; God gave him a promise, HIS OWN SEED! Wow what a covenant of Love… 'For God so loved the world', says John 3:16…wow!

CHAPTER ELEVEN

THE COVERING AND COVENANT OF INTIMACY

THE COVERING OF INTIMACY: "A WOMAN SHALL COMPASS A MAN" (Jer. 31:22)

"Good Afternoon Dr. Simmons~

I have been listening and speaking to God on your behalf today. In doing so I am reminded of something the Lord directed me as I have been going before Him regarding financial issues, resources, etc. The Lord spoke that I should begin to pray for the person who is RESISTING releasing the blessing. He showed me that many are able, and have more than sufficient funds to give; however, what they do not have is Him. They possess financial resources, but they do not possess the Love of the Lord. In fact, they truly know Him not. Some who hold the blessing of resources believe they have security in Him; yet they have never given their very heart to Him and therefore cannot conceive of giving their earthly "riches" to further His kingdom. So, I am praying for the one or more who are to release to you and to the one or more who are to release to me. I am praying for the one or more who will release to Apostle Stacy Slaughter and Apostle Adrienne Williams in particular. I KNOW beyond any doubt that these ladies are on Kingdom assignment and I KNOW beyond any doubt you are too. Somewhere I am on assignment as well, and part of that is to pray and believe in total committed faith that OUR GOD does and will supply to meet the desires HE has placed in our hearts. We will continue to pray for those who do not know Him yet for as they come to know Him they will Love what He loves and who He loves. They WILL give! Did you meet that one today?" -**Prophetess Holly Sharp -August 8 2010 @2:29pm**

THE COVERING ACCEPTED:

"You see correctly. This is what God has shown me. And yes I did meet him. Once, upon entering church; Again leaving the lobby area and coming down a hallway; And third, he sat beside me in service, a stranger in a five hundred member church, to meet him three times. I've never crossed paths with anyone in that church twice let alone three times and then to sit next to him in worship. That's not coincidence. We just have to see what God says now. Lol…Lol…Lol!!"
Dr. Randy E. Simmons - August 8 2010 @2:49pm

REJOICE O COMPASSING WOMAN…REJOICE:

"We shall worship.
We shall praise.
We shall give thanks.
We shall pray.
We shall believe.
We shall rejoice.
We shall give testimony…"
-Prophetess Holly Sharp -August 8 2010 @2:53pm

A PROPHETIC WORD:

"This is a prophetic word the Lord dropped in my spirit early one morning last week. He was speaking in regards to those who have the prophetic inside, yet they carry it rather than wear it. There are so many who desire to "put it on" when it will bring attention to themselves and "take it off" when they don't want to be bothered or do not want the responsibility of the lifestyle required. It is a beautiful word. Just wanted to share.

The Lord says, "You carry the garment but you won't wear it. You refuse to put it on ~ for in doing so, you are cloaked with the responsibility of the mantle. You lay your cloak down to be stepped on, trampled upon, in the assumption of keeping others clean ~ yet you disrespect the garment in doing so. Do not lay down your gift to be walked upon. Do not be deceived into allowing others to trample and dishonor that which I have given you to wear and place upon you. Carry the garment no longer ~ yet wear the garment I have provided, supplied, selected and hand fitted for you. Allow not man to alter the garment ~ allow only my provision and revision ~ for I AM God sayeth the Lord and I call my men and women out ~ I display them and clothe them in righteousness for they are to resemble and represent me. Made in my image, conformed in and to my Spirit. Listen to the voice of the Spirit, not the voice or influence of the flesh. Let no man say it doesn't fit."

The more I have read this and understand He is speaking to each of us who He has placed a cloak upon. I am humbled at His instruction. I will wear the garment He has tailored for me regardless if even those who have been the closest to me say it doesn't fit. God already says "it fits....wear it!" You too Man of God. The cloak He has designed for you fits; do not hesitate to wear it. Blessings ~ Prophet Holly. - **Prophetess Holly Sharp -August 8 2010 @2:47pm**

'Amen. So be it!" -**Dr. Randy E. Simmons - August 8 2010 @2:49pm**

A BEAUTIFUL WORD SHARED:

"I will share a beautiful word the Lord gave May 4, 2003 between 12:10 a.m. and 1:10 am... I will send it via personal email as you have provided. You are a writer, I am a scribe. I record the word the Holy Spirit speaks exactly as He is speaking it. No additions, no deletions, no changes. I have been hearing from the Holy Spirit this way, and writing since about 1990 probably. The intimacy with the Spirit is incredible. Even tonight as I drove alone and through detours I thought, wow, God, you are always with me...the pull was so intense I could barely contain myself. As we have talked and opened conversation about intimacy with Him something is stirring with intensity and it is exactly where God wants me to be. Exactly! Thank you Man of God for pushing and pressing me to brink of even speaking of such intimacy with the Father. I am overwhelmed by His gentle love and holding back from weeping. I am raining on the inside....totally drenched. I pray God will minister to you through the words He has spoken to me. Blessings upon you Man of God ~" **Prophetess Holly Sharp -August 8 2010 at 8:52pm**

THE COVENANT OF INTIMACY: IT'S A LONELY WALK-DAVID AND JONATHAN

"And Jonathan caused David to swear again, because he loved him: for he loved him as he loved his own soul" (1 Sam.20:17)

"Woman of God...I will speak with you later...how are you tonight?"
-11:00pm Dr. Randy E. Simmons

"I am well thank you. And you?" Yes Man of God. Attend to the people. They are seeking you and drawing from you. Return when you desire to be filled. I cannot monopolize your time sir, for others wait as well.
-11:04pm Prophetess Holly Sharp

"I love to give you time because of the depth of our conversations". You dear prophetess have become a covering. God spoke and said "a woman shall compass a man" **-11:10pm Dr. Randy E. Simmons**

"Awwww....interesting. I am glad to hear from you always; yet I do know the pull others have on you for you freely give. Just reading Zephaniah 3:20.....God will reverse our captivity! Hallelujah!" **-11:12pm Prophetess Holly Sharp**

"Yes... powerful. It seems the enemy has so many in captivity" **-11:13pm Dr. Randy E. Simmons**

"All the more reason we must remain free Man of God....for how can one lead another to freedom if they remain in chains themselves. Sometimes speaking is not enough...we must walk with another." **-11:14pm Prophetess Holly Sharp**

"Yes. But so often we are not in agreement. How can two walk together if they are not in agreement?" **-11:15pm Dr. Randy E. Simmons**

"So true. The Warrior Princess seeks to walk in agreement with the Man of God in all our spiritual and God driven ways..." **-11:16pm Prophetess Holly Sharp**

"There is a union of spirits just like comrades in arms. Warrior Princess; Warrior Prince; Prophet; Prophetess; what a union! It is a walk of covenant. David and Jonathan understood this. It is a walk of intimacy. Jesus understood this and tried to teach twelve men from different backgrounds the same." **-11:22pm Dr. Randy E. Simmons**

"Warriors do not give up. The Prophet and the Prophetess bring comfort to one another. Like applying the balm. The two see wounds and tender spots and they attend one to another to restore strength.
The Prophet and the Prophetess do not jockey for position, for they walk side by side with the same commander and Kingdom assignments. Each desiring the health and wellbeing for the other.
Reminding when to rest and when to walk; When to rest and when to speak; When to sup together and when to feed others. Do what you must do on tonight Dr. Simmons. The Father

attends to His princess..." **-11:25pm Prophetess Holly Sharp**

"It is a walk of power and Paul taught this to Timothy in 2 Tim 1:7. Not fear...but love, power and a sound mind." **-11:27pm Dr. Randy E. Simmons**

"Yes. For the walk is not for the weak of spirit." **-11:28pm Prophetess Holly Sharp**

"So you see...to walk with one you must agree with him...spirits of like nature walk together." **-11:29pm Dr. Randy E. Simmons**

"Spirits of unlike nature limp! To limp is to become impaired, lack energy, lack vigor and excitement, to be jerky and uneven; ineffective. I cannot want a limp! LOL! Every part of the body, physical and spiritual is affected when we limp. When our walk is off balance, everything tends to hurt. People can be delivered from their limping conditions....Psalm 116:8-9" **-11:34pm Prophetess Holly Sharp**

"Gideon sent thousands away because they were either afraid, weak or of a different mindset...it's better to go into battle with a few than to be distracted by a thousand of a different spirit...spirit is love, covenant, and reliability. More than that, men must be willing to stand...even if it's only with an amour bearer as in the case of Jonathan, willing to fight to the death as long as Jehovah God was with them." **-11:36pm Dr. Randy E. Simmons**

"You are always teaching me the Word. Thank you. Not many realize that." **-11:39pm Prophetess Holly Sharp**

"It's a covenant of love, a banner of friendship; even Elijah the greatest prophet needed Elisha. Moses needed Joshua. Deborah needed Barak. Covenant that is what warfare requires." - **11:40pm Dr. Randy E. Simmons**

"Even life requires…" -**11:42pm Prophetess Holly Sharp**

"God is the greatest covenant maker of all and the greatest warrior. He made a covenant with another warrior Abraham; and because he could swear by no other he swore by himself. That is an ultimate covenant. He made a covenant with Adam; one given to subdue the earth and when he was defeated by Satan; God gave him a promise, HIS OWN SEED! Wow what a covenant of Love… 'For God so loved the world', says John 3:16…wow! - **11:45pm Dr. Randy E. Simmons**

"Yes it is. None other…You do have such understanding of the Word of God. I humbly admit I pale in comparison." -**11:42pm Prophetess Holly Sharp**

"My dear Holly; the word is revelation, not knowledge. Let it come alive. That is the covenant God also made with his warriors. Jesus the word, promised never to leave us or forsake us. He was the greatest warrior and conqueror; after all he conquered death, hell, and the grave…I would walk with him any day!" -**11:50 pm Dr. Randy E. Simmons**

"…and you already do. I seek revelation daily. Some days God is quieter than others so I learn too to be quiet. I learn to wait. I learn to listen and not be overly disappointed if there is silence....The most difficult part is the sense that I should be "prepared" for something at any given moment." **-11:52pm Prophetess Holly Sharp**

"Many say they do. Peter thought he did. Jesus asked him; "Peter, lovest thou me more than these?" I wonder how many can truly answer that? Would you die for Him!!!!!!???????????? Hmmmmmmm!
Well shall we continue another time?" **-11:55 pm Dr. Randy E. Simmons**

"Today I know I am dying to self. I have asked myself would I REALLY die for Him. Yes I believe for I am physically very tired this evening.
Was up very late last night then went to bed and still wide awake at 4 am then up at 8:00 with my daughter." **-11:59pm Prophetess Holly Sharp**

"Well good thing we don't have to; he already did. But if it came to that, Wow! How many people would? God made the greatest covenant with his church. Jesus said I will establish it and the very gates of hell shall not prevail against it...that took a covenant! Took a covenant!" **-11:55 pm Dr. Randy E. Simmons**

"....well, you know I am honest at least. I can never repay Him for what He has done in my life. While I begged to live many times over the last seven years often I have been reminded of what He went through for me. Still makes me weep. Very, very tender this past week or so. Hmmm." **-12:04am Prophetess Holly Sharp**

"Holly; no repayment necessary and to seal the covenant he gave us himself; in the form of the holy spirit living within us...what many of us fail to understand, is a covenant can only be made by two equal partners; two equal soldiers can fight together. We are not equal with God, therefore we cannot make covenant or repay him for his." **-12:05 am Dr. Randy E. Simmons**

"Nor can we negotiate with Him, for we have NOTHING to negotiate with...for it ALL belongs to Him anyway. I see why you are a busy man in demand on FB. You teach you fill up; you give truth of the Word." **-12:09am Prophetess Holly Sharp**

"My question is...why would we want to negotiate? Something you have taught me this week is the intimacy of God; and in order to appreciate a walk with him, surrender is necessary!" **-12:11am Dr. Randy E. Simmons**

"Most people do not understand that and many attempt to wheel and deal with God. I have said for years, 'surrender early...but not to the wrong camp!' Do you ever sleep? LOL!" - **12:12am Prophetess Holly Sharp**

"Well God is not a gambler, and if he is he already holds the winning cards. Once we see that; we can rest, walk, and enjoy his company. Should a fight arise we know he has our back. That is what covenant is all about. The stronger swears to even protect the weaker and no wounded left behind! I get very little sleep lately, but God knows!" **-12:14am Dr. Randy E. Simmons**

"I have been seeking God regarding the man at church whom you met three times. Amen. No wounded left behind. I know that FB has you hopping tonight. We will speak again soon as the Lord allows and you are so leads. I believe you will be up into the wee hours. I am going to rest for circle under these eyes just simply are not a pretty thing. Thank you for investing time with me on tonight." -**12:17am Prophetess Holly Sharp**

"Yes, perhaps finish this thought. It was my pleasure again WOG.
Lol...Lol...Lol...Rest well WOG, and God bless. The exchange was quite inspiring" -**12:19am Dr. Randy E. Simmons**

"Yes; as always. Forgive me for not participating to a greater extent. We will speak as you are lead, for the princess shall remain a lady and wait upon the timing of God and the Man of God." -**12:22am Prophetess Holly Sharp**

"Yes...we will...be blessed!" -**12:23am Dr. Randy E. Simmons**

"Until next time....peace to your heart. Affectionately in Christ. Good night Gentleman of God." -**12:24am Prophetess Holly Sharp**

"Yes, and with you also." -**12:26am Dr. Randy E. Simmons**

PROPHETIC DELIMA AND DESPAIR: WHEN GOD DOESN'T MAKE SENSE – 'WHAT DOEST THOU HERE, ELIJAH?'

"And he came thither unto a cave, and lodged there; and, behold, the word of the Lord came to him, and he said unto him, what doest thou here, Elijah?
And he said I have been very jealous for the LORD God of hosts: for the children of Israel have forsaken thy covenant, thrown down thine altars, and slain thy prophets with the sword; and I, even I only, am left; and they seek my life, to take it away." (1 kings 19:9-10)

"Dear WOG;

I've heard many Prophets over the years and must say that you are among the best of the best that I've heard. I seek only the will of God.

For months now I've sought his will and have found much with him. I've inspired and encouraged thousands. I give of my gifts. I reflect on the word you gave on Sunday August 8th and again found it to be true after putting so many to the test. Many do not know of my financial dilemma, because as a gentleman I wear it well. When I moved back to Brunswick a few months ago doors had opened that now seem closed, a career door God had reopened had closed again the month of July due to new management takeover. My income was lost.

I've not left this apt or mingled with anyone except to go to worship. Yet in my distress I ministered unto many. Yet none heard or listened to God. The resources were prophesied; God had spoken; but none listened; even in the church. I tried to get loans to no avail. I did my part. Woman of God I write this to you because I believe that you had a sincere desire, and still have for truth.

Years ago after the laying on of hands by Rod Parsley, I was in the same position. Ready to take the world for Jesus but the financial resources didn't come, so I turned back to corporate America (Egypt) and for many years my voice was silent in the church and Egypt benefited from my anointing as it did Joseph's. Why must the financial resources be the hardest thing in the kingdom of heaven to come by? We see every other miracle but that; and then so called Prophets speak a perverse word and say: "it must not be God's will" or something even more stupid like: "don't love mammon". Many stupid things just to show their prophetic ignorance.

Do they not know that God will do nothing except he reveals his secrets unto his Prophets? Shame on them. Yesterday I heard this word in my spirit: "My son, step outside of the body of Christ now for a small season. Look to the world...become a Joseph. There are things coming upon my church that will require men like you to reset the order. Make friends with the mammon of this world for therein will you secure your future and the future of them that hear you. Your place is secured. Use GVMI as a world embassy to the USA". Afterwards I formed a new corporation: THE AMBASSAOR AGENCY, a business for profit to go after the resources of the world. Just as I did with Deshan Intl. Years ago.

I don't know where it will take me, but today I start a new journey back towards Egypt. The church and its people have disheartened me. They have not believed nor heard God. If I deal with anyone in the future it will not be here in America. I will not cast my pearls before swine. I leave you with this because I believe that you have the heart of God. But ask God for me why every time Randy Simmons was ready to obey him and do his will and poured out of his gifts into thousands, the money, even to pay the simplest bill never seems to come? Answer this question honestly WOG and I will believe that there is a prophet in America. My last endeavor took me before the council of hell in negotiation with Satan and his hoards. I know not where this one will take me. And unless God intervenes in my finances I will break. So WOG you are a Prophetess, you hear from God, you are intimate with him, then ask him and may you bring back a good answer. I wait!" -**Dr. Randy E. Simmons, August 12th 2010**

"Your transparency is stunning! The humility of a man truly after God's own heart. I will take this to God and seek Him more diligently on your behalf. Upon reading this I - IMMEDIATELY heard "I love you" tell him - said "I love you" that was none other than God and not the empty phrase the flesh speaks to comfort or console. This is a true word from the throne room. "I love you" He says.

Allow me time amazing Man of God. I will seek Him on your behalf for His word instructs us that out of the right of necessity and on the authority of His word He invites us to come to Him. I go to Him with these words on my very lips. I was awake at two three and four o'clock this morning interceding for you. I already was well aware of your present financial condition for God hath revealed days ago. I thank Him for the revelation so that I may pray accurately and with passion before our God. Dear Sir, Man of God, I too have lived in a tent (literally) for a brief period and have found myself in wilderness experiences nearly to despair, but God always knew the condition of my heart and used the wilderness to bring me even closer. Naked I was before him, stripped of pride and even stripped as a woman of womanly outside characteristics such as breast, uterus, ovaries, all hair on body including lashes and eyebrows...everything! Bare and naked. So He began to rebuild me. He began to reshape me into His likeness all the while I was in pain and pushed to the edge of the ledge, however falling off only brought me once again into the arms of Jesus. Oh we must speak. Perhaps soon by phone as God leads - will contact you if He so allows." –
Prophetess Holly Sharp; August 12th 2010

PROPHETIC PRAYER COVERING:
WE PROTECT EACH OTHER!

"The Lord watch between me and thee while we are absent one from another." (Gen 31:49)

"Father God, I do thank you for this Man of God you have allowed me to connect with on a unique and spiritually sound level. God you are so generous and precise in placing your children together. I ask Father that you embrace your son Randy Simmons, that you hold him closer to your heart tonight. I ask that you love him a little deeper on tonight. Father, reveal to this Man of God, your man, what it is that is deep within and pressing its way to the surface.

Father, there IS a seed in him. There is growth under the surface that he may know nothing about at this time. Release the seed to germinate and to spring forth into life. Allow the seed to grow at an amazing pace Father.

Define for your son what it is that he is truly experiencing during this winter season.

Not driven to despair, he still clings to you, leans on you, depends on you, and seeks your face in all things, in all places, in all things. Father I ask you in all humility and all sincerity to act quickly on his behalf. Lord, by your authority, we do call finances forward. We do call anything that is lacking to be filled. We do declare and decree that this season of famine in the land is over as of tonight. Father provide as only you can Lord.

Do not allow your servant to turn in any direction contrary to your will. Father, keep his mind sound and stable. Reveal his opportunities Lord...and Father, we ask that YOU announce this man to others. We ask YOU to introduce him to others and then upon meeting, YOU do the talking, YOU make the divine connections, YOU secure the position and position your son in security in you. Provide for his home Father, his expenses, and the needs of his children.

Father, the man of God says he is not discouraged....protect him Father. For Satan does circle round and round him looking for that moment of opportunity. Secure your son I ask in your name Father.

Use his gifts for they are simple, YOU placed them in his vessel. Reverse the finances....IMMEDIATELY....Father Your child is pressed in from all angles, Father we beg you to make a way of escape. We come to you in the name of your son Jesus...by whom there is no other name greater or more powerful.

Breathe on your son, Randy Simmons tonight. Even in the darkest part of the night may he sense your very presence. We command that this start to change immediately and without hesitation.

In Jesus name...amen.

I know the spirit will awaken me sometime in the middle of the night tonight on your behalf. I pray you will dare to go even deeper with him into even greater transparency.

I must close for tonight. This is only a thimble of what is to come.

Blessings and good night friend." –**August 8TH 2010 @11:39pm-12:00am -Prophetess Holly Sharp**

"Amen...Amen!" - **August 9TH 2010 @12:01am –Dr. Randy E. Simmons**

CONCLUSION

IT IS FINISHED:
"DON'T CAP THE FLOW!"

IT IS FINISHED: - "DON'T CAP THE FLOW!" I found the source of my communication today. It's like an oil well that gushes. Jeremiah likened it to fire, mine is like the oil spill in the gulf that is not easily capped. Working on the cap. But how do you cap God when you know he is exposing truth. And really why would anybody cap God. Paul spoke till the man fell out the window, than raised him up.

CONCLUSION

IT IS FINISHED:
"DON'T CAP THE FLOW!"

"Doc, for two days I have labored to reply to your messages. Yesterday I started to reply to a message at 6am. It was after noon when I got done (smile...it was long because he took me through noting his word with pictorial snippets). When I thought I was done the system would not post, so I had to get pen and paper to jot key notes that wowed me.

Today I made the mistake of trying to reply to "Calling those things that be not". I am literally exhausted. I felt restrained by God (but at will, I so enjoy that intimate time with him, but this was sparked by your note).

Doc, I have been home for two days from work as God; just poured into me. This usually only happens when I'm taking classes. The Word was rich. It was a life changing word that would capture an audience. I'm so being honest right now. He took me back to scripture he had shown me years ago. Prophecies still actively going on and some things still to come not so good. I'm not upset because I learned so much and was made to revisit truth.

Yes, I talk a lot. No surprise. But I found the source of my communication today. It's like an oil well that gushes. Jeremiah likened it to fire, mine is like the oil spill in the gulf that is not easily capped. Working on the cap. But how do you cap God when you know he is exposing truth. And really why would anybody cap God. Paul spoke till the man fell out the window, than raised him up (smile).

Doc, God is showing me things about "birthing" I have not heard talked about in the manner he is showing me. And I have you to thank for that. Sidebar, one of the pastors talked about birthing from a different take last night. Confirming it's the season.

Doc, I' m still so pregnant feels like twins. Any who....after much writing, I thought I was done and what is noted below flowed out. I can only assume you will understand what God is saying to you.

Doc, I thank God for you. You have (us, the body of Christ) positioned around the globe. Like Miriam was positioned to guide Moses to safety till his appointed time. God has given you womb-baskets that you have been depositing the "Birthing" and we know there is one Spirit that is the self-same spirit speaking out the will of God in the earth today. Hezekiah prayed because he was worried about the children coming to birth and the carrier not having strength to bring forth. Your book will be a source of joy that will reconcile souls back to God. And he that wins souls is wise and they shall receive wages...setting you financially straight. Shalom, shalom!" -**September 9 2010 at 5:35pm**

"Dear Wendy;

How rich and timely is this word from you, **and no, do not cap the oil well**. This word is inspiration. I have been searching for a way to end and present this book to the body and this word from you is it. Whether you believe in Prophetic Birthing; Spiritual Impregnation; The Womb Man; the Hand Maid or Spiritual Connections, is not the most important thing. What is important is that God's people began to feel an Intimacy with Him again; they begin to Know Him again; they began to feel His presence again; and indeed many who thought that their 'wombs' were barren are now learning that it is God who brings to the birth.

Wendy, Generations to come, even into the Millennium, will remember this time; countless numbers of souls saved will remember the birthing of Wendy Young and countless other Hand Maids just like you. Because you came to the birth; because you allowed the Holy Spirit to impregnate you in the spirit, as He did Mary in the natural. Sons and daughters were born into the kingdom. Know this; you will never be the same; you will never think the same; your walk with God will never be the same; All because you had this one encounter with the Lord of all the earth; and as a result you said, as did Mary: 'so be it unto thy Handmaid'. Bring to birth...the nursery is prepared!" –
Sept. 9th 2010 @ 7:04pm Dr. Randy E. Simmons

"So be it and Amen! The nursery is prepared...and I shall birth kings and priest for my God. Below is what God closed this night out with for now...

'HIS FOUNDATION is in the holy mountains. The LORD loves the gates of Zion more than all the dwellings of Jacob. Glorious things are spoken of (me), O city of God. Selah. I will make mention of Rahab and Babylon to them that know me: behold Philistia, and Tyre, with Ethiopia; this man was born there. And of Zion it shall be said, this and that man was born in her: and the highest himself SHALL ESTABLISH HER. The LORD shall count, when he writes up the people, that this man was born there. Selah. As well the singers as the players on instruments shall be there: all my springs are in there'. (Psalms 87:1-7).

'Go forth, O ye daughters of Zion, and behold the king Solomon with the crown wherewith his mother crowned him in the day of his espousals, and in the day of the gladness of his heart.' (Song of Sol. 3:11).

'WHEREFORE SEEING we also are compassed about with so great cloud of witnesses, let us lay aside every weight, and the sin which does so easily beset us, and let us run with patience the race that is set before us. Looking unto Jesus the author and finisher of our faith; who for the joy that was set before him endured the cross, despising the shame, and is set down at the right hand of the throne of God.' …You are come unto mount Zion, and unto the city of the living God, the heavenly Jerusalem, and to an innumerable company of angels, to the general assembly and church of the firstborn, which are written in heaven, and to God the judge of all, and to the spirits of just men made perfect. And to Jesus the mediator of the new covenant, and to the blood of sprinkling, that speaks better things than that of Abel. See that you refuse not him that speaks. For if they escaped not who refused him that spoke on earth, much more shall not we escape, if we turn away from him that speaks from heaven....Wherefore (I) receive a kingdom which cannot be moved, let (me) have grace, whereby (I) may serve God acceptably with reverence and godly fear: For (my) God is a consuming fire. (Heb. 12:1-2, 22-29).

'For the LORD, whose name is Jealous, is a jealous God... (Exodus 34:14). 'And on my servants and on my handmaidens I will pour out in those days of my Spirit; and they shall prophesy.' (Acts 2:18). –**Wendy Young Sept. 9 2010 @10:11pm**

"He which testifieth these things saith, SURELY I COME QUICKLY. Amen. Even so, come, Lord Jesus.
The grace of Our Lord Jesus Christ be with you all. Amen." (Rev.22:20-21).

Dr. Randy E. Simmons
Contact Info.

981-302-363

Global Visions Ministries Intl Inc.

Dr. Simmons @ reshofa1@gmail.com

Another Book = Prayer Confession = Two = Decree and Declare $12.23 Amazon

---

Prophetic words to Know & Use by John Eckhardt

Hagar - slave woman, law, legalism, mockery Gen 21:9

Haman - Wicked plots Esther 3

Hammer - to smash, a strong weapon Jer 23:29

Hannah - birthing, intercession and travail 1 Sam 1:20

Heart - mind, spirit, inner man Prov 4:23

Hedge - restrain, protection Isa 5:5

Horn - power and strength Psalm 89:17

Horse - strength, swift, pride Job 39:19

Hour - A present time, A time quickly approaching John 4:2